THE INSIDER'S GUIDE TO

NEW ENGLAND

THE INSIDER'S GUIDES

AUSTRALIA • BALI • CALIFORNIA • CANADA • CHINA • EASTERN CANADA • FLORIDA • HAWAII •
HONG KONG • INDIA • INDONESIA • JAPAN • KENYA • KOREA • NEPAL •
NEW ENGLAND • NEW ZEALAND • MALAYSIA AND SINGAPORE • MEXICO •
RUSSIA • SPAIN • THAILAND • TURKEY • WESTERN CANADA

The Insider's Guide to New England
First Published 1992
Moorland Publishing Co Ltd
Moor Farm Rd., Airfield Estate, Ashbourne, DE61HD, England
by arrangement with Novo Editions, S.A.
53 rue Beaudouin, 27700 Les Andelys, France
Telefax: (33) 32 54 54 50

© 1992 Novo Editions, S.A.

ISBN: 0 86190 279 3

Created, edited and produced by Novo Editions, S.A.
Editor in Chief: Allan Amsel
Original design concept: Hon Bing-wah
Picture editor and designer: Jane Pinel
Text and artwork composed and information updated
using Xerox Ventura software

Printed by Samhwa Printing Co Ltd, Seoul, Korea

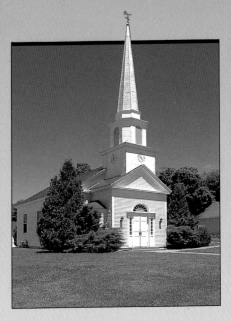

THE INSIDER'S GUIDE TO
NEW ENGLAND

By Richard Bond
Photographed by Robert Holmes

MPC

Contents

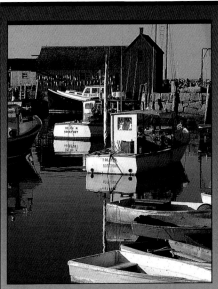

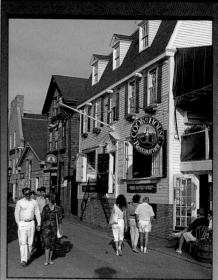

NEW ENGLAND

SYMBOLS

⊖	RIVER, LAKE, SEA
▬▬▬	CONTROLLED ACCESS/DIVIDED HIGHWAY
	PRINCIPAL ROAD
─··─	INTERNATIONA BOUNDARY
─·─	STATE BOUNDARY
⬟	URBAN AREA/CITY
⛷	ALPINE SKI AREA
✈	AIRPORT

CANADA

Isle La Motte
Grand Isle
St Albans
North Troy
Newport
Derby Line
CA
Champlain
Jeffersonville
Burlington
Shelburne
Long Trail
Craftsbury Common
91
Charlotte
Stowe
Coleb
Bristol
Long Trail
VERMONT
Lyndonville
Middlebury
Montpelier
St Johnsbury
Lancaster
GREEN MOUNTAIN
2
Barre
ittleton
WH MOU NATIC FORE
NATIONAL
Randolph
Woodsville
93
7
FOREST
Chelsea
2
Proctor
Gorham
Fairhaven
Pittsfield
Orford
WHITE MOUNTAIN
Rutland
Woodstock
Appalachian Trail
NATIONAL FOREST
Long Trail
White River Junction
NEW HAMPSHIRE
North Conw
Dorset
Ludlow
Windsor
Caanan
Plymouth
3
Manchester Center
GREEN
Moultonborough
Arlington
MOUNTAIN
Chester
Newport
Sunapee
93
NATIONAL
Bellows Falls
Laconia
Bennington
FOREST
Townshend
Newfane
Franklin
Wolfeboro
Williamstown
Wilmington
Gilsum
99
Canterbury
North Adams
Brattleboro
Keene
Hillsboro
Concord
Adams
Hoosac Tunnel
Winchester
Hancock
Rochester
Sanfor
Pittsfield
Dalton
Harrisville
202
Lenox
Greenfield
Manchester
Kennebunk
Housatonic
Lee
Becket
River
Athol
Milford
Dover
Great Barrington
Stockbridge
Northampton
202
202
Nashua
Derry
Portsmouth
Ogunqu
Sheffield
BERKSHIRE HILLS
Amherst
Fitchburg
Exeter
Kittery
Caanan
Easthampton
MASSACHUSETTS
Lawrence
Haverhill
Hampton
Norfolk
Holyoke
Chicopee
Leominster
Lowell
495
Newburyport
7
Litchfield
44
Springfield
Ware
90
Concord
93
95
202
202
Worcester
495
Reading
Rockport
84
Waterbury
Windsor
84
Marlbourgh
95
Lynn
Gloucester
Danbury
Hartford
6
395
95
BOSTON
Marblehead
New Britain
CONNECTICUT
Webster
Framingham
93
Winthrop
Meriden
Middletown
6
Milford
93
Quincy
MASSACHUSETTS BAY
Derby
Wallingford
Putnam
Pascoag
395
Norwood
Shelton
Willimantic
6
Smithfield
Woonsocket
95
Scituate
Stamford
New Haven
495
RHODE ISLAND
Attleboro
Brockton
Norwalk
Bridgeport
Stratford
Chester
West Warwick
Providence
Middleboro
Duxbury
Greenwich
Darien
Ivoryton
Norwich
Warwick
Barrington
44
Plymouth
Provincetown
LONG ISLAND SOUND
Old Lyme
New London
Bristol
Fall River
495
Cape Cod National Seashore
Groton
Westerly
Portsmouth
Tiverton
Fairhaven
CAPE COD BAY
6
Wellfleet
Mystic
Stonington
Wakefield
Newport
New Bedford
Sandwich
Brewster
Orleans
RHODE ISLAND SOUND
Sakonnet
Falmouth
6
Hyannis
Dennis Port
Chatham
MARTHA'S VINYARD
NANTUCKET SOUND
Nantucket

NEW YORK

Lake

30 miles
50 km

N

Pittsfield

Conneticut River

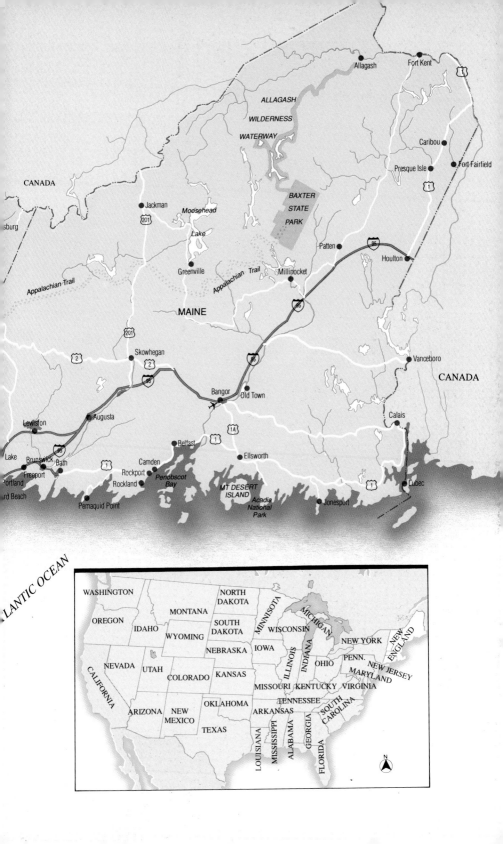

New
England

A PLACE APART

There are so many reasons to visit New England that no book can enumerate them all. It is truly a place apart, an often-beautiful land of lakes, seashores, mountains, river valleys, villages, towns, and bustling cities. Not only the best of America's past, it is also much of the cultural, educational, and technological promise of its coming centuries. In a nation bereft of a long historical tradition, New England keeps a way of life, architecture, and culture linked to America's earliest days, and to the Europe which preceded them.

Composed of six states, including five of the original thirteen colonies, New England is so steeped in the history and culture of the United States it is difficult to imagine an America without New England. Although geographically small when compared to the rest of the nation, New England has had perhaps the strongest impact of any region on the country as a whole.

Named "New" England by the early explorer Sir John Smith, it is the New World's strongest link, historically and culturally, to the Old. Yet it is also profoundly American, from its colonial villages, farmsteads, and elegant Victorian city streets to the bold commercial vigor of its modern skylines. And if New England is the land where American liberty was born, it has also nurtured this liberty with its continuing commitment to education and culture, expressed today in a concentration of many of the nation's best colleges, universities, museums, theaters, and concert halls.

But these are not the best reasons to come to New England. The best reasons are countless, and include the multicolored splendor of the autumn hills, the crystalline purity of the northern lakes, the salty smell of the sea, the beauty of villages couched in emerald pastures and peaceful river valleys, the glitter of trout streams emerging from spring snow, the towering granite peaks, the vast forests of spruce and pine, the taste of America as once it truly was.

A LAND FOR ALL SEASONS

And New England is a land for all seasons. In winter the earth lies beneath a blanket of white; wood smoke rises from the chimneys; skaters flit across the frozen ponds while on the lakes fishermen huddle in their huts and drop their lines through holes in the deep ice. Children sled on steep back streets and country slopes; the hills are alive with skiers; snowshoers and cross-country skiers wander back-country

trails through forests whose silence is broken only by the occasional chatter of a chickadee.

Spring, the rebirth of life, is magical in New England. After months of cold, the warm March winds melt the snow and in April the buds burst forth, transforming the gaunt gray branches to brilliant green. The geese, ducks, and first songbirds begin to return; boys follow the thawing trout streams, and early blossoms paint the apple orchards.

Summer brings hot days, and the lakes fill with swimmers, water skiers, and boaters. Fishermen cast and troll for trout, lake salmon, pickerel, bass, and other game fish. The ocean bays are a kaleidoscope of sails and spinnakers; surf and sandy beaches glimmer in the warm sun. Rafters, kayakers, and canoers ride the rivers and hikers wander the peaks, hills, and forests.

Ocean fog OPPOSITE and rolling hills ABOVE characterize New England's scenic charm.

But it is fall that is the glory of New England. From north to south the woodlands blaze with countless shades of scarlet, crimson, vermilion, yellow, gold, and orange; as the leaves fall the white birches and tan beeches and oaks stand out against the darker firs, spruce, tamaracks, and pines. Hunters go forth to seek deer, pheasant, moose, and other prey to stock their larders. The rural air has a scent of apples and coming snow, and families draw closer round the hearth, conscious of the ending of the year.

PEAKS, BAYS, AND RIVERS

New England occupies an area of only 66,672 sq miles (172,680 sq km) in the northeast corner of the United States, bordered by New York to the south and west, by Quebec and New Brunswick to the north, and by the Atlantic Ocean to the east. In size it is somewhat smaller than Great Britain, less than half the size of California, and slightly larger than Michigan or Illinois.

New Hampshire's White Mountains are ideal for river fishing ABOVE, and in the autumn display an array of vivid fall colors OPPOSITE.

Maine is the only New England state which was not part of the original thirteen colonies, because it was part of Massachusetts until 1820. At 33,265 sq miles (86,156 sq km) Maine is also half the total area of New England, and more than three times the size of Vermont, New Hampshire, or Massachusetts, and nearly six times the size of Connecticut. At 1,212 sq miles (3,139 sq km), Rhode Island is New England's, and the nation's, smallest state.

The Appalachian chain dominates much of western New England, from Mt Katahdin in northern Maine down through Maine's Rangely Mountains and the White Mountains of Maine and New Hampshire. Further west, the lower, forested Green Mountains span the entire length of Vermont and continue into Massachusetts as the Berkshires, and on across Connecticut to join the Taconic Mountains of New York.

Like New England's mountains, its rivers run primarily north to south, swinging east to meet the sea at wide, island-filled bays from Maine's Bar Harbor to Connecticut's shores of Long Island Sound. Many of New England's rivers keep the names given to them by the original New Englanders — the Merrimac, Penobscot, Kennebec, and the 400-mile (644-km) Connecticut, which runs almost the entire length of western New England, separating Vermont from New Hampshire and bisecting Massachusetts and Connecticut to reach Long Island Sound.

Because eras of glaciation have given it relatively poor, rocky soil, New England has never been an agricultural center, although its sheep-raising industry was a significant national resource in the nineteenth century, and Maine's potatoes remain the nation's best. Endowed with a magnificent coastline and hundreds of bays and harbors, New England first derived its prosperity from ship-building and fisheries. In the nineteenth century, New England's textile, leather, and other manufacturing became the nation's most predominant. In recent years, electronics, computer and data communications technologies, weaponry, banking, and a growing tourist industry have become major aspects of New England's commercial vitality.

THE NEW ENGLANDERS

New Englanders have learned to live with the various stereotypes which have been assigned to them—the shrewd Connecticut Yankee, the imperturbable Boston Brahmin, or the terse and taciturn inhabitant of Maine, New Hampshire, or Vermont. These characterizations, once more valid, have become blurred over the years by the mixing of Irish, Italian, Polish, and other European genes. The beliefs and traditions that these immi-

whose ancestors came to the region in southward migrations from the Bering Straits about 12,000 to 15,000 years ago. These people hardly modified the land in which they lived, finding adequate sustenance in the forests, lakes, rivers, and ocean. Some tribes also grew pumpkins, beans, corn, and other vegetables.

As human migration from Europe turned from trickle to torrent between the seventeenth and twentieth centuries, the ecological diversity and bounty of the land was diminished and in many areas totally de-

grants added to a population traditionally English and ethically Puritan brought a welcome infusion of renewed vigor and broader cultural tolerance.

The population of the six New England states is unevenly distributed. A majority inhabits the southern half of the region, in cities such as Boston, Providence, and Hartford, swelling their hubs and sprawling suburbs to house almost three-quarters of New England's 13 million inhabitants. In the three northern states, the cities and towns are smaller with greater distances between them, and there remain large areas of wilderness, particularly in Maine.

The original settlers of New England's wilderness were the Algonquin Indians,

stroyed. Once flocks of geese truly darkened the sky, covering it in a solid cloud from one horizon to the other. Fish were so plentiful in the streams they could be literally scooped out by hand or net. The forests were filled with animals that are now legend: caribou, wolf, eastern buffalo, and panther.

But the Europeans, with their conviction that anyone not a Christian was a "Devil," had little interest in or respect for New England's inhabitants, or for its wildlife. The environment took a back seat to buccaneering. Whenever possible, the colonists cheated the Indians out of title to their lands by devious and meaningless agreements; when the Indians refused such stratagems, the colonists simply overwhelmed them with their firepower, leaving smallpox and alcohol to further reduce their numbers. Today, the names for lakes and rivers, for islands and mountains, are almost all that connects New England with its tribal past.

By the late seventeenth century, the English Puritans had established a theocracy that imposed upon their new world, and was to impose upon their descendants, a prevailing sense of order, discipline, and frugality. These qualities were to remain strong in the New England Yankee temperament until the spiritual earnestness that had

and Virginia and the Carolinas, moved ever westward, its numbers increased by a steady flow of immigrants from across the sea. By the late 1840's, after worsening English repressions and "the great hunger" in Ireland, the Irish came to New England in great numbers. In time, their political and oratory skills and gave them a strong hold on local governments, particularly in Massachusetts, where they have continued to exercise an active role.

French Canadians, too, emigrated from neighboring Canada to work in the many textile mills that rose beside New England's

accompanied them diminished in the eighteenth century. Under the influence of the practical elements of the Puritan ethic, fleets of merchant and fishing ships, including slavers and privateers, expanded and brought increasing prosperity to New England and with it the accumulation of wealth.

This wealth, and the independence derived from it, caused bitter resentment toward the "mother country" when England arbitrarily imposed a number of trade edicts and taxes upon this, her most affluent North American possession.

In angry response, the colonists rose up in successful rebellion, drove the British into the sea, and formed a new nation. This fledgling nation, born in New England

rivers, bringing with them their own language and customs. Portuguese fishermen augmented the region's fishing fleets, Italians came to labor on construction sites and formed a "little Italy" of their own in many a New England town. The Jews came, so did the Poles, the Russians, and the Swedes, all forming distinctive communities where, for a time, their cultural heritages could be celebrated and preserved. Although they have been long since absorbed into the mainstream of New England life, their ways and the ways of those who came before them together create the human pageant that is now New England.

Faces of today's New Englanders display a warmth and friendliness at odds with the taciturn reputation of their forebears.

TRAVELERS AND TOURISTS

Among the millions who visit New England every year are both travelers and tourists, those who come to enjoy it as it is, and those who are contented with the largely superficial attractions of its tourism industry. Needless to say, the traveler, he or she who is willing to investigate beyond the cliche, who is willing to change a little in order to learn, will have more fun and profit more from a visit than will the simple tourist.

trails, or to wander the beaches, promenades, scenic villages, and historic city tours. Like Europe, New England was built at a different pace than today's — before the automobile came to endanger the pedestrian and fill the cities with clamor and pollution.

And rather than seeing New England as a 66,000-square-mile shopping mall, attempting to validate one's visit by what one carries home, it is simpler to see it as New Englanders do — as a place to *be* at home, to most of them the best place on earth. Thus there's wisdom in avoiding the tourist

Like many popular areas, New England has created a tourism industry that portrays it not as it is, but as it would like to seem, or as it thinks the visitor would like to see it. Because tourism is much the same everywhere, the tourist is therefore deprived of many of the unique resources and fascinations of this extraordinary, beautiful, and historic place.

Thus there are better and worse ways to visit New England. If possible, one should avoid the main highways except for transit, take as much time as possible, and avoid the noise and hubbub of the cities for the relaxation and harmony of country life. To the extent feasible, it's wise to walk as much as possible, to enjoy a few of the many hiking

trinket zones, the high-priced shops and restaurants dedicated to the superficial distracting of the summer crowds, and instead go for the heart and soul of New England, the back roads and quiet country inns, the shores, peaks, and vistas, a way of life that was born with America.

Many people come to New England to "get away from it all", the stress, urban ugliness, crowded conditions, and discord that characterizes much of the late twentieth century. Others come to revisit the birthplace of American liberty and culture, to seek a common heritage, a place that reminds us of what America was once and hoped to be.

Because New England truly has it all — ocean, beaches, islands, mountains, rivers, streams, lakes, Indian memories, American history, colonial and Victorian architecture, education, museums, music, art, hiking, fishing, hunting, skiing, swimming, boating, canoeing, and a hundred other recreations — one's visit should be predicated on what one wants to see and do.

NEW ENGLAND ITINERARIES

Although small by comparison with the rest of the United States, New England is so

are simply too many interesting roads, towns, and byways to list them all here.

THE FULL CIRCUIT

The best of all New England: Connecticut's **Litchfield Hills**, crossing into Massachusetts and traveling north up the **Housatonic River** into the **Berkshires** and the western **Mohawk Trail** to the Vermont border. From here one can swing northwest to **Lake Champlain** then east through the **Green Mountains**, across New Hampshire, with a stop in

topographically and culturally diverse that one could not hope to know it in detail without spending many weeks, if not months, there. But a series of highlights, itineraries to discover the best of New England, can give the visitor a marvelous sense of the beauty, complexity, and history of this land.

To be sure, your itinerary will naturally be based on your place of entry. The most common entries to New England are by car from New York state, often from the greater New York City area, by plane at Boston, or by car from Canada. Depending on your entry, you may want to try one or a combination of the following itineraries. In each case, general areas only are noted here, with detail provided in the following text. There

its stunning **White Mountains**, and then east to the Maine coast. Continuing northeast along the coast, with a stop at scenic **Portland**, to **Camden** or **Bar Harbor**, one can then turn inland toward **Mount Katahdin State Park** and back south through the villages and forests of the **Rangely Mountains** and Maine's rolling southern hills.

From southern Maine one hops the border for a look at historic **Portsmouth** and lower New Hampshire, then crosses into Massachusetts to explore the **Boston** area and **Cape Cod**, and from there south along

The attractive Atlantic shores OPPOSITE and lakes ABOVE of New England provide livelihood and recreation for the millions of inhabitants and visitors.

the coast into **Rhode Island** and back along the coast of Connecticut.

This circuit can be begun at any point, and can take anywhere from several weeks to as long as you want. For outdoors people, the best season is summer, for the swimming, beach strolling, boating, fishing, and hiking. For those who love the fall colors, this entire itinerary is resplendent in September and October.

THE BERKSHIRES

Nationally famous music, art, architecture,

and history among the superb green hills and precipitous granite crests of western Massachusetts. Enchanting country inns, exhilarating hiking, rafting, fishing, swimming, and a host of other activities are possible in one of the most beautiful areas of the United States.

SAILING THE COAST

For boating afficianados, New England's 6,130 miles of shoreline, its thousands of islands, and its lovely bays and many harbors all provide unique opportunities for summertime sailing. Bring your own boat if you have one, or, providing you can attest to your abilities, rent or lease a craft at one of New England's many yacht basins.

A HISTORICAL TOUR OF NEW ENGLAND

It's all historic, so you can hardly go astray. But from the old cities of **Boston, Portland, Portsmouth, Providence**, and **New Haven**, to the thousands of centuries-old towns from

southern Connecticut to northern Maine, there is more than enough history to fill a library and a lifetime of travels.

A TOUR OF NEW ENGLAND'S FINEST ART MUSEUMS

Among the best areas for art museums are **Boston**, **Providence**, **Portland**, **Williamstown** and the **Berkshires**, **Hartford**, and **New Haven**, as well as many smaller towns with both international and regional collections.

DOWN THE HISTORIC CONNECTICUT AND HOUSATONIC VALLEYS

Both the Connecticut and Housatonic Rivers flow north to south across wide areas of natural beauty and historic interest.

THE WILDERNESS

A Week in Maine's Baxter State Park

One of the finest parks in the eastern United States, Baxter is centered around magnificent Mt Katahdin. In addition to climbing the main peak, there are many smaller peaks and miles of hiking trails through superb pine, spruce, and fir forests. Mt Katahdin is also the northern end of the Appalachian Trail, which can be followed down through New Hampshire, Vermont, Massachusetts, and Connecticut.

VERMONT'S LONG TRAIL

Considered one of the world's ten best hiking trails, the Long Trail is situated in Vermont's Green Mountains. They are less precipitous and therefore easier hiking than the White Mountains of New Hampshire. A mix of hardwood and conifer forests and open meadows, with plenty of water, camping places, and vistas, this area makes a fine excursion.

WANDERING THE COAST OF MAINE

Maine has 3,500 miles of shoreline, more than any other Atlantic state, and even more than California! Much of the southern section, between the New Hampshire border and Portland, has been developed, but north of Portland to the Canadian border it is often completely undeveloped and stunningly beautiful. Many small towns add scenic variety.

THE WOODLANDER: THE BACKWOODS OF MAINE — SWIMMING, CANOEING, HIKING

No other place east of the Rocky Mountains has the backwoods variety of Maine. With its 10,000 lakes and over 5,000 trout streams and rivers, its mountains and rocky coast-

White **Mountains**, and from there westward into **southern Vermont**, down into the **Berkshires** of Massachusetts, and back to Boston.

A TWO-WEEK ITINERARY OF NEW ENGLAND

Again, the northern half is best, from **Boston** northward through **Newburyport**, **Portsmouth**, the southern Maine coast, including **Portland** and as far north as **Acadia National Park**, across Maine into

line, Maine is the last vestige of the outdoors experience left in the eastern United States. Best choices include the **Allagash**, **Penobscot**, and **St John Rivers**, the **Moosehead Lake region**, **Mt Katahdin**, the **northeast coast** from Acadia National Park to the Canadian border, and all the top half of the state.

ONE WEEK IN NEW ENGLAND — THE VERY BEST

If you have only a week in New England, go for the northern half — a day in **Boston**, then a drive up the coast to Portland (if it's summer, continue on, to **Sebago Lake State Park**). Then turn west toward the

New Hampshire and down to the **White Mountains**, across to the **Green Mountains** and **Lake Champlain**, then down to the Berkshires and back to Boston, with stops, if there's time, in Connecticut's **Litchfield Hills** and then **Rhode Island**.

The important thing to remember about any New England itinerary is that the destination is never as important as the journey, and that sometimes wandering with no destination is the best journey of all.

OPPOSITE: The lighthouse of Eastham, Massachusetts was built at a time when the ocean was New England's lifeline to the world. ABOVE: Lake Sunapee, New Hampshire, a popular tourist destination, was once the home of Indian tribes.

Eastern Massa- chusetts, Boston and Cape Cod

THE HEART OF NEW ENGLAND

The geographical "middle" of New England, Masssachusetts is an irregular rectangle of 8,257 sq miles (21,385 sq km) bordering Rhode Island and Connecticut in the south and Vermont and New Hampshire in the north.

In the west, the rolling, and at times massive, Berkshire Hills are one of the nation's loveliest mountain regions. The Connecticut River flows from north to south across the western middle of the state, its wide channel and tree-bordered banks offering tranquility and beautiful vistas. The Massachusetts coast offers a variety of natural beauty to those who love the sea. Though not as impressive as Maine's, it is best exemplified by the sand dunes, beaches, and cranberry bogs of Cape Cod. The offshore islands, Nantucket and Martha's Vineyard, have a unique charm that draws many thousands of visitors each year.

But it is to the Massachusetts villages and towns, with their superb colonial architecture, and to modern and historic Boston, that the visitor is drawn.

TOURIST INFORMATION

The **Massachusetts Office of Travel and Tourism** (13th floor, 100 Cambridge Street, Boston, MA 02202; ℤ (617) 727-3201, toll-free (800) 623-8038) provides a free travel kit that can be useful in planning a vacation in its historic cities or picturesque countryside. For travel information, call toll-free (800) 624-MASS.

BACKGROUND

Long before Europeans reached the shores of Massachusetts, a variety of Indian tribes, belonging mostly to the Algonquin federation, peopled the land. They first welcomed these strange, white-skinned people, sheltered them from the cold winter, and fed them in times of hunger. But it soon became clear that these European guests did not intend to go home, would not respond with friendship in kind, but rather intended to take over the Indian lands, betray and enslave the tribes, and force them to accept this strange religion which insisted that humans had crucified the Great Spirit. Courageous and independent, the Indian tribes one by one chose annihilation in war over serfdom, or died pitiably by the thousands from diseases introduced by the new immigrants.

THE FIRST EUROPEANS

Probably someday archaeologists and historians will discover incontrovertible proof that Scandinavian or other European explorers reached New England well before Columbus came to the New World. Some now claim it was the Viking Eric the Red, or his son, Leif Ericsson, who was the first European to reach Cape Cod. Records do show that the English explorer John Cabot visited the Massachusetts coast in 1497, only five years after Columbus discovered the New World. Yet it was well over a century before there were any permanent settlements here.

PILGRIMS AND PURITANS

Four days before Christmas, 1620, a shipload of pilgrims from Southampton, England, weighed anchor off what is now Plymouth. They had left England on September 15, intending to go Jamestown, but had first reached land at Cape Cod on November 19. Before disembarking at what they were to call Plymouth Rock, they drew up a charter which they termed the Mayflower Compact. This document established a temporary government based on the principle of the will of the majority; as such it set the stage for the American Revolution and the writing of the Constitution of the United States 150 years thereafter. Little could these first settlers have imagined that by the end of the century nearly 100,000 men, women, and children would have crossed the ocean from England to settle in the Massachusetts wilderness.

In 1630, a second settlement, based on theocratic principles, was founded at Massachusetts Bay by John Winthrop and his

OPPOSITE: On July 4, Bostonians dress up to commemorate their Colonial past.

hard-working, God-fearing Puritans. It was in this spirit that "the good town of Boston" was established — a town which quickly became, as the city remains today, the hub of New England business, cultural, and intellectual life.

THE SEEDS OF REVOLUTION

In subsequent years, British mismanagement of its American possessions created mistrust and anger in the colonies. Nowhere was this more notable than in Massachusetts. A stubborn king and a politically unwise Parliament burdened the colonies with unreasonable taxes. The Acts of Trade required that the colonies trade only with England and its markets. The Tea Act, the Stamp Act, the Townshend Acts, and the Intolerable Acts — all were perceived in the colonies as either oppressive or punitive, and created reactions of increasing defiance. "No taxation without representation" became the rallying cry that carried the colonists to revolution.

By 1775, under the uncompromising leadership of Bostonians like Samuel Adams, James Otis, and John Hancock, Massachusetts had become a catalyst uniting the thirteen colonies. Their speeches provoked protests that eventually exploded into action and bloody revolution. Indeed, "the shot heard 'round the world" and the first battle of the revolution took place on Massachusetts soil.

On April 19, 1775, British soldiers fired on the minutemen, as the patriot soldiers were termed, on the green in Lexington, Massachusetts — the first time mutual hostility became open warfare. Two months later on June 17, the Battle of Bunker Hill was fought, actually not on the hill for which it was named but on nearby Breed's Hill. In this battle, the colonial militia were defeated by British regulars. Nonetheless it fired the fighting spirit of the Continental soldier and the determination of the colonists to sustain the revolution until independence was achieved.

As a consequence of this revolution a new nation was born in 1776, a nation that was to name itself the United States. Its cornerstone was laid in Massachusetts.

OPPOSITE: A replica of the *Mayflower*, the clipper that brought the pilgrims to Plymouth in 1620, is anchored in the Plymouth harbor.

THE MARITIME MERCHANTS

Although Massachusetts experienced some political problems after the Revolution, it survived economically by exploiting the seas. Fishing, whaling, and the China trade made fortunes for daring seafarers and enterprising merchants. Those fortunes stood the state in good stead when the nineteenth century saw a decline in the maritime economy. Fortunes brought home to Boston in the sleek hulls of sailing ships were, during the industrial revolution, wisely invested in new industrial endeavors, notably textile manufacture. Textiles were to become the state's economic backbone as mill towns were quickly built along Massachusetts rivers. By 1850 the city of Lowell was a world leader in textile production.

THE TWENTIETH CENTURY

When, in the early years of the twentieth century, cheap labor in the southern states and abroad began to draw the textile industry away from New England, Massachusetts sought out new sources of income. By mid-century, the state regained economic stability in electronic and related industries — the high-tech revolution.

Since its earliest beginnings, Massachusetts has been the cultural and intellectual center of New England. In politics and government, its statesmen, once pre-eminent in the struggle for independence, became active thereafter in the affairs of the new nation. For more than two hundred years Massachusetts statesmen have continued to exert creative leadership in the nation's subsequent existence, as recently as the Presidency of John F. Kennedy and the Presidential campaigns of Robert Kennedy and Michael Dukakis.

Massachusetts is the home of more institutions of higher learning than any other state in the Union. Among them are two of the world's most prestigious universities — Harvard University and the Massachusetts Institute of Technology (MIT), as well as five of the nation's most academically outstanding colleges — Williams, Amherst, Smith, Mount Holyoke, and Wellesley.

Throughout the years Massachusetts has retained, in some measure, the ethical standards that characterized its beginnings: a capacity for independent thinking, a strong moral sense, a consistent faith in the power of education, a capacity for hard work, and a commitment to frugality.

BOSTON

It is easy to fall in love with Boston. Beautiful and sophisticated, it represents an almost

neighborhoods — elegant Beacon Hill, fashionable Back Bay, and historic North End.

Boston's nearly three million citizens, if one includes the city's outlying suburbs, is half the population of the state. They are a mix of blue bloods and blue collars, of sixth generation "Brahmins" and first generation Irish, the wealthy and the disadvantaged, the gentry and the homeless.

Over the centuries, Boston has provided more than its share of scholars, writers, and statesmen, men and women who have profoundly influenced the life of the nation.

perfect marriage of historic preservation and economic revitalization. The union has created a marvelous skyline of contrasts. Tall skyscrapers and the imposing modern Government Center alternate with the steeple of the Old North Church, the clock tower of the Customs House, and other historic landmarks.

BACKGROUND

The city founded by the Puritans in 1630 is inextricably associated with America's first role as a British colony. It remains proud of its part in the struggle for independence. Narrow streets, much as they were in colonial times, twist and turn haphazardly through famous

Indeed, Boston could be said to combine in its history and people the classic elements of America's heritage and its promise for the future.

Shawmut Peninsula

John Winthrop and his Puritans are said to have "stolen" much of the Shawmut Peninsula from hermit preacher Reverend William Blackstone to establish the city of Boston. The city owed much of its rapid growth to its fine deep water harbor and its fishing and merchant fleet that, by the eighteenth century, was the third largest in the English-speaking world.

Settlers in ever-increasing numbers came to Boston, making it the hub of trade and

28

commerce in the English colonies and the most prosperous city in the English colonial empire. However, when the Crown and Parliament grew greedy and imposed upon the colonies a series of oppressive taxes and trade regulations, Boston led the break from the Mother Country.

Cradle of Independence

Years before the Revolution, the Massachusetts House of Representatives denied the right of Parliament to tax the colonies without representation, and it was Boston's revolutionaries whose speeches at meeting after meeting rallied their compatriots to unite against British oppression.

In March, 1770, one such group gathered outside the Old State House loudly protesting British tax policies. British soldiers fired into the crowd, killing five people. News of the "Boston Massacre" spread through New England, everywhere fanning hotter and hotter the flames of rebellion.

In meetings at Faneuil Hall and the Old Meeting House, Sam Otis and Samuel Adams continued to call for independence. One meeting, in December, 1773, led to the "Boston Tea Party," when about 90 colonists disguised as Indians boarded English ships by night in Boston Harbor and dumped more than three hundred chests of tea into the sea. In retaliation, the English closed the harbor and, in May, 1774, sent troops to occupy the city, forcing Boston's citizens to house the hated British soldiers in their homes.

The festering anger and resentment came to a head on April 18, 1775, when Paul Revere traveled to Lexington on his famous "Midnight Ride" to warn patriot leaders that British troop were on their way to nearby Concord to confiscate arms stored there by colonists. Bloody skirmishes the next day at Lexington Green and later at Concord gave the colonial militia its baptism by fire and marked the beginning of the Revolution.

George Washington, formerly a colonel of the Virginia militia, assumed general command of the Continental forces at Cambridge in July, 1775. He proved to be a brilliant soldier and politician. In less than a year he had wrested Boston from British control. The city continued free for the remaining years of the Revolution and, thereafter, exercised a major role in the affairs of the new nation.

From the time of the Revolution and well into the nineteenth century, Boston's ships sailed the seas of the world reaping great riches. Wealthy merchants transformed Beacon Hill and Back Bay into showplaces, featuring splendid mansions and elegant townhouses. The city became known as the "Athens of America" and the "Boston Brahmin," a symbol of the ultimate in human culture and refinement.

The Immigrant Wave

When, in the middle of the nineteenth century, Boston's maritime eminence began to fade, a manufacturing economy gradually took its place. In the same period, new waves of European immigrants reached the shores of America. Thousands of Polish, Irish, and Italian workers came to Boston, as well as to other New England cities, eager to begin life anew and to find work in this burgeoning industrial economy. With the rapid influx of people of different customs and nationalities, Boston's population tended to become segregated. Enclaves of Irish or Poles or Italians grew up in older neighborhoods while the "proper" Bostonians kept to themselves in their own enclaves on Beacon Hill and Back Bay.

Decline and Revival

By the end of the nineteenth century, Boston and all of Massachusetts lost much of their manufacturing base to southern states, which

OPPOSITE AND ABOVE: Boston's Fourth of July festivities.

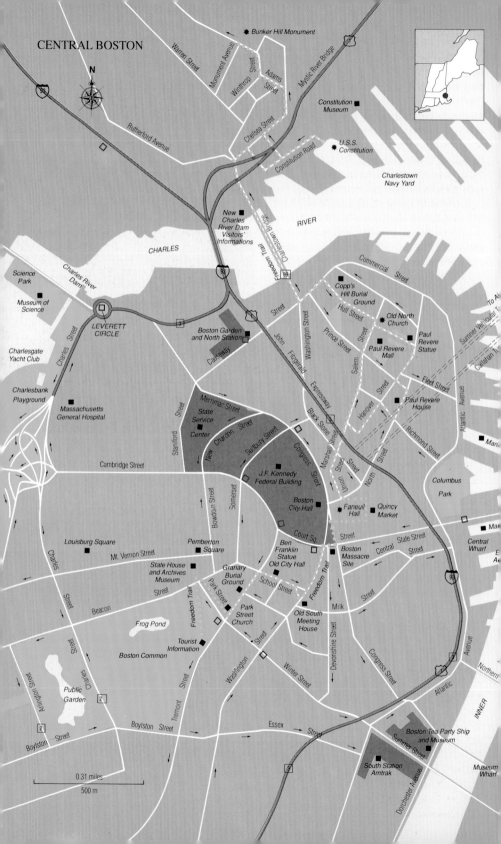

CENTRAL BOSTON

N

✹ Bunker Hill Monument

Warren Street
Monument Avenue
Winthrop Street
Adams Street
Chelsea Street
Mystic River Bridge

Rutherford Avenue

Constitution Road

Constitution Museum

✹ U.S.S. Constitution

Charlestown Navy Yard

RIVER

CHARLES

New Charles River Dam Visitors' Informations

Charlestown Bridge

Freedom Trail

93

Commercial Street

To At

Copp's Hill Burial Ground

✹ Old North Church

Hull Street
Salem Street
Prince Street

Paul Revere Mall

Paul Revere Statue

Fleet Street

Hanover Street

Paul Revere House

Sumner Vehicular T

Callahan Tu

Atlantic Avenue

Richmond Street

Science Park

Charles River Dam

LEVERETT CIRCLE

Museum of Science

Charlesgate Yacht Club

Charlesbank Playground

Charles Street

Massachusetts General Hospital

Cambridge Street

Boston Garden and North Station

Causeway

John Fitzgerald Expressway

Merrimac Street

State Service Center

New Chardon Street

Stanford Street

Sudbury Street

Somerset Street

Bowdoin Street

J.F. Kennedy Federal Building

Boston City Hall

Congress Street

Black Stone Street

Marshall Street

Union Street

North Street

Faneuil Hall

Quincy Market

Columbus Park

Washington Street

Street

Court Sq.

Ben Franklin Statue Old City Hall

Boston Massacre Site

State Street

Central Wharf

Ma

E A

Louisburg Square

Pemberton Square

Mt. Vernon Street

State House and Archives Museum

Beacon Street

Park Street

Freedom Trail

Granary Burial Ground

School Street

Old South Meeting House

Milk Street

Devonshire Street

Congress Street

Central Street

Frog Pond

Park Street Church

Tourist Information

Boston Common

Washington Street

Winter Street

Tremont Street

Public Garden

Arlington Street

Charles Street

Boylston Street

Essex Street

Boylston Street

Atlantic Avenue

Northern

INNER

Boston Tea Party Ship and Museum

Summer Street

South Station Amtrak

Dorchester Avenue

Museum Wharf

0.31 miles

500 m

93

93

93

2

2

3

could offer cheaper labor and lower taxes. The city's decline continued well into the twentieth century. In the 1960's, the area's incredible reserve of "brain power" at Harvard and MIT attracted high technology industries and research and development, which in turn fueled an urban revolution. Under the leadership of MIT-alumnus and architect I. M. Pei, Boston began to regain part of its former splendor. Expansive skyscrapers, government centers, and office complexes mingled with the historic buildings to create a "new" Boston look — one of urban sophistication infused with the charm of an earlier era.

Today Boston is one of America's most livable cities. It remains the financial, commercial, intellectual, and cultural hub of New England. The cobbled streets twist and turn, while an emerald necklace of parks and greenbelts (designed last century by the renowned landscape architect Frederick Law Olmstead) encircles the city. Ethnic neighborhoods break up any tendency toward urban sprawl, with each enclave having its own distinct appeal.

Tourist Information

In advance of your trip the **Greater Boston Convention and Visitors Bureau** (Prudential Plaza, P.O. Box 490, Boston, MA 02199. ☎ (617) 536-4100, telefax (617) 424-7664) will send its free planning guide. After your arrival, you can pick it up at the **Prudential Visitor Center** in the Prudential Center Plaza, open daily from 8:30 am to 5 pm, or at the **Boston Commons Visitor Information Center** at Tremont and Winter Streets, also open daily, from 8 am to 5 pm. In the downtown historic center, the National Park Service, which manages the Freedom Trail, keeps its Visitor Center at 15 State Street open from 9 am to 5 pm.

Touring Boston

The Freedom Trail

Boston is a city to be explored on foot and the **Freedom Trail**, a three-mile (five-kilometer) walking tour has been laid out by the National Park Service. It winds through the city and across the river into Charlestown, passing along its route 16 major historic sites and buildings related to the Revolu-

tionary era. It also goes through the varied neighborhoods that characterize the city: the Italian North End, the "Old Boston" section of Beacon Hill, and the Irish community in Charlestown. Do not worry about getting lost; signposts and a red line painted on the sidewalk point you in the right direction. It takes about half a day to see all the sights if you are in a hurry; allow an entire day for a leisurely stroll.

To start your Freedom Trail tour, go to the information kiosk on the Boston Common off Tremont Street. This is an area with souvenir

vendors hawking Boston memorabilia and food carts offering hot-dogs, ice-cream, and sweets. Inside the kiosk you can pick up a map of the Trail, along with information about the city's other attractions.

Now follow the red line into the **Boston Common**. This handsome, 45-acre (18-hectare), city green was purchased for $150 by the Puritan city fathers in 1634 as a militia "trayning field" and for the "feeding of Cattell." Under law, the Common can still be used for these purposes.

The Common has always been the pride of the city, even though in the beginning it was used for public hangings and punishments. In fact, the Puritans had a pillory built here to make an example of transgressors; the first to be pilloried was the carpenter who built it, who was accused of charging too much money for his work.

During the Battle of Bunker Hill, the British used the Common as an encampment and

Swan boats for rent at the pond in Boston Commons.

embarked for Charlestown from its grounds. Today, the Common is filled with hilly knolls and winding paths, statues and gurgling fountains. Noontime office workers often stroll through the park to enjoy the open space; in summer, outdoor concerts are held here. Sadly, however, like most urban open spaces in the United States, the Common is decidedly less appealing at night; even in daytime panhandlers and drunks are a common sight, and one should, needless to say, be on guard against pickpockets.

teenth-century granary that used to stand here. Established in 1660, it contains the graves of several notable Americans, including John Hancock, who signed the Declaration of Independence; the Revolutionary leader and orator Samuel Adams; the revolutionary Paul Revere; Peter Faneuil, who gave the city Faneuil Hall; and the victims of the Boston Massacre. Also interred here is Mary ("Mother") Goose, who concocted nursery rhymes to entertain her grandchildren.

Farther along the Trail at Tremont and School Streets is **King's Chapel**, completed

You can follow the Trail across Beacon Street to the "new" **State House**, designed by Charles Bulfinch and completed in 1795 on land that originally belonged to John Hancock. Its golden dome gleams like the harbor beacon that once topped this hill, and gave the neighborhood its name. The archives here contain valuable historic documents, including the original Charter of the Massachusetts Bay Colony.

Across the street from the Common is the lovely **Park Street Church**, its tall steeple a familiar Boston landmark since it was built in 1809. Abolitionist William Lloyd Garrison gave his first anti-slavery speech here in 1829.

Next to the church is the **Old Granary Burying Ground**, so-named for the seven-

in 1754; it was the first Anglican church in New England. In pre-Revolutionary times, the church was graced with gifts of silver and vestments from Queen Anne and King George III. The old cemetery next to the church contains the graves of John Winthrop, the first Puritan governor of the colony, and Elizabeth Pain, a seventeenth-century woman accused of adultery and said to have inspired Nathaniel Hawthorne to write his classic novel, *The Scarlet Letter*. Also on School Street is the statue of **Benjamin Franklin**, the first portrait statue erected in Boston, and the **Old Corner Bookstore**, a red brick house dating to 1712 that was the center of literary Boston in the nineteenth century. Noted authors, including Hawthorne,

Longfellow, and Emerson, gathered here to discuss their craft.

The **Old South Meeting House**, built in 1729, was the largest building in colonial Boston. It frequently hosted town meetings, especially in the years leading to the Revolution, when men such as Samuel Adams and John Hancock rallied the townspeople against the British. One of those meetings (held December 16, 1773), called to discuss the new British tea tax, led to the famous Boston Tea Party.

The **Old State House**, at Washington, Court, and State Streets, is located in the heart of downtown Boston, overshadowed by the towering steel and glass behemoth of **Government Center**. Built in 1713, it was the seat of colonial government and public life. In 1761, James Otis railed against unfair British regulations, prompting John Adams later to write, "then and there, the child Independence was born." And on July 18, 1776, from the east balcony, the Declaration of Independence was first proclaimed to the citizens of Boston.

A circle of cobblestones in the street just outside the Old State House marks the site of the **Boston Massacre**. Paul Revere's famed engraving helped to make the Massacre a key event in the growing popular resistance to British rule.

Follow the red line into **Dock Square**, with its boutiques, food-stands, markets, and bricked plaza. Also located here are **Faneuil Hall** and the **Quincy Markets**.

It is ironic that the Hall known as the "Cradle of Liberty" — because its second-floor meeting house hosted several important (and vociferous) protests against British colonial policies — was donated to the city in 1742 by Dutch slave trader Peter Faneuil.

The first floor of the Hall has always been a market; however, stalls that once offered fresh meat, vegetables, and dairy products to colonial Bostonians have been transformed into modern boutique stands and food booths catering to tourists.

Note the grasshopper weather-vane atop the hall dome; for over two centuries it has been the symbol of Faneuil Hall. Fashioned in 1742 and a fine example of colonial artistry, it was inspired by similar weather vanes on the Royal Exchange building in London

and is the only part of the original Faneuil Hall which remains totally unmodified.

The Trail passes next through riotous **Haymarket Square**, a sprawling open-air food market with booths offering everything from fresh meats to hand-polished fruits and vegetables. Use the pedestrian underpass to cross Fitzgerald Expressway. This brings you to the **North End**, Boston's famed Italian neighborhood.

The North End, not Back Bay, is the city's oldest neighborhood. In fact, until the nineteenth century, this section of

narrow, twisting streets was about all there was to Boston. When landfill and reclamation projects created new city dwellings, wealthy Boston families moved out of the crowded North End, and waves of immigrants moved in.

Today, it is a colorful area with its streetside restaurants featuring noontime plates of homemade pasta, sausage, and pizza. It also contains two of the most revered historic shrines along the Freedom Trail.

If **Paul Revere** were alive today, he would still have a **home** in Boston. That home, in North Square, is where the Revere family

Faneuil Hall OPPOSITE and Paul Revere's House ABOVE are preserved as memorials to America's fight for independence.

lived from 1770 to 1800. The clapboard building was built in 1680 by a wealthy merchant on the site of Puritan minister Increase Mather's home, which was destroyed by fire in 1676. In its time a fashionable townhouse, it is today the oldest wooden house in Boston.

While living here, Revere produced his famous Boston Massacre engraving, took part in the Boston Tea Party, secretly carried important revolutionary dispatches to Philadelphia, and participated in numerous other radical causes.

On April 18, 1775, Revere left his house, slipped out of the city in a rowboat, borrowed a horse in Charlestown, and rode to Lexington to warn revolutionaries there that the British were marching from Boston to seize munitions hidden in Concord.

The interior of the house has been restored, and many Revere artifacts — including some of his exquisite silversmith work, his old rocking chair, and saddlebags — are displayed.

"One if by land and two if by sea" is a phrase familiar to all American schoolchildren. It was the signal to be given from the **Old North Church** (at the foot of Hull Street near the end of Paul Revere Mall) to warn revolutionaries of a British invasion aimed at Lexington and Concord. In April 1775, a church sexton hung two lanterns from the steeple's highest windows to indicate British troop movements.

The 190-ft (58-m) white steeple has been a city landmark since the church — the oldest in Boston — was built in 1723. Inside the church, pew 54 once belonged to Paul Revere's son,

and was occupied several times by Revere himself. The church bells were cast in Gloucester, England, the first made for Britain's North American empire; they sound now only on Sunday mornings before services.

Up Hull Street is **Copp's Hill Burying Ground**. The earliest graves here date from 1660 and include those of Increase, Cotton, and Samuel Mather, important figures in early Boston history. One of the more interesting graves is that of the revolutionary Daniel Malcolm, who defiantly requested that "he be buried 10 feet deep, safe from British Musket Balls." He got his wish, but six years later, British soldiers got the last laugh when they used his tombstone for target practice. Even today you can see the marks on the stone.

Copp's Hill was also the site of a British cannon, which was trained on Bunker Hill across the Charles River during the battle. You can see the same view of Bunker Hill that British General Burgoyne had when he directed cannon fire at the entrenched revolutionaries.

Here you cross the Charlestown Bridge, and then either walk up Monument Avenue to Bunker Hill, or keep to the waterfront along Constitution Avenue to visit the SS *Constitution*, the Navy's oldest fighting ship.

A 221-ft (67-m) white granite obelisk stands as a memorial to the men who fought at the Battle of Bunker Hill. The **Bunker Hill monument** is actually on Breed's Hill, where the misnamed clash took place on June 17, 1775. About 1,200 Americans and 3,000 British troops took part in the battle. The first English attack failed, and British troops twice required reinforcements.

The revolutionaries eventually were forced to withdraw; colonial General Prescott ordered a retreat only after all ammunition had been used. The toll: for the Americans, 140 killed, 271 wounded, 30 captured; for the British, 226 killed, 828 wounded.

Even though the revolutionaries were defeated, the Battle of Bunker Hill proved to the revolutionaries that they measured up well in battle against the British regulars. Said General Washington of the clash: "I am content. The liberties of the country are safe."

The monument's observation tower offers a panoramic view of Boston, the harbor, its islands, and the *SS Constitution*; its spiral staircase has 294 steps leading to the top, with no elevator. An excellent audiovisual presentation explaining the battle in detail, as well as the events leading up to it, can be seen at the **Bunker Hill Pavilion** on Hoosac Pier, just off Constitution Avenue.

Along the harbor front is the **Charlestown Navy Yard**, one of the first naval shipyards in the nation, and the last stop on the Freedom Trail.

A tour of the yard's exhibits spans nearly 200 years of maritime history. At the Visitor Information Center, you can view a 10-minute slide show, and receive information on guided walking tours.

Beginning in 1800, the yard built, serviced, and supplied ships for the Navy. Workers swarmed over the dry docks, rope walks, and shipways cluttered with maritime equipment. The yard reached peak operation during World War II, when it employed more than 50,000 men and women who built and repaired a record number of vessels. You can tour the *SS Cassin Young*, a destroyer of the type built here, which saw extensive action in that war.

Attractions include Pier 1 (one of the 11 original wharves that serviced ships), the 1833 dry dock (one of the first of its kind in the country), the Maritime Society Museum, and the Commandant's House.

But the centerpiece of the yard is the magnificent *SS Constitution*, the oldest commissioned warship in the Navy. ((617) 426-1812; admission free; open daily from 9:30 am to 3:30 pm. The foundations of the U.S. Navy were established by Congress in 1794 upon authorization of six new frigates. One of these was the *SS Constitution*, a 44-gun warship built at the nearby Hartt's Shipyard and launched in 1797.

She sailed against the Barbary pirates, fought the British in the war of 1812, and engaged in 40 sea battles without a loss. When a British sailor saw shots bounce off the *SS Constitution*'s planking, he shouted, "Her sides are made of iron!" Thus the ship gained its renowned nickname, "Old Ironsides."

The *SS Constitution* is still a commissioned warship; members of its present crew take visitors on tours of the spar deck with its huge cannons that fire 32 lb (15 kg) shells, the gun deck with its 30 24-lb (11-kg)-long guns, the captain's quarters below decks, and the berthing deck where the crew slept in hammocks. At the rear is the ship's wheel, which required the strength of four men to control. Sailors also climbed the ropes to the "fighting tops" positioned on each mast to fire on enemy ships.

Beacon Hill

The Beacon Hill neighborhood, with its narrow gas-lit streets, elegant townhouses and tall shade trees, is like a city-within-a-city

with turn-of-the-century splendor. This has not always been the case. In the late seventeeth-century, the Trimount neighborhood (Beacon Hill's old name) was a wild no-man's land referred to by some Bostonians as Mt Whoredom. But when the State House was built here in 1798, many of the city's wealthiest families rushed to commission State House architect Charles Bulfinch to design Federal mansions and elegant bow-fronted Greek Revival row houses. Beacon Hill had arrived, and it remains one of the most desirable districts in which to live.

OPPOSITE AND ABOVE: Clapboard and red-brick houses, typical of Boston's Colonial architecture, are much admired for their style.

Today, a walk along the bumpy side-walks of Beacon Hill is reminiscent of a more elegant, peaceful era. It is a splendid oasis of fine period architecture and tranquil surroundings yet within a stone's throw of busy downtown Boston.

Start your tour at the Common on **Beacon Street**. Numbers 39 and 40 are Bulfinch-designed twin mansions that house the Women's City Club of Boston; guided tours of the homes' elegant Greek Revival interiors are by appointment only. Also note the Beacon Hill "purple glass" in the windows, caused when sunlight reacted with impurities in the imported English glass, turning it a distinctive purple color.

Go north on Spruce, past old servants' houses, to **Mount Vernon Street**. This is

arguably the most beautiful street on "the Hill," as locals now call it. The **Nichols House Museum**, another 1804 Bulfinch design, is typical of Beacon Hill's architecture from its golden era. It is one of the few private homes on the Hill open to visitors, and is lavishly furnished in period decor.

Just off Mt Vernon is **Louisburg Square**. Its ornate homes frame the elegant green, creating the ultimate in traditional Boston-style charm; a home in this idyllic enclave remains the dream of many Bostonians. Louisa May Alcott, author of *Little Women*, lived here, as did novelist William Dean Howells. One of Howells' books, *The Rise of Silas Lapham*, relates the life of Boston's wealthy in the mid-nineteen hundreds.

Christmas is a great time to visit Beacon Hill, when strolling carolers are a holiday tradition. With its nineteenth-century ambience, you almost expect Whittier or Longfellow to pop up on the green.

Other Beacon Hill streets of interest to visitors are narrow, cobblestoned **Acorn Street** and, for its coffee houses, galleries, and chic shops, **Charles Street**.

If you prefer a guided tour to simply wandering around, Boston By Foot, ((617) 367-2345, offers one-and-a-half hour walking tours of the Hill, as well as walks along the Freedom Trail and through historic Copley Square.

Back Bay and Copley Square

Back Bay's wide Commonwealth Avenue is fashioned after the grand boulevards of

Paris, while the streets are lined with beautiful Victorian brownstone row houses. Since the 1870's, a Back Bay address has been a coveted status symbol.

Copley Square is the heart of Back Bay, and displays some of Boston's best nineteenth- and twentieth-century architecture.

The 1877 **Trinity Church**, designed by Henry Hobson Richardson, is a magnificent Romanesque design some consider the best church architecture in America. Inspired by the great cathedrals of France and Spain, it is massive in scale. Inside, the intricate details include rich wall murals, carvings, and friezes.

Across Dartmouth Street is the **Boston Public Library**, the world's oldest free library. The Library, with its collection of six million books, is approached through an elegant central courtyard with a fountain and a spectacular entry fashioned after a Greek temple and graced with a grand Siena marble staircase. The library is enriched by murals, bronzes, and paintings by some of the world's most renowned artists and is a tranquil retreat from the bustle of Boston.

Cross St James Avenue to reach the **John Hancock Tower**, a striking, glass-covered 60-story skyscraper designed by I. M. Pei. New England's tallest building, it is the corporate headquarters of the John Hancock Mutual Life Insurance Company. It often acts as a giant mirror, reflecting the Back Bay cityscape in its tall glass walls. It has long been plagued by the not insignificant problem of its glass sheets falling off; this however, seems to have recently been remedied.

One of the best ways to see Boston is from the Tower's 60th-floor **observatory**. High-speed elevators carry visitors the 740 ft (226 m) from the street to the observatory in about 30 seconds, from where they can see a panorama embracing the gold-domed State House, the gracious townhouses of Beacon Hill, Boston Harbor's islands, Cambridge, the North and South shores, and the distant White Mountains of southern New Hampshire. Observatory exhibits include "Boston 1775," a light and

During the summer, Bostonians are drawn to the city's many parks and pedestrian walkways.

Eastern Massachusetts, Boston and Cape to Cod

sound show about Revolutionary Boston. ☎ (617) 247-1976.

Down Stuart Street is **Copley Place**, a $500 million shopping and eating emporium. Along Huntington Avenue are the 22-acre (nine-hectare) grounds of the **Christian Science Center** (the 1894 Mother Church here has a square-shaped bell tower) and the offices of the *Christian Science Monitor*, the highly respected national daily newspaper.

Backtrack to reach the **Prudential Center**, another corporate insurance headquarters skyscraper with its own 50th-floor Skywalk, an observation tower from which 360-degree views of the city with accompanying historical commentary can be enjoyed. Sunset is the best time to visit.

Government Center

Rising in the middle of the city like a fortress of brick, steel, and glass is Government Center, an urban renewal program designed by I. M. Pei that transformed 60 acres (24 hectares) of tattoo parlors and girlie stores which only a decade ago dominated the squalid Scollay Square district, into some of the most imposing buildings in Boston, and created a new focus for the city. The district's centerpiece is the new **City Hall**, designed by Kallman, McKinell, and Knowles. It is a massive inverted pyramid resting on a plaza of brick resembling "an Aztec temple on a brick desert."

Surrounding the Hall are several modern buildings that add to the district's futuristic feel: the tall twin towers of the **John F. Kennedy Office Building**, the **Center Plaza Building** with its contours that curve to the slope of Beacon Hill, and the **State Service Center**, whose sharp architectural lines cut the horizon northwest of the Hall.

In fact, the only historic nineteenth-century building that survived Government Center's transformation is the **Sears Crescent**, notable for the huge 200-gallon (909-liter) steaming tea pot that hangs from one corner of the building to mark the site of what was the largest tea store in Boston.

The district's display of modern architecture is on a grand scale and its huge open spaces a welcoming oasis from the crowded city neighborhoods.

The Harborwalk

Harborwalk is a two-mile (3.2-km) trail that loops around Boston's historic waterfront, providing a bird's-eye view of the wharfs, boats, and islands. It begins at the National Park Service Visitor Center (on State Street near the Old State House) and ends at the Boston Tea Party Ship and Museum. Along the way are some interesting historic and commercial buildings, as well as sights and sounds of maritime Boston. Highlights include:

The **Boston Children's Museum** (300 Congress Street; ☎ (617) 426-8855; admission $6.00 with reductions for children and senior citizens; open every day but Monday, 10 am to 5 pm, Friday until 9 pm), on Museum Wharf across the Fort Point Channel, has been called "the country's best museum for kids." Its varied displays, exhibits, and special events are guaranteed to entertain children of all ages. Toddlers jump over steps and slide down platforms in Playspace; older kids climb like monkeys from platform to platform within a futuristic sculpture; and teens can even try out the latest dance steps at the Clubhouse. There are replicas of an Indian wigwam, a country street, a two-story Japanese house, and a television studio equipped with TV monitors.

The **New England Aquarium** (Central Wharf, off Atlantic Avenue; ☎ (617) 742-8870; admission $7.00 with reductions for children and senior citizens; open Monday, Wednesday, and Friday, 9 am to 5 pm) contains a four-story ocean coral reef glass tank filled with sharks, turtles, and more than 600 other sea creatures. Dolphin and sea lion shows are offered daily on the *Discovery*. One of its newest exhibits, "Wired for Sound," demonstrates just how noisy the underwater world can be. From here you can board whale-watching cruises on the wharf, which head to Stellwagen Bank, one of the East Coast's prime whale habitats.

The **Computer Museum** (Museum Wharf; ☎ (617) 423-6758; admission $5.00 with reductions for children, students, and senior citizens; open every day but Monday, 10 am to 5 pm, Friday until 9 pm) features state-of-the-art computer technology

OPPOSITE: Boston's high-tech Computer Museum captivates visitors of all ages.

in interactive displays. You can play games, create art, write music — in fact almost anything is possible here, including a computer that not only talks, but can carry on a "conversation."

Another pleasant option is the **Boston Tea Party Ship and Museum** (near South Station at Congress Street Bridge; ((617) 338-1773; admission $5.00 with reductions for children, students, and seniors; open daily 9 am to dusk). It is a full-scale replica of the British brigantine *Beaver*, and costumed guides relate the history of the 1773 Boston

Tea Party. Museum artifacts include a tea chest reputed to be among those tossed into the water on that fateful night.

CULTURAL ATTRACTIONS

Museums

The best known of Boston's museums is the **Museum of Fine Arts** (465 Huntington Avenue; ((617) 267-9300; admission $6.00 adults, $5.00 seniors, free to children under 16, free to all on Saturday 10 am to 2 pm; open Tuesday to Saturday, 10 am to 5 pm, Wednesday 10 am to 10 pm). It was originally beneficiary of artifacts gathered by Boston's wealthy Brahmins as they traveled the world in the nineteenth century; those objects still form the centerpieces of its varied collections.

It is today considered one of the world's great museums. The handsome 1909 Greek temple-style building contains more than 200 galleries. The Oriental collection is one

of the most remarkable in the country, with Buddhist paintings and sculptures, some dating to the twelfth century, dominating the Japanese displays; ceramics, including objects from the Han dynasty (third century), highlight the Chinese section.

The Egyptian artifacts are largely the bounty of a 40-year Middle East expedition sponsored by the Museum and Harvard University. It is reputed to be the finest collection of 4,000-year-old antiquities outside Cairo.

The European galleries display a large selection of Monets; in the American collection are Gilbert Stuart's portraits of George and Martha Washington. Twentieth-century art is displayed in the museum's new glass-roofed wing.

Just a short walk away is the **Isabella Stewart Gardner Museum** (The Fenway; ((617) 566-1401; admission $5.00 with reductions for children, students, and seniors; open Wednesday to Sunday, noon to 5 pm, Tuesday noon to 6:30 pm), a Venetian-style palazzo which houses the personal collections of the eccentric nineteenth-century millionairess. Isabella Stewart Gardner commissioned agents to travel the world in search of fine art, and they purchased six million dollars worth which included Matisses, Whistlers and Titian's *Rape of Europa*, painted for Phillip II of Spain. Other treasures include beautiful tapestries, centuries-old mosaics, and sculpture. Its courtyard, with Venetian-style windows and balconies, flowering plants and trees framing a Roman floor mosaic from Livia that dates to the second century, is a delight.

The **John F. Kennedy Library and Museum** (Columbia Point, off Morrissey Boulevard; ((617) 929-4523; admission $3.50 for adults, $2.00 for seniors, free under 16; open daily from 9 am to 5 pm) is another of architect I. M. Pei's designs and some consider the sleek concrete and glass structure to be one of his best.

Nine exhibit halls, filled with family and presidential memorabilia encircle a central room containing the president's desk as it was on November 22, 1963 when he was assassinated during a motorcade ride through the streets of Dallas. A 35-minute film chronicles his life and times. Other displays feature artifacts from his PT-109 days and the

---

ABOVE: In downtown Boston, American history is at your fingertips. OPPOSITE: The John Fitzgerald Kennedy Library and Museum.

Cuban missile crisis. An eight-story gray glass contemplation pavilion contains only an American flag, a bench, and a Kennedy quotation engraved on the wall.

Another **Kennedy** museum is his **birthplace** in suburban Brookline, Z (617) 566-7937. The house has been restored to the way it looked in 1917, the year Kennedy was born, and offers audio guided tours narrated by his mother, Rose Kennedy.

The **Museum of Science** and the **Charles Hayden Planetarium** (Science Park, along the Charles River; ((617) 723-2500; admission $6.00 with reductions for children and seniors; open Tuesday to Sunday, 9 am to 5 pm, Friday 9 am to 9 pm) are hands-on delights, and feature a life-sized model of an Apollo space capsule, a 20-ft (six-meter) plastic tyrannosaurus rex, and a "lightning-making" machine.

Finally, **Fenway Park** is also a museum of sorts. Located just off Brookline Avenue, in Back Bay, it is home to the Boston Red Sox, the city's major league baseball team. Fenway is also one of the oldest, most charming, and intimate of baseball stadiums, which brings the fans so close to the action that they can almost reach out and touch the players.

Music

The world-famous **Boston Symphony Orchestra** performs in **Symphony Hall** (Massachusetts Avenue; ((617) 266-1492); and the **Boston Pops** performs outdoors at the **Hatch Memorial Shell** on the Charles River Esplanade during the summer, as does the **Boston Ballet Company**. Theaters and performing arts centers are found throughout the city.

SHOPPING

If you were born to shop, get your credit cards ready, because Boston has it all. **Back Bay** is one of the leading shopping districts; its **Newbury Street** is the city's equivalent to New York's Fifth Avenue with its ultrachic boutiques, clothiers, and galleries. Alan Bilzerian, Divino, Daree, Martini Carl, Settebello, and Parachute offer the latest fashions from designers such as Gianni Versace, Kendo, and Armani. Also down the street is Burberry's, makers of the renowned British

trench coat that helps to keep Bostonians warm during their often-bitter winters.

Copley Place, a new $500 million shopping and dining palace, showcases the international fashions of Gucci, Louis Vuitton, Jaegar, and plenty of others. New England's only Neiman-Marcus department store offers a Texas-sized selection of high-quality merchandise. And if you are in the mood for something gold, try Tiffany's. Just down the block is the **Prudential Center**, for Saks Fifth Avenue and Lord and Taylor.

Downtown Crossing is unquestionably the city's most popular shopping area for all walks of Boston society. Jordan Marsh, the venerable 135-year-old Boston department store, offers designer-label clothing for both men and women, not to mention a fine selection of silver and china.

Then there is **Filene's**, a sophisticated fashion emporium whose basement sales are a Boston tradition. All sorts of designer items are sold here at bargain-basement prices, with prices further slashed at regular intervals until the remaining merchandise is sold or finally donated to charity.

Beacon Hill's Charles Street is the neighborhood's commercial center. Its many art galleries, antique stores and coffee houses make it an interesting place for browsing.

Finally, **Bloomingdales**, of New York City fame, is located in nearby Newton, Massachusetts, just west of Boston.

WHERE TO STAY

As in most major American cities, Boston hotels tend to be expensive and many cost over $150 for a double. However, Boston does offer value for the price. By shopping around you can frequently book a weekend package that includes a room on Friday and Saturday night for about two thirds the weekday rate. These offer vary with the season, but don't hesitate to ask about weekend rates when you call for reservations. You can find yourself in Boston without a room if the Red Sox are playing or during graduation time at the numerous colleges in and around the city.

OPPOSITE TOP: Boston's Red Sox baseball team has an avid local following. OPPOSITE BOTTOM: Food stands and boutiques line Quincy Markets.

Super Luxury Hotels

For elegant old-style Boston hospitality, one cannot beat the **Copley Plaza Hotel** (138 St James Avenue; Z (617) 267-5300, toll-free (800) 225-7654; 394 rooms), the **Ritz-Carlton** (Arlington and Newbury Street; Z (617) 536-5700, toll-free (800) 241-3333; 287 rooms), and the Omni Parker House (60 School Street; Z (617) 227-8600, toll-free (800) 843-6664; 541 rooms). These are "luxury" hotels with double room rates in excess of $150.

A very classy luxury hotel, decorated with murals by N.C. Wyeth (the father of Andrew), is the **Meridien** (250 Franklin Street; ((617) 451-1900, toll-free (800) 223-9918; 326 rooms), now owned by Air France. Another superb hotel is the new **Four Seasons** (200 Boylston Street; ((617) 338-4400, toll-free (800) 268-6282; 228 rooms).

In this same category is the European-style **Bostonian Hotel** (Faneuil Hall Marketplace, Dick Square; ((617) 523-3600, toll-free (800) 343-0922; 153 rooms) which is centrally located near Faneuil Hall, Government Center, and the open market; children under 12 stay free. Toward the waterfront is the ultra-modern **Boston Marriott Hotel at Long Wharf** (296 State Street; ((617) 227-0800, toll-free (800) 228-9290; 400 rooms).

Expensive

More moderately priced, but still on the high end of expensive, are **Back Bay Hilton Hotel** (40 Dalton Street; ((617) 236-1100; 367 rooms); **The Westin Hotel at Copley Place** (10 Huntington Avenue; ((617) 262-9600, toll-free (800) 228-3000; 804 rooms) and **Lafayette Swissotel** (1 Avenue de Lafayette; ((617) 451-2600, toll-free (800) 992-0124; 500 rooms).

Located near the Prudential Center is **The Lenox Hotel** (710 Boylston Street; ((617) 536-5300, toll-free (800) 225-7676; 225 rooms).

If you are attracted to large-scale hotels, there is the **Marriott at Copley Place** (110 Huntington Avenue; ((617) 236-5800; 1,147 rooms).

The **Holiday Inn — Government Center** (2 Blossom Street; ((617) 742-7630, toll-free (800) 238-8000; 304 rooms) is attractive for families as children under 18 stay free.

Moderate

Howard Johnson's operates three establishments in the city that are among the best of the moderately priced hotels: **Howard Johnson's Motor Lodge** (Andrew Square; ((617) 288-3030, toll free (800) 654-2000; 180 rooms); **Howard Johnson Lodge Fenway** (1271 Boylston Street; ((617) 267-8300, toll-free (800) 654-2000; 94 rooms); and **Howard Johnson's Hotel Kenmore Square** (575 Commonwealth Avenue; ((617) 267-3100, toll-free (800) 654-2000; 179 rooms).

If you are flying out early in the morning

or arriving late at night, the **Ramada Inn — Boston Airport** (225 McClellan Highway; ((617) 569-5250; 209 rooms), is a good standby.

Inexpensive

Finding an inexpensive hotel in Boston is not an easy task. In fact, I hesitate to suggest any. However, there is an alternative — a bed-and-breakfast. A double room will cost between $45 and $90. You can book a bed-and-breakfast through the **Bed and Breakfast Associates Bay Colony, Inc.** (P.O. Box 57166, Babson Park Branch, Boston, MA 02157; ((617) 449-5302; telefax: (617) 449-5958).

OPPOSITE: Sightseeing buses tour elegant downtown Boston. ABOVE: Downtown dining out of doors.

EATING OUT

In Boston you can find a bit of everything when it comes to cuisine, but no one should visit New England without tasting its seafood specialties — creamy clam chowder, fresh lobster, fish chowder, fried or steamed clams, and fried cod. These are served at several of the moderately priced restaurants listed below. Reservations are advised for evening meals at all restaurants.

It may come as a disappointment, but you will be hard-pressed to find the famous Boston baked beans in a restaurant. Once the staple of the New Englander's diet, this wholesome, tasty dish is now considered low-brow and uncouth. Also sadly absent from the menus is the traditional New England boiled dinner — a joint of ham boiled for hours with cabbage, carrots, onions, turnips, and potatoes.

Expensive

Most of the top-of-the-line restaurants in Boston specialize in European fare except for the **Hampshire House** (84 Beacon Street;

((617) 227-9600). It was known for its fine cuisine long before its Bull & Finch Pub, which inspired the television series, *Cheers*, thrust it into the national spotlight. Here you can dine on New England clam chowder and lobster, or steaks and chicken prepared with a French or Italian twist.

For French cuisine, Boston has several restaurants from which you can choose. **Another Season** on Beacon Hill (97 Mount Vernon Street; ((617) 367-0880) has a weekday (Monday to Thursday) fixed price, four-course menu that is moderately priced. Downtown at **Maison Robert** (45 School Street), weather permitting, one can lunch or dine outside. Here you can order New England food, such as a New England lobster in champagne sauce. **Aujourd'hui** in the Four Seasons Hotel (200 Boylston Street; ((617) 338-4400) and **Le Marquis de Lafayette** in the Lafayette Hotel (1 Avenue de Lafayette; ((617) 451-2600) also serve French-style meals.

For a change of pace, **Cafe Budapest** in the Copley Square Hotel (47 Huntington Avenue; ((617) 266-1979) serves, as its name suggests, Hungarian meals. **Jasper** (240 Commercial Street; ((617) 523-1126) prepares superb Continental meals in an elegant ambiance.

Moderate

Along the waterfront are the best seafood restaurants. Recommended are **Anthony's Pier Four Restaurant** (140 Northern Avenue; ((617) 423-6363), and **Jimmy's Harborside Restaurant** (242 Northern Avenue; ((617) 423-1000). Nearby is the **Ye Olde Union House** (41 Union Street; ((617) 227-2750).

Famous for its "fresh" lobster stew is **Durgin Park Market Dining Room** (340 Faneuil Hall Marketplace), which also claims to have been established "before you were born." As no reservations are accepted here, it is wise to arrive early on weekends.

In Boston, you can also find excellent Italian restaurants. **Cricket's** (Faneuil Hall Marketplace; ((617) 720-5570) and **Davio's Ristorante and Cafe** (269 Newbury Street; ((617) 262-4810) are highly recommended.

For good food served with elegance at a reasonable price, there is the **Cafe Plaza** in the Plaza Hotel (138 St James Avenue; ((617) 267-5300).

ABOVE: Street chess challenger in Cambridge. OPPOSITE: The Colonial buildings of Harvard University dominate Cambridge.

Inexpensive

Like its hotels, Boston's restaurants are pricey. However, many of the above establishments serve a lower price luncheon menu, and the thrifty traveler, who wants to sample the "high life" of Boston, would do well to eat a late lunch and a light dinner.

For lighter meals, Boston abounds with establishments serving Italian sandwiches and pizzas. The Italian sandwich, originally a long hard roll filled with salami, tomato, lettuce, onions, black olives, and topped

Massachusetts Institute of Technology

MIT, situated along the Charles River just off the bridge, is world-famous for its research in science and engineering, and for the Nobel laureates among its numbers. Tours of the campus are offered daily. Two of the most interesting buildings are the triangular-roofed Kresge Auditorium and the moated **MIT Chapel**, both designed by Eero Saarinen.

with olive oil, now comes in a wide variety of fillings. Some have even become so "yuppie" as to include bean sprouts. An Italian sandwich is a meal in a bun. Along the same line are meatball and Italian sausage sandwiches, which are filling and tasty.

CAMBRIDGE

Cross the Harvard Bridge from Boston and you will enter Cambridge, a small and unassuming industrial city that is home to two of the world's greatest institutions of higher learning: the Massachusetts Institute of Technology and Harvard University.

Harvard

Continue down Massachusetts Avenue and you will head directly into **Harvard Yard**. This is the heart of **Harvard University**, the oldest college in the United States, established in 1636 to train young men for the ministry. Six American presidents graduated from Harvard and its alumni include countless statesmen and renowned thinkers in every field and from every corner of the world.

The Harvard Information Center (1350 Massachusetts Avenue; ((617) 495-1573) provides maps and materials outlining the campus highlights; guided tours are offered from June through September.

Harvard itself, with more than 400 buildings, resembles a small village rather than a typical campus. **Massachusetts Hall** is the oldest building on campus, dating to 1720; its handsome red brick walls adorned with ivy provided the architectural inspiration for other buildings on the grounds. During the Revolution, the Hall headquartered colonial troops.

Nearby are **Harvard Hall** (1776) and the very English Holden Chapel (1744), complete with its own coat of arms. But **University Hall**, a white granite building completed in 1815 from a Charles Bulfinch design, is one of the most striking structures

on campus. In front of the building is Daniel Chester French's statue of university namesake John Harvard, a seventeenth-century minister who willed a large sum of money to the fledgling college. (The model for the work was not actually Harvard at all, but rather a nineteenth-century student whom Chester thought fit the ideal of what John Harvard should have looked like.)

The many-columned **Widener Memorial Library**, containing more than 10 million volumes in its collections, is an imposing building.

Do not overlook Harvard's fine museums. Van Goghs, Renoirs, and Picassos can be found at the **Fogg Art Museum**; in the **Sackler Museum**, just across the street from the Fogg, are one of the finest collections of Chinese jade in the world; and German Expressionists dominate at the **Busch-Reisinger Museum**.

Other interesting displays include the **Peabody Museum of Archaeology and**

Phoning home from Harvard Square.

Ethnology (North American Indians, with relics from Lewis and Clark's 1803 explorations), and the **Botanical Garden's** German glass-blown flowers, depicting nearly 800 different species of flowering plants. However, the **Museum of Comparative Zoology** has the most fascinating collections, including a 225-million-year-old egg, a six-million-year-old turtle shell, the 25,000-year-old Harvard Mastodon (found in New Jersey), a 180-million-year-old dinosaur, and a genuine giant sea monster.

For a break from touring, head to **Harvard Square**, with its fine selection of coffee houses and bookstores. Don't leave Cambridge without a brief walk through its historic district. The handsome **Common** was the encampment site for George Washington's colonial army for nearly a year. **Brattle Street** is notable for "Tory Row," named for homes built by wealthy British sympathizers during the Revolution. (Most of the houses date back to the nineteenth century.) Also on Brattle is the house of Maine poet Henry Wadsworth Longfellow, who lived here for nearly 50 years. The 1759 structure was also Washington's army headquarters during the British attack on Boston.

WHERE TO STAY

Cambridge hotel rates tend to be high and reservations will be essential during graduation season (mid-May to early June) and college registration (late August and early September).

Luxury and Expensive

For ultra-modern, luxury lodging in either Boston or Cambridge, try the **Hyatt Regency** (575 Memorial Drive; ℂ (617) 492-1234, toll-free (800) 233-1234; 471 rooms). Patterned after the Hyatt Regency in San Francisco, it has a glass elevator that carries you to the revolving Spinnaker Restaurant, which serves Italian meals.

For night life without having to leave the hotel, you can stay at the **Charles at Harvard Square** (1 Bennett Street; ℂ (617) 864-1200; 299 rooms) whose **Regattabar** is one of the top jazz clubs in Boston.

Of equal quality and price are **Boston Marriott Cambridge** (Kendall Square; ℂ (617)

494-6600, toll-free (800) 228-9290) and **Royal Sonesta** (5 Cambridge Parkway; ☏ (617) 491-3600, toll-free (800) 343-7170; 400 rooms).

Moderate

Howard Johnson's Motel (777 Memorial Drive; ☏ (617) 492-7777, toll-free (800) 654-2000; 205 rooms) is reliable. At the **Quality Inn** (1651 Massachusetts Avenue; ☏ (617) 491-1000; 134 rooms) children under 16 stay free.

EATING OUT

Cambridge, like Boston, has fine dining establishments, but the Cambridge coffeehouses, which serve food along with coffee, tea, and hot drinks, have a style of their own. They abound in the university area and rise and fall in popularity with the whims of the college crowd. Ice cream parlors are popular here. Hit Harvard Square on a hot summer's day for the best ice cream treats in Boston or Cambridge.

Expensive

Panache (798 Main Street; ☏ (617) 492-9500) serves excellent lobster as well as the best lamb in the area. At **Upstairs at the Hasty Pudding** (10 Holyoke Street; ☏ (617) 864-1933), you can get a fixed-price three-course English or French dinner. The **Spinnaker Restaurant**, atop the Hyatt Regency (575 Memorial Drive) serves Italian cuisine.

LEXINGTON AND CONCORD

BACKGROUND

"Bloody Butchery by the British Troops" screamed the headlines of the *Salem Gazette*, describing the fight that took place between 77 colonial militiamen and 700 regular British troops on April 19, 1775. These were the "shots heard round the world."

Word of the battles at Lexington Green and at Concord bridge and of the skirmishes back along the 20-mile (32-km) road to Boston spread quickly through the American colonies, uniting the colonists as no words could do, in a resolve to fight for their independence.

What had begun as a struggle between English authorities determined to enforce the will of Parliament, and the people of Massachusetts, who were just as determined to retain their rights as English citizens, soon escalated into a war for independence which lasted more than eight years. By 1775, Britain's oppressive economic policies had transformed America into a seething powder keg of discontent.

The English government suggested that General Thomas Gage, governor of Massachusetts and commander of the British forces, jail revolutionary rabble-rousers like Sam Adams and John Hancock. But Gage knew where such actions would lead and decided on what he thought was a less inflammatory engagement: to seize the revolutionaries' arms supplies stored in Concord. His mission's success depended on secrecy to ensure little resistance by the townspeople. Despite his precautions, Boston's revolutionaries knew of Gage's plan before his troops left the city, and sent Paul Revere and William Dawes to Lexington with news of the advancing soldiers.

In Lexington, revolutionaries gathered at Buckman's Tavern on the Common to await the arrival of the British troops. When the 77 minutemen saw the Redcoats, they formed two long lines. Militia Captain John Parker exhorted his men, "Stand your ground. Don't fire unless fired upon. But if they mean to have a war, let it begin here!"

Soon British officer Major John Pitcairn ordered the patriots to disband; in the face of more than 700 British regulars, there wasn't much else they could do. As the militiamen slowly obeyed, a shot rang out, no one knows from which side. Then British troops, many of them inexperienced in actual combat, began firing wildly at the revolutionaries, ignoring their commanders' orders to stop. When it was over, eight Americans lay dead, and the first battle of the Revolution had taken place.

The British continued to Concord where they searched all buildings for arms; what they found they burned or tossed into ponds. When the revolutionaries saw smoke coming from Concord, they thought the British were burning the town, and advanced to attack them at Concord's North

Bridge. "Fire, fellow soldiers, for God's sake, fire!" yelled revolutionary Major Buttrick of Concord. Having been joined by minutemen from the surrounding countryside, the militia soon outnumbered the English by four to one.

The battle raged on. The British were driven into retreat along the road back to Boston, where they were attacked constantly. One British officer said it "seemed as if there was a musket behind every tree." Some of the heaviest fighting took place at Menotomy, with more than 5,000 troops on both sides. Eventually, the arrival of British reinforcements saved Gage's troops from annihilation, and they retreated to Bunker Hill in Boston.

The final toll: for the British, 73 dead, 173 wounded, 26 missing; for the revolutionaries, 49 dead, 40 wounded, five missing. Now England knew that the American rebellion ran deeper than dissatisfaction over taxes; the American people were prepared to fight for their freedom.

WHAT TO SEE

Lexington is a good place to begin your "Revolution" tour. Often called the "cradle of American liberty," nearly 100,000 visitors a year trek **Battle Green** where troops and patriots fought. The battle line is marked by a sculpture of the *Minuteman*

On the Green is the **Buckman Tavern**, where revolutionary militia gathered before the battle. The tavern's old front door has a bullet hole made by a British musket ball during the fight. Inside, you will find the original seven-foot (two-meter)-wide tap room, along with many other historic artifacts.

The seventeenth-century **Hancock-Clarke House** is where Paul Revere and William Dawes warned Sam Adams and John Hancock of the British advance. The nearby **Munro House** served as British headquarters and a field hospital for troops after the battle. Other historic sites are detailed in walking tour maps available at the Lexington Historical Society, on the Common, ((617) 861-0928.

From Lexington, you can follow the battle road down Massachusetts Avenue. At the **Fiske House** site, intense close-quarter fighting took place; it also marks the boundary of **Minuteman National Historic Park**, which encompasses the battlegrounds.

Your first stop in the park should be at the Battle Road Visitor Center (Route 2A), where a film and maps portray the skirmish. During summer months, reenactments of the battle are sponsored by the National Park Service. Up the road is the **Paul Revere Capture Site**, where Revere was taken by British troops when he, William Dawes, and Dr. Samuel Prescott were surprised by an English patrol as they rode on from Lexington to Concord to warn of the British advance. The captured Revere later escaped, Dawes fled back to Lexington, but Prescott eluded the British to carry word of their march to Concord.

Continuing west is **Bloody Angles**, so-called for two sharp turns in the road which provided ambush points for the militia. Eight British soldiers were killed here during their retreat. Just before reaching Concord is **Meriam House**, which gave cover to minutemen as they fired on fleeing British troops crossing a narrow bridge.

Finally, Concord's **North Bridge** is where the American revolutionaries first fired a volley against British soldiers. It is difficult to believe that these beautiful surroundings could have been host to such bloody undertakings. You can walk the battle route, and even cross over the North Bridge itself. Daniel Chester French's statue, the *Minuteman*, stands here, a memorial to the citizen-soldiers of 1775 who led the fight for freedom. You get a panoramic overview of the battleground from the North Bridge Visitor Center, ((617) 369-6993.

WHERE TO STAY

In Concord it is possible to stay in Henry David Thoreau's former home, now the **Colonial Inn** (48 Monument Square; ((508) 369-9200; 60 rooms; moderate to expensive). It has a good restaurant with seafood, continental specialties, and home-baked breads and pastries.

Another place to stay is the standard **Howard Johnson's Motor Lodge** (740 Elm Street; ((508) 369-6100; 106 rooms; moderate to expensive).

THE WORCESTER AREA

WORCESTER

Industrial Worcester is the second largest city in Massachusetts. Situated 50 miles (80 km) west of Boston, it is not a major tourist destination, but the **Worcester Art Museum** (55 Salisbury Street; ((508) 799-4406; admission $3.50 with reductions for students and senior citizens, free for children under 18; open year-round daily except Monday, times variable) houses one of the finest collections of art and antiquities in New England.

One of the museum's displays is that of the priceless artifacts from Antioch, dating from the second to the sixth century AD. The collection resides in Worcester because the museum sponsored a series of Syrian excavations in the 1930's which unearthed these ancient treasures.

For the serious history buffs, the **American Antiquarian Society** (Salisbury Street and Park Avenue; ((508) 755-5221; admission free; open Monday to Friday 9 am to 5 pm, closed holidays) has the largest collection of source materials covering the nation's first 250 years of history. This collection includes copies of the *Massachusetts Spy*, the inflammatory anti-British newspaper printed in Worcester between 1700 and 1776, which boldly supported the push for independence.

Tourist Information
The **Worcester County Convention and Visitors Bureau** (33 Waldo Street, Worcester, MA 01608; ((508) 753-2920) can provide information about the city.

Where to Stay
There are many hotels in Worcester, particularly in the moderate to expensive range. If you want to make reservations in advance, you can call **Howard Johnson–College Square** (800 Southbridge Street; ((508) 791-5501; 137 rooms; moderate to expensive).

"FRUITLANDS"

The youth movement's "return to nature" in the 1960's could have been inspired by a curious nineteenth-century settlement in **Harvard** Massachusetts, called **Fruitlands** about 22 miles (35 km) north of Worcester on Route 110. Established in 1834 by transcendentalist Bronson Alcott (father of Louisa May Alcott, author of *Little Women*) and English activist Charles Lane, the little farm community attracted Utopians who gave up material goods, embraced vegetarianism, and spent much time communing with their natural surroundings — the hilly beauty of the Nashua Valley. The community soon disbanded, but the old farmhouse at Fruitlands now houses a transcendentalist museum with displays of artifacts belonging to Alcott and other nineteenth-century transcendentalist writers and philosophers such as Thoreau and Emerson.

Other museums on the grounds include a 1794 **Shaker House**, moved here after Harvard's Shakers (see also THE SHAKERS, page 85) left the village in the early twentieth century. It is now filled with exhibits of handsome Shaker handiwork.

THE NORTH SHORE

SAUGUS

Many an eighteenth and nineteenth century New England sea captain harbored his merchant ship in ports along the North Shore. A trip north from Boston can be a journey through history. The **North of Boston Tourist Council** (P.O. Box 3031, Peabody, MA 01960; ((508) 532-1449) has prepared a wealth of literature on the area's museums and historic houses and public buildings.

Just north of Boston, off U.S. 1, is the **Saugus Iron Works**. A replica of an iron works built in 1650 by early Puritans, it demonstrates how settlers made and forged iron. Its workers toiled 12 hours a day, six days a week, in the white heat of the blast furnace, to the constant clanging of great hammers.

Today the iron works looks much as it did in the seventeenth century, complete with

OPPOSITE: Salem Witch Museum

water wheel pits and slag piles. You can tour the furnace, forge, iron house, and blacksmith shop; only the iron works house is original, dating to 1646.

SALEM

Background: The Witch Trials

"At first the girls would not answer, for fear of being discovered. They simply screamed and writhed or did blasphemous things, such as dashing a Bible against the wall. But gradually they began to give names."

Thus begins an inquisitor's account of Puritan Salem's 1692 Witch Trials, an American inquisition and reign of terror and hysteria. By the time it was over, 19 people had been hanged on Gallows Hill in one of the most notorious episodes in American history.

What to See

This town, settled in 1626, leans heavily on its "be-witching" legacy. (Even its tourism slogan chips in with, "Stop by for a Spell.") If witches grab your fancy, head to the **Salem Witch Museum** (admission $3.50 with reductions for children and senior citizens; open daily 10 am to 5 pm), where 13 life-sized stage settings present a historically

accurate drama examining the hysteria (Washington Square; ℂ (508) 744-1692).

The 1642 **Witch House** (on Essex Street; admission $2.50; open daily 10 am to 4:30 pm) is the restored home of Jonathan Corwin, one of the judges at the witch trials; preliminary examinations of more than 200 people accused of witchcraft were held here. The **Burying Point** (Charter Street), dating from 1637, is interesting for its seventeenth-century gravestones; the graves include those of judges of the witchcraft trials and a *Mayflower* passenger. The **Rebecca Nurse House** (in Danvers) belonged to a woman who was hanged as a witch; it overlooks a field where she is buried in an unmarked grave. And Gallow Hill is still here.

From the early eighteenth century, Salem was an important port and shipbuilding town, home of many wealthy merchants. Its seafaring legacy is apparent in the **Peabody Museum**, begun in 1799 by 22 sea captains who founded the East India Marine Society. By 1821 they had collected 2,000 items from all over the world for the growing museum; today, the collection numbers more than 300,000 artifacts and works of art exhibited in seven buildings and 30 galleries. Included are ships' figureheads and models, paintings, gold, silver, and textiles (on East India Square; ℂ (508) 745-1876).

Of Salem's seafarers, Nathaniel Hawthorne wrote, "They sailed where no others dared to go, anchored where no one else dreamed of making a trade." Native son Hawthorne was a leading celebrity in the mid-1800's during the flowering of American literature. He was fascinated by both Salem's witch and sea legacies: he harbored a brooding sense of guilt about one of his ancestor's involvement in the witch trials, and had turned to the sea for an occupation when he served as officer of the Custom House.

At one time, 40 wharves stood on Salem's harborfront; the longest was **Derby Wharf**, which still stands today. Across the street, the 1819 **Custom House** (ℂ (508) 744-4323; open 8:30 am to 5:30 pm every day of the year except Thanksgiving, Christmas, and New Year) contains restored offices, including Hawthorne's. Both Derby Wharf and the Custom House are managed by the National Park Service, which offers daily guided tours in July and August. But the **House of the Seven Gables** ((Turner Street; ((508) 744-0991; admission $5.00 adults, $2.50 children under 16; open daily 10 am to 4:30 pm) is the major Hawthorne relic. Featured in his novel of the same name, the 1668 house contains original Hawthorne furnishings, and its share of secret stairways and passages. Other houses on the grounds include the 1750 Hawthorne birthplace, and the 1655 Retire Becket house. The **Essex Institute** (Essex Street; Z (508) 744-3390) preserves six houses spanning three centuries (the earliest dating from 1627) and its museum includes original witchcraft trial records.

Salem's new **Heritage Walking Trail** maps supply an itinerary that includes most of the town's historical attractions; the path is marked by a red line drawn on the sidewalk.

Tourist Information
The **Salem Chamber of Commerce** (Old Town Hall in Derby Square; ((508) 744-0004) can provide you with maps and other information.

Where to Stay and Eating Out
In downtown Salem is the **Hawthorne Hotel on the Common** (18 Washington Square; ((508) 744-4080; 89 rooms; moderate to expensive) and nearby is the **Lyceum** (43 Church Street; ((508) 745-7665) which serves inexpensive to moderate Continental menus. It was here that Alexander Graham Bell first demonstrated his telephone.

CAPE ANN

Cape Ann's rocky promontory and wild seas lure weekending Bostonians to its coastal villages, harbors, and artists' colonies. Named for the Queen of England in 1614 by Captain John Smith, the Cape has always looked to the sea for its livelihood.

GLOUCESTER

The first settlement on the Cape and the oldest seaport in the nation (1623), Gloucester continues to be one of the busiest fishing ports in the world, with a fleet of nearly 300 boats. Huge fish-processing plants line its shores, packaging the catch for shipment across the country.

The **statue** of the Gloucester fisherman (*Man at the Wheel*), which appropriately faces the sea, is a New England landmark. The statue's inscription simply reads, "They that go down to the sea in ships."

More than 10,000 Gloucester men have been lost in three centuries of fishing, and almost every year another Gloucester boat and crew is claimed by the sea. Each June, the Blessing of the Fleet ceremony takes place during St Peter's Fiesta.

Whale-watching cruises board at the docks in downtown Gloucester. For

additional Cape Ann whale-watching cruises, contact **Cape Ann Chamber of Commerce**, (33 Commercial Street, Gloucester, MA 01930-5034; ((617) 283-1601).

For a completely different perspective of this fishing village, head to the **Rocky Neck Art Colony** (East Main Street, East Gloucester), the nation's oldest working art colony, with galleries and shops.

Where to Stay
The best hotels are along the beach on Atlantic Road. The **Bass Rocks Motor Inn** (119

OPPOSITE: Witches were taken seriously by early New Englanders, but in Salem today their legacy is a tourist attraction. ABOVE: Placid waters at the fishing village of Rockport.

Atlantic Road; ((508) 283-7600; 48 rooms) is expensive, but the view is rewarding. In the moderate to inexpensive price range is **Gray Manor** (14 Atlantic Road, East Gloucester, MA 01930; ((508) 283-5409), a large summer home converted into a guest house.

Where to Eat

For good New England seafood, stop at **The Easterly Restaurant** (87 Atlantic Avenue; ((508) 283-0140; inexpensive to moderate).

ROCKPORT

Rockport is a fishing village, artists' colony, and tourist attraction rolled into one. Its streets are busy with people during the summer season, and parking space is but a dream, and its folksy style attracts families, the elderly, and tour buses.

Rockport is well known for its shops. Galleries, crafts, and restaurants are crowded into both old and new fishing shanties along the narrow winding lanes of **Bearskin Neck**, a favorite gathering place for artists.

The quality of natural light on Cape Ann attracts artists and photographers to this picturesque village. Late afternoon is an especially popular time, as the setting sun focuses its fiery colors on the landscape and casts fleeting shadows over the craggy outcroppings along the shoreline.

A Rockport landmark is **Motif No. 1**, a weathered red lobster shack, a favorite subject for countless painters. It is actually a recent replica of the original, which was destroyed in a storm a few years ago.

Continuing around the head of the Cape, the shoreline scenery from Pigeon Cove to Annisquam is dotted with picturesque hidden bays and tiny coves.

Where to Stay

The best is the **Peg Leg Inn** (2 King Street; ((508) 546-2352; 29 rooms). It is almost as old as the town itself and has moderate and expensive rooms depending on the view.

Eating out

No alcohol is served in Rockport; it is a "dry" town. You can, however, bring your own

Picturesque Rockport Harbor.

wine into any of the restaurants that line Bearskin Neck. Seafood is the standard fare and prices are inexpensive to moderate.

IPSWICH

A colonial town about 21 miles (34 km) north of Rockport on Route 1A, Ipswich still has nearly 50 homes built before 1725, with several from the 1600s. One of the finest is the **John Whipple House** (on Main Street), which dates back to 1640.

The **Richard T. Crane Beach Reservation**, at the end of Argilla Road on Ipswich Bay, is popular with the area's artists, and the sandy beach which stretches for five miles (eight kilometers) is among the East Coast's finest. Here the **Pine Hollow Trail** leads hikers on an hour-long trek along the shore and through a red maple swamp. Follow up a walk with a feast of a regional favorite, delectable Ipswich clams, available at any restaurant in the village.

NEWBURYPORT

At the mouth of the Merrimack River, less than six miles (10 km) from the New Hampshire state line, is Newburyport. During the eighteenth and nineteenth centuries, the town's large merchant vessel fleet made local sea captains wealthy. Their Federal-style mansions lining High Street are a testament to their success. Tours around one of the finest, **Cushing House**, built in 1808 for Caleb Cushing, first U.S. envoy to China, show some of the artifacts he brought back from his tour of duty in the Orient.

Note the "widow's walks" atop many of the historic homes. Historians are divided as to their origin. Some say they were built for sea captains' anxious wives, who could gaze over the harbor and out to sea from their lofty perch, searching for their husbands' returning ships. Others contend that they were simply an affectation of style — an ornamental ironwork favored by one wealthy sea salt, and then copied by his contemporaries.

The riverside **Market Square District** is also newly restored, its cobblestoned streets lined with handsome historic brick buildings which now house shops and restaurants.

Less than three miles (five kilometers) east of Newburyport is **Plum Island**, a national wildlife refuge where more than 250 species of migratory birds stop to rest along the Atlantic Flyway each spring and fall. Vistas of the island's dunes, marshes, and its six-mile (10-km)-long beach can be enjoyed from an observation tower. In the fall, wild beach plums and cranberries can be found along the shore.

THE SOUTH SHORE

While some visitors might make a quick stop at Hingham's Old Ship Church (1681), Scituate's Lawson Tower and Light, and the Hull Lifesaving Museum, most travel the South Shore along Interstate 93 and U.S. 6 only as a route from metropolitan Boston to Cape Cod. However, there are at least three sightseeing detours that should not be missed.

QUINCY

Just south of Boston across the Neponset River, this former shipbuilding center was home to both John Adams and John Quincy Adams, the only fatherson tandem to become presidents of the United States (they were the second and sixth presidents, respectively).

The **John Adams National Historic Site** (Adams Street; ((508) 773-1177) is the home bought in 1787 by the president and his wife Abigail. The varied styles of its original furnishings are the result of occupancy by four generations of Adamses. The **John Quincy Adams Stone Library** has more than 14,000 books in nine languages. On Franklin Street, guided tours lead you through the birthplaces of the Adamses, modest seventeenth-century colonial saltboxes containing family artifacts, including some of the famous letters Abigail wrote to John when he was a member of the Continental Congress in Philadelphia and, later, a negotiator at the Paris Peace Talks. (((508) 773-1177; open daily from mid-April to mid-November.) Finally, the resting place of two presidents — John and son John Quincy — is the **United First Parish Church** (Hancock and Washington Streets; ((508) 773-1290).

PLYMOUTH

Next stop is Plymouth, about 30 miles (50 km) south. Every American schoolchild knows about **Plymouth Rock**, the boulder where the Mayflower Pilgrims first stepped onto American soil on December 21, 1620. What is traditionally regarded as "The Rock" is covered by an elaborate Greek Classical pavilion on the Water Street Harbor shore, and marked with a plaque.

Across the street, you can climb the 37 steps to the top of **Cole's Hill** to the burial place of the Pilgrims who died during that first bitter winter in the New World and to a great view of Plymouth Harbor. Also on the harbor front, at State Pier, is the *Mayflower II*, a full-scale replica of the vessel which brought the 103 settlers from England (admission $5.50 adults, $3.75 children ages 5 to 12; open daily, April to November, 9 am to 5 pm, July to August, 9 am to 7 pm). Guides, dressed in period costumes and playing the roles of the passengers and crew who made the treacherous crossing, demonstrate seventeenth-century skills, and answer questions about the first colony of Pilgrims.

Tablets on **Leyden Street** mark the sites of the Pilgrims' first houses; however, the 1666 **John Howland House** (on Sandwich Street) is the only remaining Plymouth home where original Mayflower Pilgrims actually lived. The **Richard Sparrow House** (on Summer Street) is Plymouth's oldest, dating from 1640. In nearby Kingston is the 1674 **Major John Bradford House**. Possessions of the first Pilgrims are on display at the **Pilgrim Hall Museum** (Court Street; ((508) 746-1620; admission $4.00 with reductions for children and senior citizens; open daily 9:30 am to 4:30 pm).

About three miles (five kilometers) south on Route 3A is **Plymouth Plantation** (admission $12 adults, $8 children 5 to 12; open daily, April to November, 9 am to 5 pm), a living-history museum that recreates the 1627 settlement of the Pilgrims. Men and women portray the dress, speech, and manner of actual residents of the historic community, bringing to life the routines and activities of seventeenth-century Plymouth.

You will get a good overview of the village, with its many thatch-roofed cottages, from the **Fort Meetinghouse**, ((508) 746-1622.

Plymouth County

Southern Massachusetts produces more than 50 percent of the nation's cranberry crop. **Cranberry World** (off Route 44; ((508) 747-1000; admission free; open daily, April to November 9:30 am to 5 pm, and July to August 9:30 am to 9 pm) traces the history of this tangy red berry from colonial times to the present; features include tours

of working cranberry bogs and cooking demonstrations.

Another way to enjoy the cranberry region is to board the **Edaville steam train** in nearby **Carver**, one of the state's cranberry capitals with more than 3,000 acres (1,200 hectares) under cultivation. The train takes you through six miles (10 km) of a 1,800-acre (730-hectare) cranberry plantation. The ideal time for a trip is during the fall harvest. (Rochester Street; ((508) 866-4526; admission $12.50 with reductions for children and senior citizens; open April to December, times variable.)

At Plymouth Plantation, seventeenth century lifestyles are reenacted.

Tourist Information

The **Plymouth County Development Council** (P.O. Box 1620, Pembroke, MA 02359; ((508) 826-3136) provides tourist information free of charge.

Where to Stay

The **Sheraton Plymouth Hotel at Village Landing** (180 Water Street; ((508) 747-4900; 177 rooms) is in the expensive range and offers high-quality service and rooms with a water view.

For a change of pace and an intimate look at New England living, **Be Our Guest** (P.O. Box 1333, Plymouth, MA 02360; ((508) 837-9867) will book you a room in a moderately priced guest house or bed-and-breakfast.

Eating Out

With a charm all its own, the **Lobster Hut** (Town Wharf; ((508) 746-2270) fixes simple seafood meals for less than $10.00. On hot summer days you can eat outside on the picnic tables.

NEW BEDFORD

In the second chapter of his classic novel, *Moby Dick*, Herman Melville says that Nantucket may have been the romantic home of whaling, but that it was New Bedford which made whaling an industry.

Indeed, New Bedford, a deepwater port on Apponagansett Bay, was once the greatest whaling center in the world, providing work for more than 10,000 men. By the 1850's, it harbored more than 400 whaling ships, some of whose voyages lasted up to five years. Each whaling fleet alone was valued at more than $10 million.

Whaling built New Bedford. As Melville wrote, "all these brave houses and flowery gardens came from the Atlantic, Pacific and Indian Oceans. One and all, they were harpooned and dragged up hither from the bottom of the sea."

A good example of the prosperity derived from whaling is the many elaborate mansions of sea captains and maritime merchants along **County Street**, at the crest of a hill overlooking the harbor. The **Gilbert Russel House**, built in 1800 and remodeled in

elaborate Italianate style in 1868, is one of the most spectacular.

The discovery of oil in Pennsylvania in the late 1850's marked the beginning of the end for New Bedford. With its whaling fleet badly depleted by the Civil War and losses in Arctic waters, New Bedford's whaling slowly gave way to manufacturing.

But much of the whalers' presence remains in New Bedford. The town's fishing fleet ranks first in the nation in value of fish and scallops landed. More than 200 vessels moor at the downtown waterfront.

From the New Bedford Visitor Center on North Second Street it is a short trip up Johnny Cake Hill to the world's largest whaling museum, the **New Bedford Whaling Museum** (admission $3.50 with reductions for children and senior citizens; open September to June, Monday to Saturday 9 am to 5 pm, Sunday 1 pm to 5 pm, summer hours variable ((508) 997-0046). For 175 years, New Bedford's whalers were known throughout the world, and their legacy is preserved here. Perhaps the most interesting exhibit is the bark, *Lagoda*, the

ABOVE: New England's seafaring legacy is on display in New Bedford's Whaling Museum.
OPPOSITE: Full-scale replica of the *Mayflower* moored at Plymouth.

largest ship model in the world, built in 1915. This half-scale replica of a vessel that made 12 whaling voyages is outfitted with whaleboats, harpoons, and other equipment. In the Panorama Room gallery, there are two 50-ft (15-m) sections from a quarter-mile (400-m)-long painting depicting one year aboard an 1847 whaler. The original crew list of the whaleship *Acushnet* bearing Herman Melville's name are also on display here. The museum library contains more than 1,100 logbooks from whaling journeys, and the theater shows a film of an actual whaling expedition, complete with a "Nantucket sleigh ride," or whale chase.

Across the street from the Whaling Museum is the **Seamen's Bethel**, the whaleman's chapel of Melville's *Moby Dick*. Built in 1832, it contains a pulpit resembling the hull of a ship, and memorial tablets dedicated to sailors lost at sea.

New Bedford's flourishing nineteenth-century glass industry is represented at the **Glass Museum**, housed in a 1821 Federal mansion filled with more than 2,000 pieces of Pairpoint and Mt Washington glass (Second Street; ((508) 994-0115; admission $2.00 with reductions for children and senior citizens; open 10 am to 4 pm, closed Sundays).

Tourist Information
New Bedford Visitor Center (North Second Street; ((508) 991-6200).

Where to Stay
Pineapple Hospitality (P.O. Box F821; ((508) 990-1696) operates a bed-and-breakfast booking service (open Monday through Friday from 9 am to 5 pm). It specializes in the New Bedford area but does have some listings for other parts of New England and will happily help you lay out an itinerary and bookings for each night.

On the outskirts of New Bedford are many moderately priced motels, including the **Comfort Inn** (171 Faunce Corner Road; ((508) 996-0800; 85 rooms).

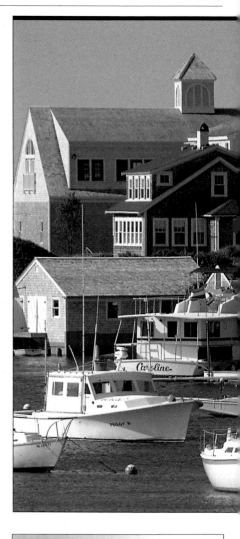

Tidy villages and natural harbors contribute to Cape Cod's summer popularity.

CAPE COD

A long spit of sand that curls out into the Atlantic Ocean for about 70 miles (113 km), Cape Cod is one of New England's premier resort areas, with 300 miles (480 km) of sandy beaches, coastal villages, and isolated islands.

The Cape extends about 30 miles (50 km) into the warm Gulf Stream before it turns up at its "elbow." The weather is much milder here than on the mainland, with summers cooled by sea winds and winters warmed by Gulf Stream air.

The peninsula was a sleepy amalgam of small colonial fishing villages before the advent of the automobile. Then mobile visitors from nearby cities (Boston is only 70 miles

or 113 km to the north and New York City is less than 250 miles or 400 km away) discovered its charm. Now swamped by visitors each summer, Cape Cod is a more intriguing destination in off-season months.

Cape Cod has preserved much of its beauty due largely to the **Cape Cod National Seashore**, 27,000 acres (10,930 hectares) of dunes and beaches, salt marshes, pine forests, and cranberry bogs set aside to protect a remnant of the fragile ecosystems of the Lower Cape.

TOURIST INFORMATION

In the summer, the **Cape Cod Chamber of Commerce** (Routes 6 and 132, Hyannis, MA 02601; ((508) 362-3225) keeps its visitors center open daily from 9 am to 7 pm. There you can pick up maps, guides, and hotel information. The **Bed & Breakfast Cape Cod** (P.O. Box 341, West Hyannisport, MA 02672; ((508) 775-2772) will help you in finding a moderately-priced room, if one is available, on the Cape.

A DISAPPEARING LAND

A succession of glacial depositions and wind and wave erosion formed Cape Cod's present hook shape. This geologic history, and ongoing ocean and climatic changes, spell a doubtful future for the Cape, one all too well known to its 175,000 residents. Studies seem to indicate that the roaring sea and northwest winds of the Atlantic are

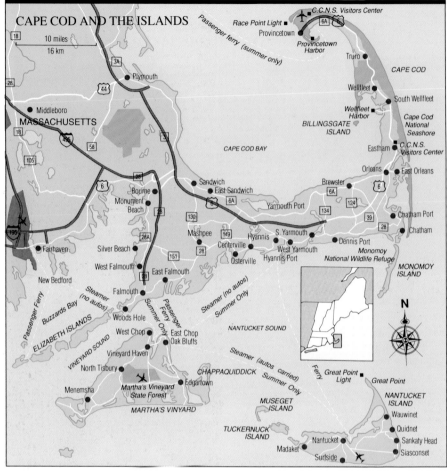

CAPE COD AND THE ISLANDS

eroding the Cape a little more each year, and that the land itself may be sinking into the sea.

Over the last century, entire communities have been lost to the ocean. One report tells of Billingsgate Island, a fishing village off Jeremy's Point that once held a lighthouse, school, and 35 family homes. By 1935, it had been completely washed into the sea. "Now all that is left of this island, which was first explored in 1620 by the Pilgrims, is a sand bar that surfaces at low tide — a grim reminder of Cape Cod's tenuous future," the report read.

Scientists say that generations from now, the Cape will be only a memory, worn away to a few sandy shoals, and that there is nothing modern-day technology can do to stop it. There are more alarming statistics: "Parts of the Cape are losing five acres (two

hectares) a year to marine erosion," wrote Greg O'Brien, an expert on Cape Cod and the islands. "Chatham, on the Mid Cape's south coast, lost 10 ft (three meters) of shoreline a day to marine erosion during a recent winter."

A greater threat to the Cape is the rise in sea level brought about by the "greenhouse effect" — automobile, power plant, and other human pollution melting polar ice caps. Scientists predict that within the next 40 years, shorelines from Provincetown to Bourne will retreat an average of 100 ft (30 m), and according to O'Brien, by the year 2100 more than 1,200 ft (366 m) of shoreline could be underwater. "Adding to this problem is the fact that while sea levels are rising, some coastal areas of the Cape, formed from silt sediments, are actually sinking—slowly compressing under their own weight."

Provincetown, at the Cape's tip, finds itself in a most precarious position; the U.S. Geological Survey in Woods Hole predicts that the town "is headed for real trouble" which can be measured "in tens of years, not hundreds."

This is happening all over the Cape. The cliffs at Falmouth Heights are washing into Vineyard Sound; West Barnstable lost 15 ft (4.5 m) of Sandy Neck beach in one recent winter storm; even the land in Wellfleet, where Marconi transmitted the first transatlantic cable 85 years ago, rests more than 200 ft (61 m) out in the sea. Geologists give Nantucket Island only 700 years before it disappears under the ocean.

PILGRIM BEGINNINGS

Cape Cod was inhabited by the Wampanoag Indians when explorer Bartholomew Gosnold landed in 1602. He named the peninsula for the great schools of cod found in the surrounding waters.

In 1620, the Mayflower Pilgrims landed at today's Provincetown before moving on to Plymouth, just across Cape Cod Bay. The Pilgrims stayed there for more than a month, exploring the area and working on what was to become the Mayflower Compact, the governing constitution of the Massachusetts Bay Colony.

By the 1630's, settlements had sprung up along the Cape, with fishing the mainstay industry. A whaling industry evolved, and the Cape's fishermen commanded a fleet of vessels that sailed out of the ports of Truro, Wellfleet, and Nantucket Island.

OVER THE BRIDGE

On summer weekends, traffic to the Cape may be backed up more than an hour at the bridges spanning the **Cape Cod Canal**, and cars line up bumper-to-bumper along U.S. 6 and 6A, which together stretch the length of the Cape.

The Cape Cod Canal, which eliminates the need for ships to circumnavigate the peninsula, took 11 years to build, and was finished in 1919 at a cost of $16 million. Because of it, there are only two road accesses to the Cape.

If you select the Bourne Bridge at the southern end of the canal, Route 28 will lead you first into the "Upper Cape," that part of the peninsula closest to the mainland, past West Falmouth and Falmouth and Marstons Mill before reaching Hyannis. If you cross at the Sagamore Bridge, at the canal's northern end, you can either continue on U.S. 6, a four-lane highway across the "Mid Cape" to Orleans, or Route 6A, a two-lane scenic road through several Mid-Cape towns. Highways 6 and 6A meet near Orleans and continue up the "Lower Cape" to Provincetown as rural Route 6.

THE UPPER CAPE

The southwestern end of Cape Cod, on Buzzard's Bay, has spectacular coastline, historic houses, and the Nobska Lighthouse overlooking Vineyard Sound. It was originally settled by Quakers in the seventeenth century; its first house was built in 1685.

Falmouth

The main town on the southwestern elbow of the cape, Falmouth expanded around its village green, where many sea captains built fine houses at the height of the whaling

Fences decrease the erosion of Cape Cod's dunes.

industry's prosperity. The **Falmouth Historical Society Museum** (55/65 Palmer Avenue; ((508) 548-4857; admission $2.00 adults, $0.50 children; open mid-June to mid-September, Monday through Friday 2 pm to 5 pm), which occupies two eighteenth-century houses on the Green records the town's whaling legacy. Also on the village green is the birthplace of Katherine Lee Bates, who wrote the lyrics to *America the Beautiful*.

Around Falmouth

From Falmouth one can bicycle along the

old railbed from Falmouth to **Woods Hole**, a principal port on the Cape, and a former whaling town from where ferries depart daily for the islands. It is also home to the **Woods Hole Oceanographic Institute** (WHOI), the **Marine Biological Laboratories**, and the **National Marine Fisheries Service** — some of the world's most prestigious marine research institutions. The successful search for the *Titanic* was planned and launched by WHOI from Woods Hole in 1986. Only the Marine Fisheries Service is open to the public, allowing visitors to view its aquarium during the summer.

From the **bluff** where Nobska Lighthouse stands, one can see the boats

traveling between Woods Hole and the islands, as well as those en route to New York and Boston.

North Falmouth's **Old Silver Beach** on Buzzard's Bay, and Falmouth's **Surf Drive Beach** on Vineyard Sound, are two of the best beaches on the Upper Cape.

Tourist Information

The **Falmouth Chamber of Commerce** (P.O. Box 582; toll free ((800) 526-8532) has a visitors center in downtown Falmouth in the Lawrence Academy building.

Where to Stay

EXPENSIVE

On the outskirts of town, overlooking a lake, is **Coonamessett Inn** (Jones Road; ((508) 548-2300; 24 rooms), a former New England farm.

More modern, and less homey, are **Holiday Inn — Falmouth** (24 Main Street; ((508) 540-2500; 121 rooms), **Sea Crest Resort and Conference Center** (Old Silver Beach; ((508) 548-3850; 266 rooms), and **Quality Inn Falmouth** (291 Jones Road; ((508) 540-2000; 98 rooms).

MODERATE

The **Capewind** (34 Maravista Avenue; ((508) 548-3400; 31 rooms) offers quality rooms on a small scale, and **New Seabury**

Resort (Rock Landing Road; ((508) 477-9111) does it on a grand scale with 368 rooms.

Eating Out

If you are not staying at the **Coonamessett Inn**, (Jones Road; ((508) 548-2300)consider having a traditional New England seafood meal there. Prices run from moderate to expensive.

Another choice is the **Regatta** (217 Clinton Avenue; ((508) 548-5400) overlooking the harbor. It specializes in seafood prepared in French and American styles. Reservations are essential at this expensive restaurant.

mill still stone-grinds cornmeal. The **Heritage Plantation** (Grove and Pine Streets; ((508) 888-3300)offers more antiquities, including the 1931 Duesenberg used by actor Gary Cooper, and a large selection of Currier and Ives paintings.

Mashpee

At Mashpee, on the southern shore, live the few surviving descendants of the Massipee Indians, who lived on the Cape before the first European explorers arrived. The **Old Indian Meetinghouse and Burial Ground** dates back to 1684, making it the oldest in the state.

Sandwich

Sandwich, on the northwestern corner of the Cape just a few miles past the Sagamore Bridge, is the oldest town on the peninsula, dating from 1637. It is renowned for its Sandwich glass, produced between 1825 and 1888 in the workshops of the Boston and Sandwich Glass Company. The exquisite, lacy patterns are collectors items and quite valuable; see also the glass displays at the **Sandwich Glass Museum** (Town Hall Square, across from the village green; ((508) 888-0251; admission $2.50 with reductions for children and senior citizens; open April 1 to October 31, daily 9:30 am to 4:30 pm).

The **Hoxie House** and **Dexter Grist Mill** (on Water Street) are two of the village's restored seventeenth-century buildings; the

MID CAPE

Barnstable

Barnstable is just over 12 miles (20 km) along the Cape's north shore from Sandwich and faces Cape Cod Bay. It has a fine beach on **Sandy Neck**, a seven-mile (11-km) spit of sand that protects the harbor. Cabin cruisers, schooners, and other boats are often docked here. The old **Custom House** (now called the **Donald G. Trayser Memorial Museum**), located on Main Street at Cobb's Hill, has interesting displays of the town's maritime history.

ABOVE: Beach huts stand like sentinels along the Cape Cod coast. OPPOSITE: Parking attendant looks out for business at a Barnstable beach.

As a county seat, Barnstable is the political hub of the Cape. The two cannons in front of its courthouse were brought by oxen from Boston during the war of 1812. The **Sturgis Library**, built in 1644, is the oldest library in the country; among its collections are genealogical records of the Cape's families.

Yarmouth Port and Dennis

Yarmouth Port has a row of sea captains' homes on Main Street; botanic trails past Miller's Pond can be found off Route 6A.

Martha's Vineyard. National attention focused on the Cape in the early 1960s when native son John F. Kennedy became President. "I always go to Hyannis Port to be revived, to know again the power of the sea and the Master who rules over it all and all of us," said the President, whose family still owns a large estate in this exclusive waterside village. The estate is protected by a tall fence and is not open to the public, but the **John F. Kennedy Memorial** is located on Ocean Street.

The **Cape Cod & Hyannis Railroad** provides daily excursions of varying time

Dennis is less than five miles (eight kilometers) to the east. From its **Scargo Hill Tower** there are fine views of both the bay and ocean; when the weather is clear you can see from Plymouth to Provincetown at the tip of the Cape. Dennis is also where Henry Hall developed commercial cranberry growing in the early eighteenth century; now cranberry bogs are common on the Cape landscape.

Hyannis

Flights to the Cape arrive here and Hyannis is the Cape's main vacation and shopping center, and a good base for visits around the Cape. Ferry services leave from here (summer season) to Nantucket Island and to

lengths around the Upper and Mid Cape's spectacular coastline, salt marshes, and cranberry bogs (Main Street, Hyannis; ((508) 771-1145).

Centerville

Just west of Hyannis, Centerville is adjacent to **Craigville Beach**, the most popular swimming spot on Nantucket Sound.

LOWER CAPE

Chatham

Located on the southeastern tip of the Cape, Chatham is protected from fierce ocean storms by Morris Island, part of the nationally-protected seashore. **Fish Pier**, off Shore

Road, is home to the large fishing fleets that unload their catches in the late afternoon.

The **Chatham Lighthouse** Beach offers panoramic views of the bay and **Nauset Beach**, the Cape's first true ocean beach and among the most popular. Just off the coast is **Monomoy Island**, a 10-mile (16-km)-long sand spit protected as a wildlife refuge, with more than 250 species of birds.

Cape Cod National Seashore

Established in 1961, this 27,000-acre (11-hectare) refuge of wind-sculpted dunes, deserted ocean beaches, spectacular cliffs, and salt pond marshes dominates the seashore from Orleans to Provincetown.

The **Salt Pond Visitor Center** in **Eastham** and the **Province Lands Visitor Center** provide literature on the Seashore, schedules for guided nature walks, and pamphlets on biking and hiking trails; the Seashore's headquarters is located in **South Wellfleet**, ((508) 349-3785.

Seashore highlights include nine scenic hiking trails, including **Nauset Marsh Trail**, a beautiful 30-minute walk among salt ponds and marshes; **Atlantic White Cedar Swamp Trail**, a 35-minute trek through a white cedar swamp, beginning near Marconi Station; **Beech Forest Trail** near Provincetown, a 40-minute walk through sand dunes and beech forests; and **Cranberry Bog Trail**, east of Truro, which leads through natural wild cranberry habitat.

Wellfleet

Historic towns also edge the seashore. One of the most picturesque is **Wellfleet**, once a great whaling port. It is still home port for a large fishing fleet. In true seafaring spirit, the downtown church tolls "ship's bells."

PROVINCETOWN

At the tip of the peninsula, Provincetown is a strange amalgam of tacky tourist shops, chic boutiques, fishing fleets manned by burly Portuguese sailors, whale-watching cruises, wide beaches, wind-swept dunes, an artists colony, and more recently, a meeting place for gays.

For all its freak-show atmosphere, P-Town, as locals call it, looks out on some of the Cape's most spectacular scenery. The **Pilgrim Monument**, at Town Hill off Bradford Street, is a 252-ft (77-m)-high Italianate bell tower commemorating the Pilgrims' "landing" at Provincetown in 1620 (they were blown off course); the view from the tower's observation deck takes in all of the Cape. Nearby hiking trails take visitors past marshes, ponds, and pine forests. **Herring Cove** and **Race Point** beaches provide a spectacular setting for swimming and sun bathing.

A tour of Provincetown begins on **Commercial Street**, the main village thoroughfare, lined with galleries, shops, restaurants, and bars. The population swells from less than 4,000 to nearly 80,000 at the height of the summer season, and it seems that everyone is walking along this street at the same time; sometimes it is simply impassable — a tangle of people, cars, and bicycles.

Once it was the third-largest whaling port in the world. Today, its fishing village legacy continues, with boats arriving during late afternoon at **MacMillan Wharf** to unload their catches.

OPPOSITE: Would-be dummies in Nantucket.
ABOVE: Memento artist in Cape Cod.

Early this century, artists and writers were drawn to this isolated outpost on the Atlantic Ocean by Charles Hawthorne's Cape Cod School of Art. In 1916, the Provincetown Players launched the careers of playwrights Eugene O'Neill, Tennessee Williams, and Sinclair Lewis.

Whale-watching

Whether sailing off Cape Ann, north of Boston, or near Cape Cod to the south, **whale-watching cruises** have been cited as a great way to "witness the miraculous." One little girl on a cruise marveled that a whale once came so close "he sprayed us when he blew." A chance to see these marvelous mammals at close range is a thrilling adventure indeed.

You will also quite likely see schools of porpoises and dolphins, sea turtles, sharks, seals, and sea birds playing very close to the ships.

However, all whale-watching operations are not alike. Some boats are no more than floating hotdog and souvenir stands that happen to ply the waters the whales frequent. Others offer marine biologist-led narrated tours of prime whaling areas, video replays of the day's sightings, and good food. A few more enterprising cruise operators "guarantee" whale sightings, claiming a 95 percent success rate; if you fail to spot any whales, you are offered a free trip to try again.

If time permits, choose a whale-watching cruise off Cape Cod. Daily morning and afternoon cruises, offered April to October, last anywhere from three to four hours. While many cruise operators vie for your dollar, the **Whale Watch Dolphin Fleet**, ☏ (508) 255-3857, of Provincetown on the tip of the Cape, likes to claim that they are the cream of the crop.

The Dolphin Fleet originated whale-watching on the East Coast, and it is also the largest and most successful of all the operations, having made more than 6,000 trips since 1975. Their boats, built especially for whale-watching, are exceptionally stable. (The boats' seating capacity is 270 passengers, but only 145 people are permitted on each cruise to ensure a satisfying trip.) Cruises are led by scientists from the Center

for Coastal Studies, one of the world's leading whale research and conservation organizations, and acknowledged authorities on the humpback whales that live in local waters. A portion of each ticket sale is donated to help "save the whales."

Dolphin Fleet ships head offshore about six miles (10 km) to the Stellwagen Bank, the main whale feeding ground in Massachusetts Bay. Through years of research, Coastal Studies scientists have identified several hundred individual humpbacks, and will offer you their individual histories, as well as stories of the finback and right whales found here. There are morning, afternoon, and sunset cruises lasting four hours; reservations are recommended.

For additional information about Cape Cod whale-watching cruises, contact **The Massachusetts Department of Commerce and Development**, Division of Tourism, (100 Cambridge Street, Boston, MA 02202; ☏ (617) 727-3201).

Getting There

By car from Boston, take Interstate 93 south to Route 3; continue south to U.S. 6, and follow that up the Cape to Provincetown at the tip.

To reach the Whale Watch Dolphin Fleet office, turn left on Conwell Street, right on Bradford, then left on Standish.

It is only 114 miles (184 km) from Boston to Provincetown, but allow at least three hours to get through the sometimes maddening traffic on the Cape.

THE ISLANDS

MARTHA'S VINEYARD

"Island in Troubled Water" screamed the headline in the *Vineyard Gazette*, the 131-year-old weekly newspaper that serves Martha's Vineyard, the bucolic island seven miles (11 km) off the Cape Cod coast. The piece was in response to a decision of the state legislature that would allow private developers to run wild over the island's South Beach.

Developers as bogeymen have always been a rallying point for the island's 12,000 full-time residents, who include celebrities such as former first lady Jacqueline Kennedy Onassis, newsmen Walter Cronkite and Mike Wallace, singer Carly Simon, and cartoonist Jules Feiffer. As a result of the concern expressed by such influential residents, the decision was reversed and the island's spectacular beauty and miles of beaches and woodlands remain comparatively unspoiled.

The triangular-shaped island was named by the explorer Gosnold in 1602, when he found wild grapes growing everywhere. The grapes are gone, but what remains is a fascinating landscape dotted with little fishing villages and summer resorts.

Vineyard Haven, the main port of entry for visitors, is an old whaling town, much of which was destroyed in the Great Fire of 1883. Some pre-1883 houses can still be found on Williams Avenue, and the Seamen's Bethel is another original harborfront building. Along Main Street, you'll find shops and cafés, along with a Daughters of the American Revolution museum.

Two of the Haven's most familiar landmarks are the **West and East Chop Lighthouses** on the cliffs at the entrance to the harbor.

However, many visitors head straight for **Edgartown**, the oldest town (1642) on Martha's Vineyard. This whaling port of the early-nineteenth century is charming, with elegant sea captains' houses (complete with widows' walks) and weathered saltboxes lining North and South Water Streets, overlooking the harbor.

Other architectural delights include the 1840 **Fisher House** on Main Street, called by many the most elegant residence in town; the 1843 **Methodist Church**, with its massive pillars and tower; and the **Cooke House**, a 1765 shipbuilder's house that is now home to the Dukes County Historical Society.

Board the *On Time* ferry (an island joke — it has no regular schedule, and can transport only three cars at a time) at Edgartown to reach **Chappaquiddick Island**, 200 yds (180 m) across the harbor. The island is a paradise of thick woodlands, wildlife refuges, and unspoiled beaches.

Oak Bluffs, located between Vineyard Haven and Edgartown, has a unique history. In the 1830's, Edgartown Methodists came to Trinity Park each summer to meet and pray at extended revival meetings. By 1850, the revival, held in an oak grove at the town's north end, was drawing 12,000 people. Soon tents were replaced with small cottages — the so-called **Cottage City.** Today, these colorful cottages with their gingerbread turnings, fish scales, and lacy fretwork remain one of the most charming symbols of Vineyard living.

Up-island towns are few and far between. **Chilmark** offers excellent views of Vineyard Sound; and **Menemsha** is largely a working fishing village, but renowned for its picturesque moors.

Martha's Vineyard State Forest, in the center of the island, has hiking paths through dense stands of pines.

However, the westernmost tip of the island is the most spectacular. The brilliantly colored **Gay Head cliffs** rise 150 ft (45 m) above the stormy Atlantic. Ripples of blue, red, white, and orange run through the clay, whose strata contain fossils of camels, whales, and other animals millions of years old. Because of erosion problems, one can no longer walk down the face of the cliffs to the beach below, but a winding path eventually gets you there.

The small towns around Gay Head are peopled by Wampannoag Indians, descendants of the island's original inhabitants.

Getting There

Access to Martha's Vineyard is by the **Steamship Authority** ferry, ((508) 540-2022, which provides daily services between Woods Hole and the harbor at Vineyard Haven; the trip takes about 45 minutes. (Car ferries fill up quickly, so you should call well in advance to reserve space on the boat.) Or you can fly with the **ProvincetownBoston Airline,** ((508) 693-2070.

NANTUCKET ISLAND

Some 30 miles (50 km) south of Cape Cod is Nantucket Island, for almost 100 years — until the 1830's — the world's greatest whaling port. Today it is one of the most charming and picturesque destinations on the East Coast, its streets lined with well-preserved houses, and its landscape graced with long stretches of lovely beaches and open green moors.

Visitors arriving by ferry from Woods Hole (a three-hour ride) are often confronted with a mysterious, fog-shrouded island seascape that obscures the main port, **Nantucket Town**. But once ashore the beauty is astounding. As one writer put it, "This is not just an island; it is an experience."

Early Nantucket settlers were taught by the Indians how to harpoon whales from the shore, and soon the settlers were setting out to sea to do their whaling.

By the early 1800's, Nantucket Town had more than 10,000 residents. Its cobblestone streets, elegant houses, and tall elm trees were testament to the successes of its sea captains, shipowners, and merchants.

When the new, larger ships could no longer dock in shallow Nantucket Harbor, the island lost many of its whalers to the deep port in New Bedford. After the Pennsylvania oil boom hit in the 1840's, Nantucket's fortunes declined even further, along with the whaling industry's. Today, its year-round population numbers around 3,500.

Fine seventeenth- and eighteenth-century houses can be seen on Main Street. The local **Historical Association**, ((508) 228-1894, provides pamphlets outlining a self-guided walking tour of the town.

One of the best preserved is the **Hadwen House** (Main and Pleasant Streets), a Greek Revival mansion built in 1845 for a whale oil merchant; it contains original furnishings of the whaling era.

The oldest existing house in the village was built in 1686 by **Jethro Coffin** on Sunset Hill. This **saltbox** is a fine example of seventeenth-century colonial architecture. The horseshoe-design in the chimney brick was meant to ward off witches and other evil spirits. And the **Old Mill**, on Mill Hill, built in 1746 by wood salvaged from wrecked ships, is still used to grind corn.

To learn more of Nantucket's seafaring legacy, visit the **Whaling Museum** (Broad Street; admission $3.00 adults, $1.00 children; open daily 10 am to 5 pm, May 28 to October 12), located in a factory that once made candles from whale oil. On display are excellent collections of harpoons, ship and whale models, and other artifacts from the town's whaling days.

At **Straight Wharf**, at the beginning of Main Street, is the *Lighthouse Nantucket*, a double-masted lightship formerly moored offshore to guide ocean vessels around the island's dangerous shoals. The wharf's fishing sheds have now been transformed into shops and restaurants.

Around the Island

Just outside the town, the **Nantucket Moors** are windswept hills of bayberry, wild rose, heather, and brambles that burst into vibrant color in summer and fall. Nestled among these hills are the villages of Wauwinet, Quidnet, and Siasconset.

Wauwinet is the gateway to the **Coatue**, a 10-mile (16-km) sand spit that protects Nantucket Harbor from the more turbulent Nantucket Sound. One can walk along the spit to its northern tip, where the 1818 **Great Point Lighthouse** marks the site of treacherous sandbars in the Sound.

Siasconset sits on the easternmost edge of the island. By the end of the nineteenth century, this village, which became a popular destination for both artists and tourists, was linked to Nantucket Town by a railroad.

Nantucket beaches offer something for everyone — **Jetties Beach**, located near the channel leading into Nantucket Harbor, has warm Sound swimming and gentle surf; **Children's Beach**, with broad shallow flats, is a protected swimming area for bathers.

The beaches of the island's south shore are often washed by powerful breakers. **Surfside** and **Cisco Beaches** are popular with surfers; **Madaket Beach**, at the island's western end, is good for surf casting.

OPPOSITE TOP: Many of the Cape's vacationing visitors take advantage of its relatively undeveloped shorelines and relaxed atmosphere. OPPOSITE BOTTOM: A short distance off the coast of Cape Cod, the island of Martha's Vineyard is a world unto itself.

Central Massa- chusetts and the Berkshires

CENTRAL MASSACHUSETTS

Leaving historic Boston, the coastal region, and Cape Cod, central Massachusetts offers a quite different ambiance. An area of lakes, trails, colleges and cornfields, it stretches north to New Hampshire and west to the foothills of the Berkshires.

SPRINGFIELD

Springfield is a sprawling industrial city, home to more than 200 factories and manufacturing plants. The city is located in the geographical center of the state at the crossroads of two interstate highways (Interstate 90 and Interstate 91).

Springfield is best known as the home of America's largest weapons arsenal, **Springfield Armory**. The Armory manufactured the first American musket in 1795, supplied Union weapons during the Civil War, and produced the famous Springfield rifle. It now houses the **Benton Small Arms Museum**, with displays of weapons dating from the fifteenth century.

The Armory, on the Quadrangle (Chestnut and State Streets), is part of a cultural complex that includes the **Museum of Fine Arts** (European and American primitive paintings) and the **Smith Art Museum** (Oriental and American art and furnishings).

Also worthy of attention is Springfield's massive **Eastern States Exhibition**, or "Big E" as it is called, which is held each September to display the year's agricultural and industrial achievements.

In 1891, Dr James Naismith of Springfield College invented a game whose object was to toss a ball into a peach basket. He called it basketball, and after he realized that removing the basket bottoms would add momentum to the game, it became wildly popular.

Now basketball is part of the American way of life and its heroes and their hours of glory are the pride of The **Basketball Hall of Fame** (Springfield Center, off Interstate 91; ℂ (413) 781-6500; admission $5.00 with reductions for children and senior citizens; open year round, times

variable) which is the nation's shrine to hoops.

The inventor is honored with a large memorial and a replica of the original YMCA gymnasium where the first game was played. It differs from other major sports' halls of fame in that it honors great players from amateur, college, and professional ranks —not just the professional. Besides old balls, jerseys, trophies, and videos, the hall offers a "shooting gallery" with basketballs delivered on a conveyor belt to visitors who stand behind a rail and "shoot some hoops."

Tourist Information

Always willing to provide information on the area is the **Greater Springfield Convention and Visitors Bureau**, (56 Dwight Street, Springfield, MA 01101; ℂ (413) 787-1548).

Where to Stay

For reliable quality with a little personal attention, try the **Best Western Black Horse** (500 Riverdale Street, West Springfield; ℂ (413) 733-2161; 50 rooms; moderate to expensive). One can also count on **Howard Johnson's Motor Lodge** (1150 Riverdale Street, West Springfield; ℂ (413) 739-7261; 112 rooms; moderate to expensive), **Quality Inn and Conference Center** (296 Burnett Road, Chicopee; ℂ (413) 592-7751; 185 rooms; moderate to expensive), and **Sheraton Inn — Springfield West** (1080 Riverdale Street, West Springfield; ℂ (413) 781-8750; 265 rooms; expensive) for comfortable lodgings.

OPPOSITE: Flower market in the Pioneer Valley.
ABOVE: Picnicking near the Mohawk Trail.

AROUND SPRINGFIELD

Old Sturbridge Village

Just 30 miles (48 km) east of Springfield is **Old Sturbridge Village** (℄ (508) 347-3362; admission $14.00 adults, $6.00 children; open daily 9 am to 5 pm, closed holidays and Mondays from November to April), a living-history museum that recreates life in an 1830's rural New England town. More than 200 acres (81 hectares) of rolling landscape, woodlands, country pathways, a

working historical farm, and more than 40 historic buildings form part of the village, which opened in 1946. Guides in historical dress demonstrate nineteenth-century skills, and share the customs, work, and celebrations of early Massachusetts with visitors.

Center Village is the heart of Old Sturbridge. Its Common is lined with historic homes such as the rustic 1704 Fenno House, the 1740 Richardson House Parsonage of a saltbox design, and the Center Meeting House, which dominates the head of the Common with its Greek Revival columns and tall white-clapboard spire.

The living-history museum of Old Sturbridge Village in central Massachusetts recreates nineteenth-century New England life.

Take one of the footpaths leading off the Common to the **Pliny Freeman Farm**, which demonstrates typical 1830's community life in New England. It is one of the liveliest spots in the entire village, with costumed men and women performing daily farmstead tasks. The seasonal rhythms are also very evident — with the birth of baby lambs and calves and the plowing and planting of fields each spring; crop harvesting in the fall; and preparations for the long New England winter.

In addition to their daily tasks, village residents recreate special events such as the festive Fourth of July celebrations which include a parade, music, and a reading of the Declaration of Independence. There are also programs, seminars, and workshops for those with an interest in field archaeology, spinning, and blacksmithing.

Where to Stay

Hotels here are more reasonably priced, and smaller, than in Springfield: **Old Sturbridge Village Motor Lodge** (U.S. 20; ℄ (508) 347-3327; 59 rooms; moderate) and **Quality Inn Colonial** (U.S. 20; ℄ (508) 347-3306; 64 rooms; moderate).

QUABBIN RESERVOIR

The Quabbin Reservoir covers 128 sq miles (332 sq km), and supplies drinking water to the Boston area. To build the reservoir, engineers dammed the Swift River, flooding four river valley towns and in the process, created a recreational wonderland offering fishing, hiking, and scenic shore drives along U.S. 202, Routes 9 and Alt. 32. From an observation tower off **Windsor Dam** (Route 9, two miles or just over three kilometers from Belchertown) there is a wonderful view of nearly 50 reservoir islands, created by valley hills that rise above the water line.

THE PIONEER VALLEY

Several well-known college campuses can be visited in the Pioneer Valley.

In **Amherst**, the Amherst College campus is a tree-shaded green; the high-rise University of Massachusetts towers above the

surrounding corn fields. The town itself was home to three celebrated American poets — Robert Frost, Emily Dickinson, and Eugene Field. One University of Massachusetts French professor is reputed to have the state's most extensive private library.

In nearby **Northampton**, Smith College, founded in 1875 to produce "intelligent gentlewomen," is now co-educational. Just north of town are many restored homes, including the 1658 Parsons House and 1796 Shepherd House. With Hampshire and Mount Holyoke colleges as well, the Pioneer Valley is blessed with cultural attractions and college-style nightlife.

THE MOHAWK TRAIL

The Mohawk Trail follows the trace of an ancient Indian footpath from New York's Finger Lakes to central Massachusetts. One of the first historical references to the trail notes that the Pocumtuck Indians, under pressure from the expanding colonists, retreated from their villages on the banks of the Connecticut River near what is now Greenfield, Massachusetts, in 1663 to invade the lands of the Mohawks, in the area of what is now Troy, New York. In the ensuing war, the Mohawks annihilated the Pocumtucks, virtually wiping out their legacy in North America. Later, pioneers traveled along the Mohawk Trail from the Massachusetts Bay Colony to the Berkshires, then on to Dutch settlements in the Mohawk and Hudson valleys.

The Mohawk Trail became a major path for moving colonial forces to New York to defend British outposts during the French and Indian wars. These troops included a young Paul Revere, then making his first trip away from his Boston home.

Soon after Independence, the Mohawk Trail was used by covered wagon trains moving west, as it provided the easiest way over the mountains. In 1786, it became America's first toll-free interstate road.

The nineteenth century brought stagecoaches to the trail, as more and more settlers moved westward. But it was not until

After wiping out nearly every Indian in the state, Massachusetts now attempts to capitalize on its native American heritage.

1914 that the Mohawk Trail was opened to automobile travel.

Today, the Mohawk Trail extends 63 miles (100 km) along Massachusetts Routes 2 and 2A, from Millers Falls on the Connecticut River to Williamstown, near the Massachusett–New York state line. It is one of the nation's prettiest highways, ascending from the Connecticut River valley past farms and orchards into the rugged forested slopes of the Berkshires, and ending, at Williamstown, in one of New England's most renowned villages.

ALONG THE TRAIL

Millers Falls
Spanning the Connecticut River just west of Millers Falls is the **French King Bridge**, 750 ft (228 m) long and 140 ft (43 m) above the water. The northern side of the bridge provides an excellent view of the River and of **French King Rock**, supposedly the site of the first planting of the French flag in this region by French explorers.

Greenfield
Farther west, Greenfield is known for its involvement in the Indian wars and for its fine colonial architecture. There is a panoramic view of the lush Greenfield Valley from the **"Poet's Seat Tower"** on Greenfield Mountain (east on Main Street toward High Street, then follow the signs). The town also has a covered bridge over the Green River.

Deerfield
South of U.S. 5 and settled in the mid-1600s this famous colonial town has Indian and Revolutionary War monuments and pre-Revolutionary War houses lining its Main Street, with many open to visitors. Deerfield was the site of two attacks in the French and Indian wars, the Massacre of Bloody Brook in 1675, and the Deerfield Massacre in 1704.

The restoration of Deerfield's historic structures was the first project of its kind in the United States. Period artifacts can be viewed at **Old Deerfield Village and Memorial Hall Museum**. The Museum also offers guided tours of a street lined with 12 colonial-era houses.

Back on the Mohawk Trail, you can stop in **Shelburne Falls** to see the **"Bridge of**

Flowers," an arched trolley bridge that has been maintained as a "hanging garden" by the Shelbourne Women's Club since 1929. Flowers cover the bridge from spring to fall. The 400-ft (122-m), five-arch concrete bridge was built in 1908 across the Deerfield River to carry trolley tracks between Shelburne and Buckland, but was abandoned in the late 1920s as transportation patterns changed.

Also worth seeing are the geologically impressive glacial potholes visible at **Salmon Falls** (follow the signs from the bridge), reputed to be some of the largest in the world.

Charlemont

The trail's half-way point, this town, settled in 1749, offers "Mohawk Trail concerts" featuring classical American and European chamber music (May to October) in the historic, yet acoustically perfect, **Charlemont Confederated Church**.

Charlemont's landmark is the 900-lb (409-kg) bronze cast statue (at Indian Bridge spanning the Deerfield River) "Hail to the Sunrise," depicting an Indian with arms outstretched to the "Great Spirit," a 1932 memorial to the Mohawks. Unfortunately, commemoration of America's original inhabitants occured only long after they had been annihilated.

Bissell Bridge, a recreated covered bridge built in 1951 across Mill Brook, is just off Route 2 on Heath Road.

Charlemont to North Adams

West of Charlemont, the Mohawk Trail climbs into rugged **Hoosac Range**, a wall of granite

ABOVE: Deerfield's historic church has long been one of the town's most prominent attractions.
OPPOSITE: Fall colors on the Mohawk Trail.

(once nicknamed the "Berkshire Barrier") that isolated the northern Berkshires from the rest of Massachusetts until 1875, when the Hoosac Tunnel was blasted through the rock. Soon after, one enters the superb mountain scenery of the **Mohawk Trail State Forest**. There are plenty of excellent hiking trails, including an easy one to the top of Forbidden Mountain, as well as picnic areas and campgrounds.

Whitcomb Summit, just north of the town of Florida, offers the Trail's highest viewpoint (2,200 ft or 670 m) with a panorama of the Deerfield River and the Hoosac Tunnel.

Built to reduce the grade for trains traveling between Boston and Troy, New York, the **Hoosac Tunnel** is four miles (six kilometers) long. It took 25 years to complete, finally opening in 1873 after taking the lives of nearly 200 men and costing more than $15 million. It had to be blasted through solid granite, and involved the first working use of nitroglycerin; constant accidents earned the Tunnel the nickname of the "Bloody Pit." It is now considered by many local residents to be haunted by the ghosts of the men who died building it.

To reach the Tunnel's eastern entrance, take Whitcomb Hill Road south to the Deerfield River, then turn left on River Road until you reach the railroad tracks.

Just west of Florida is the **Western Summit**, with fantastic views of North Adams, Williamstown, the Hoosac Valley, and the Green Mountains, along with Mt Greylock, the highest mountain in the Berkshires. Hang gliders launched from the summit often reach altitudes of more than 3,500 ft (1,067 m).

As the Trail descends toward North Adams, be careful to slow for the Hairpin Turn, a 180-degree curve memorable for its configuration and its spectacular views of the surrounding countryside. Off-the-road parking provides access to an observation platform. Here the Golden Eagle Restaurant has a second-story, outdoor veranda with panoramic views of three states: Massachusetts, Vermont, and New York. The Trail continues down to the factory town of North Adams.

North Adams

Once a busy nineteenth century mill town, North Adams has seen its commercial prominence vanish with the textile industry. It is now a year-round recreation center, with **ski**

areas minutes away, and abundant summer activities. It also puts on a **Fall Foliage Festival**, when the surrounding hills are a palette of scarlet, gold, and crimson.

Its 150-year-old **Cider Mill**, one of the largest restored mills in New England, makes tasty golden apple cider. The **Natural Bridge**, located on Route 8 North, is another North Adams attraction. A rock formation about 550 million years old, it is a marble chasm 475 ft (145 m) long and 60 ft (18 m) deep. This unique geological feature is the only natural, water-eroded bridge in North

WILLIAMSTOWN

Williamstown is only five miles (eight kilometers) west of North Adams on Route 2, but it is a universe apart. Hawthorne once remarked that Williamstown is "a white village and a steeple set like a daydream among the high mountain waves." In the late nineteenth century, it was a spa and summer resort. Set in a hollow of the surrounding Berkshires and in the shadow of Mt Greylock, Williamstown remains one of New England's

America, and can be traversed from May through October for a small admission charge. North Adams has also recently created the $72 million **Massachusetts Museum of Contemporary Art**, located in a 28-building industrial complex.

High over the town looms the magnificent granite bulk of **Mt Greylock**. At 3,491 ft (1,064 m), it is the highest point in Massachusetts. From its rocky barren summit the hiker is rewarded with a fine vista of the Berkshires and western Massachusetts, the Green Mountains of Vermont, and the Hudson River Valley of New York. The surrounding peaks and forests have many well-marked hiking trails, including part of the Appalachian Trail, which crosses Mt Greylock.

loveliest villages. The 1793 **Williams College**, long rated the country's best liberal arts college, is situated in this town. Known for its stringent intellectual requirements and brilliant, demanding professors, Williams College is well worth a visit by those whose children might someday seek the best American education has to offer.

Williamstown's **Sterling and Francine Clark Art Institute** (South Street, just west of the town center) houses one of the world's largest private collections of Renoirs, as well as works of other Impressionists, and is one of the finest small art museums in the country.

At the information booth, Main and South Streets, you may obtain a self-guiding map to explore Williamstown's rich past. On Main

Street, many of the large and lovely homes date from the 1750's. One of the most interesting college buildings is Lawrence Hall, part of the **Williams College Museum of Art**, an octagonal Grecian rotunda inspired by Thomas Jefferson's *Monticello.*

The **Williamstown Summer Theater Festival**, founded in 1955, is an annual event featuring some of the country's most celebrated actors.

The main venue is at the nation's finest summer theater, Williamstown Theater on Main Stage. In addition there is Williams

Pittsfield, Massachusetts, Shakespeare & Company in Lenox, Massachusetts, and the Berkshire Theater Festival in Stockbridge, Massachusetts, to name a few. You can watch a different theater production in Williamstown or one of its neighboring towns every night of the week, at less than half the cost of a ticket to one of New York's Broadway shows.

Where to Stay and Eating Out

Williamstown has many hotels and restaurants for a college town. Reccommended

College's Adams Memorial Theater on Main Street. The festival has featured actors such as Christopher Reeve and Richard Thomas, directors such as Joanne Woodward, and playwrights like John Guare. Other choices include: Adams Memorial Theater's "Cabaret," which presents an early revue and a late cabaret that often includes stars from the Main Stage, Thespis Productions, now almost 10 years old, at the Clark Institute; the Calliope Theatre Company; a women's theater group; and the Spring Street Ensemble Theatre, which showcases experimental productions.

Just a half-hour drive away are the Oldcastle Theatre Company in Bennington, Vermont, The Theater Barn in New Lebanon, New York, the Berkshire Public Theatre in

hotels are **The William's Inn** (on the Green; ☏ (413) 458-9371; 103 rooms; expensive), and the **Four Acres Motel** (213 Main Street; ☏ (413) 457-9731; 30 rooms; moderate). The best restaurant is **Le Jardin Inn** (777 Cold Spring Road; ☏ (413) 458-8032) which specializes in lamb and duck meals.

THE BERKSHIRES

"There's no tonic like the Housatonic," said Oliver Wendell Holmes about the river that snakes through the Berkshire Hills and winds into Connecticut. It creates an idyllic setting for the well-preserved little towns that dot the **Berkshires** in the westernmost county of

Massachusetts. Village greens are surrounded by stunning colonial architecture; white clapboard church steeples pierce the blue skies; and tall shade trees line quiet residential streets. A plethora of cultural activities include nationally-renowned theater and music festivals.

However, its extraordinary variety of landscapes — open meadows and rolling farmlands, valleys dotted with shimmering lakes, wooded hills and green mountains, rushing rivers and plummeting waterfalls—is a major ingredient of the Berkshires' magic; this area is also the heart of Massachusetts' ski country.

Stretching from the Vermont border in the north, down the old "York State" line to the south, the Berkshire Hills remained a wilderness until 1725, when pioneer Matthew Noble erected a log cabin in what is now the town of Sheffield. Soon dense forests were cleared for farmland, and towns appeared along the Housatonic River. In the nineteenth century, the Berkshires were mined for iron used on the railroads. Marble was also quarried here and transported to construct such edifices as the Capitol dome in Washington, D.C.

The Berkshires attracted urban dwellers wishing to "escape" into the country, including some of America's wealthiest families (such as the Carnegies and the Vanderbilts), who built elegant mansions (quaintly called summer "cottages") and used them for less than three months of the year.

From Williamstown you can continue north to Burlington, Vermont, or turn south on Route 7 toward the lower Berkshires.

Along the way you will pass the popular **Jimmy Peak** and **Brodie Mountain** ski areas near the town of Hancock.

THE SHAKERS

A detour off U.S. 7 onto U.S. 20 at Pittsfield brings you to **Hancock Shaker Village**, an authentic community of the Shaker religious sect that thrived from 1790 to 1960. It is today a living, working museum of Shaker rural life, with 20 restored buildings on 1,000 acres (405 hectares).

The Shaker movement started in England in 1747 as an offshoot of Quakerism. Manchester's Ann Lee first led eight followers to the American colony of New York and founded a settlement near Albany.

For a time, they were known as "shaking Quakers" because "dances" during religious services made their bodies shake and tremble. Eventually, the Shakers' pronouncements and beliefs in four principle doctrines (separation from the outside world, common property, confession of sins, and celibacy, with separation but equality of the sexes) took hold. By the mid-nineteenth century, the Shaker movement reached its zenith, with 19 communities in the United States.

Strolling through the village on a guided tour, you will notice that the buildings are

austere but elegant and the craftsmanship outstanding. Shaker ways of coping with the material world are sometimes ingenious, while their keen grasp of the concepts of purity and functionalism have raised the design of their buildings, furniture, and common utensils to an art form.

The village's finest example of Shaker architecture and genius is the magnificently restored **Round Stone Barn**. Built in 1826, the barn's upper level could be accessed by horses and wagons, which unloaded their harvest into a central haymow and then proceeded around a track to another exit. This eliminated the problem of backing hitched teams out of the barn, an often difficult task. Cows were stabled on the ground floor.

It is also interesting to note how separation of the sexes was carried to an extreme. **The Brick Dwelling** (community dining room, sleeping rooms, and kitchen) which

OPPOSITE: The Chapel of Williams College, one of the nation's highest-ranked liberal arts colleges.
ABOVE: Hancock Shaker Village is a study in simplicity.

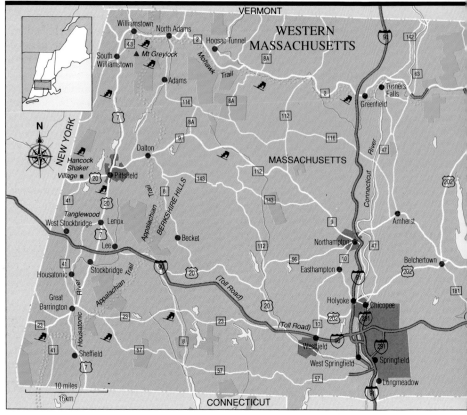

housed 100 brothers and sisters, is divided exactly in half; it is also very light and airy, with more than 3,000 windowpanes.

Hancock tours also include nineteenth-century **craft demonstration** and a walk through the site's farm and herb garden (the seed industry was a Shaker specialty).

PITTSFIELD

Returning toward U.S. 7, you will arrive at **Pittsfield**, whose **concert hall** has been the scene of distinguished music since 1918 and is now home to the South Mountain Concerts series. Artists who have appeared here include Leonard Bernstein, Leontyne Price, Rudolf Serkin, and the Tokyo Quartet. Concerts are held during late summer and fall. The Berkshire Ballet offers a six-week series of classical, modern, and contemporary dance at the **Koussevotzky Arts Center** on the Berkshire Community College campus.

Pittsfield is also home to the **Berkshire Museum**, a fine collection of nineteenth- and twentieth-century American paintings and Hawthorne memorabilia. The **Berkshire Athenaeum's Melville Room** has a unique selection of books, letters, and pictures of the author. Melville's home, "Arrowhead," in Pittsfield, is filled with personal artifacts from his time in the house (18501863). Melville wrote part of *Moby Dick* here, where he could gaze out over the Berkshire Hills, which he said reminded him of rolling waves and gray humpback whales.

Where to Stay

The **Berkshire Hilton Inn** is on Berkshire Common (((413) 499-2000; 175 rooms; expensive) or you can stay at the smaller, cozy **Heart of the Berkshires Hotel** (970 West Housatonic Street; ((413) 433-1255; 16 rooms; moderate).

LENOX AND TANGLEWOOD

Lenox became popular as a summer resort when the Boston Symphony Orchestra

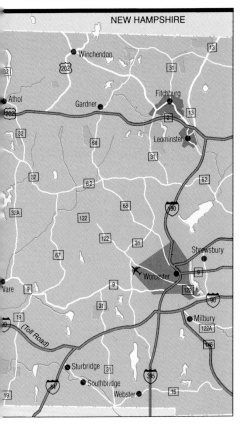

NEW HAMPSHIRE

One can enjoy, as well, one of the many non-Boston Symphony concerts, recitals, and full orchestra presentations; nearly 50 of these performances are held throughout the summer. The **Popular Artists' Series** consists of rock, pop, and folk concerts, while the **Stockbridge Chamber Concerts** at Seven Hills offers a year-round program of music in the great estates, halls, and historic churches of the Berkshires.

On Lenox's Main Street is the 1805 "Church on the Hill." Several other streets offer glimpses of mansions once owned by business and industrial magnates (Harrimans, Biddles, Stuyvesants) who had summer "cottages" in Lenox. Most of these houses are not open to the public, although one — Wheatleigh — now operates as an elegant country inn and restaurant.

Where to Stay

Wheatleigh (West Hawthorn Road; ((413) 637-0610; expensive), **Village Inn** (16 Church Street; ((413) 637-0020; 28 rooms; moderate to expensive) and **Quality Inn** (330 PittsfieldLenox Road; ((413) 637-1100; 120 rooms; moderate to expensive) are recommended in the area.

Around Lenox

Nearby the **Pleasant Valley Wildlife Sanctuary** is a Massachusetts Audubon preserve of native plants and landscapes, including beaver ponds, open meadows, and more than seven miles (11 km) of walking trails.

BECKET

Jacob's Pillow Dance Festival, which takes place in Becket over 10 weeks each summer, offers some of the country's best dance and music. Since its inception more than 50 years ago, the program has commissioned new dance works from many innovative and renowned choreographers. Performers have included Martha Graham, Merce Cunningham, and the Alvin Ailey Repertory Ensemble. Besides main theater performances, the Pillow's "Inside/Out Series" presents a free, hour-long show on an outdoor stage that includes works in progress, discussions with dancers and choreographers, and audience questions.

chose it in 1939 as the site of its annual **Berkshire Festival of Music**. The festival is held at **Tanglewood**, one-and-a-half miles (just under three kilometers) southwest on Route 183. The 210-acre (85-hectare) estate is where Hawthorne once lived and wrote *The House of Seven Gables*. The site takes its name from *Tanglewood Tales*, which he also wrote here.

The Boston Symphony and guest artists perform here every July and August. The main "Music Shed," designed by Eero Saarinen, seats only 6,000, but an expansive lawn allows thousands more to enjoy the evening's music.

During Boston Symphony concert nights, Tanglewood is a mass of traffic and humanity. It is best to arrive early to find a spot in the parking lot, and maybe bring along a picnic meal; it is not unusual for people to arrive more than three hours before a scheduled performance. Special bus excursions to Tanglewood concerts are offered by a number of local tour agencies.

STOCKBRIDGE

Stockbridge is a stately New England town with fine houses, quaint shops, historical attractions, and a lively arts community. Established as an Indian mission by preacher and theologian John Sargeant (whose 1739 home, the **Old Mission House**, is open for tours), the town has evolved into a grand summer resort. The **Norman Rockwell Museum**, a restored eighteenth-century mansion in the Old Corner House (on Main

Street; ((413) 298-3822; admission $4.00, children $1.00; open year-round except January 15 to 31, times variable), exhibits a large permanent collection of his paintings.

Other attractions worth visiting include **Chesterwood**, off Route 183 in Glendale, the summer estate of Daniel Chester French, sculptor of the Lincoln Memorial in Washington, D. C., and the *Minuteman* in Concord, Mass. His mansion, studio, barn gallery, and period garden are open to guided tours, along with nature trails that offer views of Monument Mountain.

ABOVE: The studio and estate of reknowned sculptor Daniel Chester French in Stockbridge. OPPOSITE: Antiques and objets d'art can be found in New England's many antique shops.

The **Berkshire Theatre Festival**, one of the nation's top summer theaters, has performed here for more than 60 years. Classical works with name actors are staged June through August in the large Playhouse; new plays and children's theater from around the world are set in the barn, as part of the Unicorn Theater Company.

Where to Stay

The antique-filled rooms, flower-laden courtyard, and front porch lined with comfortable rocking chairs of the **Red Lion Inn** have made it a regional favorite for years. (Main Street; ((413) 298-5545; 100 rooms; moderate to expensive). Smaller and of equal quality is **The Inn at Stockbridge** (U.S. 7; ((413) 298-3337; 7 rooms; expensive).

Around Stockbridge

Just west off Interstate 90, **West Stockbridge** is a replica of a New England town, as if there were not enough real ones in the area. Its Main Street is lined with 1800s-style storefronts housing galleries, specialty stores, antiques, and other tourist traps. A number of fairs and festivals are held here during the year. The **Williamsville Inn** (Route 41; (9413 374-6118; expensive) has an excellent dining room.

Berkshire Scenic Railway is a "rolling museum" that operates over a portion of the historic New Haven Housatonic Valley Line with vintage railroad equipment and comfortable 1920-vintage coaches. It rambles at a leisurely 10-mph (16-kph) pace for 15 miles (24 km) between **Lee** and **Great Barrington**. With an open or round trip ticket you can stop anywhere you wish along the line and board a later train to complete your journey. The train follows the path of the Housatonic River, past mills, waterfalls, meadows, and mountains. Although the train is stationed at Lee, you can also board in Stockbridge, Housatonic, and Great Barrington.

Tyringham, about five miles (eight kilometers) south of Lee along Tyringham Road, is noted for its **Gingerbread House** and **Tyringham Art Galleries**. The thatched cottage with rock pillars and grottoes, built in the 1930's by sculptor Sir Henry Hudson Kitson, now houses several art galleries. There are also beautiful sculpture gardens and woodland walking trails.

GREAT BARRINGTON

A short scenic drive south on U.S. 7 leads to Great Barrington, the largest town in the southern Berkshires resort area. The Mohican Indians built their "Great Wigwam" at a ford here in the Housatonic River. The village gained prominence in 1774 when its residents seized the courthouse from the British, committing the first act of open rebellion in the colonies against the Crown. And William Stanley (founder of General Electric) helped to light up the town with electricity as early as 1886. A booth on Main Street in the center of town provides visitor information.

Great Barrington was a station on the Underground Railroad transporting fugitive slaves to freedom. W.E.B. du Bois, the author and editor, lived here, as did James Weldon Johnson, co-founder of the National Association for the Advancement of Colored People (NAACP).

This part of the southern Berkshires is an antique hunter's delight. Scores of antique shops can be found in Great Barrington, South Egremont, Sheffield, New Marlboro, and along the winding backroads of the Berkshire farm country nestled cozily in gentle hills. As with all antique shops, beware of fakes and inflated prices.

Where to Stay

The best of Great Barrington's hotels are **Wildflower Inn** (Route 23; ((413) 528-2720; 12 rooms; moderate to expensive); **Monument Mountain** (249 Stockbridge Road; ((413) 528-3272; 18 rooms; moderate to expensive); and **Briarcliff Motor Lodge** (U.S. 7; ((413) 528-3000; 16 rooms; moderate to expensive).

Around Great Barrington

Sheffield, founded in 1733 and the oldest village in the Berkshires, is the only Massachusetts town with two **covered bridges**.

Farther south, off Route 7A, is **Ashley Falls**, location of Berkshire County's oldest home, the 1735 **Ashley House** (open for tours May to mid-October), and **Bartholomew's Cobble**, a national natural landmark renowned for its native ferns and wildflowers.

There are also six miles (10 km) of hiking trails skirting the banks of the Housatonic River.

About 12 miles (19 km) past South Egremont (off Route 41, then follow the signs almost to the New York state line) is **Bash Bish Falls**, a 275-ft (84-m) waterfall plunging down a steep gorge. Legend has it that an Indian girl jumped to her death here; her spirit is said to haunt the pool beneath the falls.

Less than five miles (eight kilometers) north of Great Barrington off Route 7, is

Monument Mountain. Two trails lead to the summit. An easy two- to three-hour round trip offers spectacular views of Squaw Peak. Monument Mountain is also known as the site of an 1850 meeting between Melville and Hawthorne, which began their friendship.

ANTIQUE HUNTING IN THE BERKSHIRES

The Berkshire Mountains offer some of the best antique-hunting grounds in the region. Colonists who settled in New England in the seventeenth century tried to duplicate those styles which were popular back home in England. But very few had the skills or services of a master carpenter or furniture maker. Thus, you will find that the earliest "early American" antiques might be rudimentary pieces of furniture — often large, squared-off pine and oak cupboards, broad flat tables, and smaller boxy furnishing, (see SHOPPING in TRAVELERS' TIPS Chapter).

Maine

BY FAR the largest New England state, Maine is also in many ways the purest remnant of the old New England spirit of hard work, honesty, thrift, and personal ethics — in a word, the "soul" of New England. Looking down on its neighbor states as too soft, too modern, too flamboyant, and too money-oriented, Maine has been hardened by its long, cold winters and constant battle with the sea.

Although the state's stunning beauty, lovely architecture, and largely undeveloped back country continue to draw more and more visitors (and new residents) each year, native Mainers still retain a certain sense of privacy which seems to exclude newcomers — a newcomer being anyone whose family has not lived in the state for at least several generations. And although in recent years there has been a rise in "anti-outsider" sentiment, the traveler is still welcomed for himself more than for the money he might spend.

"DOWN EAST"

A fabulous landscape of 10,000 lakes and 10,000 offshore islands, Maine is as far east as the traveler can go without leaving the United States. For a Maine resident, to travel northeast toward Canada is to go "down east" a term that has come to be identified with the state itself. Maine's coastline juts north and east into the cold, stormy Atlantic; to the north Maine is bounded by the endless spruce and fir forests of the Canadian provinces Quebec and New Brunswick. Only on its western border does Maine touch the United States, along the state line with New Hampshire.

In his famous journal of exploration, *The Maine Woods*, Henry David Thoreau termed the state the last remaining wilderness east of the Mississippi. Even then, however, most of the towering white pines that gave the state its nickname had been cut down for ships' masts. Today, nearly 90 percent of Maine remains uninhabited spruce, fir, and pine forests, which are, however, heavily overlogged by the paper industry, furnishing, as one Maine conservationist complained, "half of America's toilet paper."

THE MAINE ETHIC

Maine's wild coastline is the longest and most varied in New England, stretching for 3,500 miles (5,600 km). A jagged panoply of inlets, islands, peaks, peninsulas, bays, reefs, and stony headlands washed by the cobalt sea and hammered by white surf and crashing winter storms, the Maine coast has given rise to countless legends and tragedies of the north Atlantic, and has prepared many thousands of young fishermen and sailors for a life at sea.

Similarly so, the back woods of Maine, which gave rise to generations of lumberjacks, woodsmen, trappers, and guides, remain a marvelous experience for the more adventurous and hardy visitor — the largest undeveloped forest area in the United States east of Montana. For those willing to take the time and trouble, Maine's extensive northern river system offers perhaps the best long-distance canoeing in the lower 48 states, where the traveler can lie at night under the undimmed stars and hear the lonely, half-mad laughter of the loons across vast and silent lakes.

OPPOSITE: At anchor in Rockport, one of many excellent harbors along the Maine coast.
ABOVE: Local flair at the Fryeburg Fair.

Less well known is Maine's major, though lessening, agricultural role. Before the United States took over the Indian lands west of the Mississippi, Maine provided sheep and cattle for much of the northeast. And until federally-subsidized irrigation projects made it possible to grow potatoes cheaply on arid western farmlands, Maine potatoes were known as the nation's finest — which indeed they still are.

As with most unique places, Maine suffers from numerous cliches: rough-and-tumble lumberjacks and log cabins, salty lobster fishermen and tight-lipped natives whittling wood on the porch of a century-old general store while they talk about the "comin' nor'easter," of wandering moose, howling wolves, and L.L. Bean.

But the lumberjacks have been largely replaced by huge belching combines that grind their way through the north woods, uprooting trees and snipping off their tips and roots. Like most of their fellow Americans, unfortunately, the natives are more likely to be watching television than whittling wood, and the general store is probably filled with trinkets for the tourist trade. The moose still wander, except in hunting season when they try to keep their heads down, but no wolves have howled in Maine for nearly a hundred years — although their ecological niche is being taken over by coyotes, wilier and less afraid of man.

And sadly, L.L. Bean, once the purveyor of fine outdoors gear for Maine hunters and fishermen, is now a catch-all, trendy cloth-

downhill ski, skate, or ice fish. And in spring again there is fishing, hiking, wandering, and enjoying the outburst of blossoms and flowers that foretells the coming summer.

For warm-season vacationers, late June through August is best, when the temperatures generally hover between 70 °F and 80 °F (21 °C and 27 °C) during the day, and slightly lower at night. For skiers, Maine's cold winter weather is a blessing, for it brings heavy falls of snow. Western Maine's ski retreats, mountains surrounded by lush forests, provide a magnificent wilderness setting in which to enjoy the slopes.

TOURIST INFORMATION

To help plan your trip, the **Chamber of Commerce & Industry** (126 Sewall Street, Augusta, ME 04330) will provide free maps and brochures. For travel information, call (out of state) toll-free (800) 533-9595, or (in-state) ((207) 289-2423.

BACKGROUND

THE DAWN PEOPLE

Maine's first known inhabitants were the tribes of Paleo and Algonquin Indians who, 10,000 to 25,000 years ago, wandered down from what is now Canada and the western United States, probably along the St Lawrence River, until they reached the sea. Called "the dawn people" because they had traveled so far east, toward the dawn, they were divided, in Maine, into roughly Algonquins in the south, Penobscots in the middle, and Micmacs and other coastal tribes in the north.

They tended to winter along the coast and travel inland in the late spring, summer, and fall for hunting and gathering. The Penobscots, whose name means "the rocky place," describing a bouldered series of rapids on the river of the same name, spent their winters along Penobscot Bay, where they lived off the shellfish, fish, and shore animals. In warmer months they traveled in

ing mall and catalog store full of high-price goods for those who prefer the image of the back woods to the reality of being there.

YEAR-ROUND VACATIONS

For vacationers, the 33,215 sq mile (86,050 sq km) Maine offer unique experiences on a year-round basis. In summer one can swim in its crystalline, unpolluted lakes, swim and sail on the coast, fish the lakes, streams, and ocean, visit its lovely colonial towns, canoe its rivers, or hike its mountains. In the fall there is Maine's wonderland of autumn colors to enjoy, as well as hiking, hunting, and fishing. In winter the visitor can cross-country or

The Fryeburg Fair is a "Maine" event in late September or early October of every year.

small clans and hunting groups far up into the vastness of the Allagash and upper Penobscot watersheds, even into what is now Canada, returning with moose, caribou, and deer. Although they apparently lived in relative peace among themselves, the Maine tribes were threatened by raiding parties of fierce Mohawk warriors from upper New York state, and later by the colonists, who massacred them with the efficiency befitting Christian religious superiority.

EUROPEAN EXPLORERS

Tenth-century Norsemen were probably the first European explorers to land on Maine's shores. But the region was largely ignored until John Cabot passed in 1497. In the 1600s, colonists began to move north from what is now Massachusetts, and the French started to travel south from Acadia into Maine; there were soon frequent skirmishes between British and French troops, which continued until an eventual British victory in 1763.

The colony of Massachusetts bought what is now Maine for $6,000 in 1677; and this area remained part of Massachusetts until 1820, when it entered the Union as a free state under the Missouri Compromise. The young state quickly distinguished itself in its opposition to slavery, its commercial power, and the contribution which its brave regiments made in several major Civil War battles. It had some moral surprises in store for its sister states as well: in 1851, Maine became the first state to enact a law prohibiting the manufacture of alcoholic beverages; the law remained in force until 1934. More recently, in 1949, Maine voters sent their Congresswoman Margaret Chase Smith to the Senate, making her the first woman to serve in both houses of Congress.

THE SOUTH COAST

Maine's south coast draws many of the state's visitors to its wide beaches and sparkling surf. There are many lovely beaches along the coast, with the water gradually

Kittery, just north of the New Hampshire border, is Maine's oldest community.

getting colder as one moves northeast. Well-known is the 11-mile (18-km) **Old Orchard Beach**, a traditional haven for families from Quebec; it is the smoothest, hardest sand beach in Maine.

KITTERY

Most travelers enter Maine at its southernmost point, from Portsmouth, New Hampshire. The first town on the Maine side of the border is Kittery, once the home of pioneers and Revolutionary War heroes. This sea village — Maine's oldest community, established in 1623 — was once the backbone of the young nation's shipbuilding industry. Its legacy can be traced to Kittery's Portsmouth Navy Yard, which built John Paul Jones' ship, *Ranger*, in 1775. The *Ranger* was the first ship to fly the Stars and Stripes, and took to France the news of General Burgoyne's surrender, thus receiving the first salute ever given an American ship by a foreign power.

Today, the shipyard builds primarily submarines, and no visitors are allowed. But at the private boat yards on the Piscataqua River, the visitor can watch pleasure craft being built. The **Kittery Historical and Naval Museum** (Rogers Road, off U.S. 1; ((207) 439-3080; admission $2.00 with reductions for children, families, and senior citizens; open Monday to Saturday, 10 am to 4 pm, closed October 15 to Memorial Day except Saturdays, 1 pm to 4 pm) has an interesting collection of artifacts from Kittery's past.

Another Kittery landmark is **Fort McClary** (1809) on Kittery Point, which defended the townspeople against Indian attacks. A restored hexagonal blockhouse and the original granite sea walls remain standing.

The **Isles of Shoals** can be seen just off shore. They once harbored pirates who plundered ships after luring them to their doom along the rocks by placing false lights near the shallows.

Around Kittery

Historic sites north of Kittery include the **Sarah Orne Jewett House**, birthplace and home of the noted nineteenth-century novelist, and the **Hamilton House**, a fine 1787 Georgian mansion overlooking Salmon

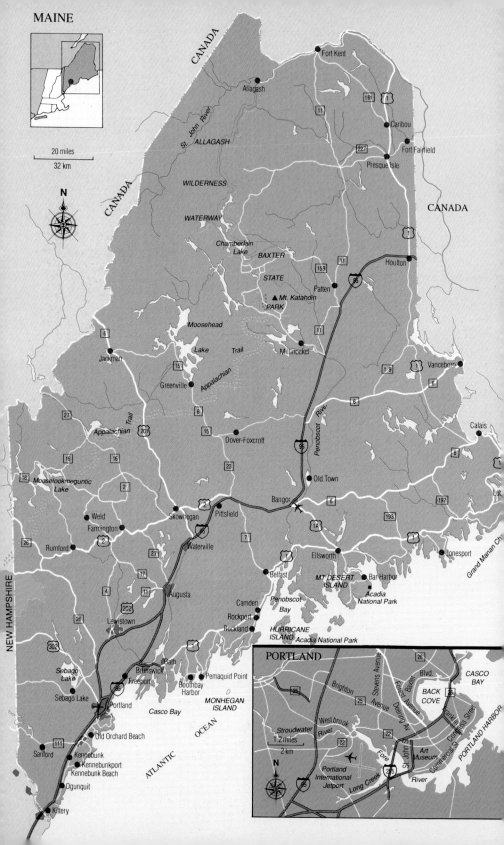

Falls River, both in Berwick. But perhaps the most notable historical complex is **York Village** (York StreetU.S. 1ALindsay Road; ((207) 363-4974). A self-guided tour includes several historic buildings and a colonial-period cemetery.

Well worth a visit is the **Old Gaol**, a stone jail built in the 1600s on a knoll overlooking York, complete with dungeons, cramped cells, jailers' quarters and a most gruesome pit—an oozing, wet hole in the ground used for unruly prisoners. It continued to be used as a jail until the 1860s.

Other local attractions include one-mile (1.6-km) **York Beach**, **Wild Kingdom Amusement Park**, and a never-ending string of fast-food seafood restaurants.

On leaving York, you have the choice of touring Maine via Interstate 95, making quick loops at various exits to harbor towns and other attractions, or taking U.S. 1, a two-to three-lane highway that bisects the commercial districts of most coastal communities.

Where to Stay
Hotels in the area are usually booked in the summer season. However, several days in advance you can usually reserve a room: **Charter House Motor Hotel** (Route 1, Kittery; ((207) 439-2000; 56 rooms; expensive); **Days Inn** (Route 1, Kittery; ((207) 439-5555; 108 rooms; moderate).

Eating Out
Fresh seafood is the standard fare at Kittery's restaurants. There are good restaurants in each price category: **Warren's Lobster House** (Route 1, Kittery; ((207)439-1630; expensive); **Bill Foster's Down East Lobster and Clambake** (Route 1A, York Harbor; ((207) 363-3255; moderate); and **Weathervane** (Route 1, Kittery; ((207) 439-0330; inexpensive).

OGUNQUIT

Going north on U.S. 1 along the coast, the next major community is Ogunquit, whose Indian name means "beautiful place by the sea." The name is well-suited, as the beach here is a three-mile (five-kilometer) stretch of white, inviting sand. The town itself is also lovely, with shady streets and fine colonial architecture.

Not to be missed is **Marginal Way**, a one-mile (1.6-km)-long path along the ledges high above the Atlantic. It follows the 100-ft (30-m) crest of Bald Head Cliff, linking the promontory with **Perkins Cove**, a fishing port with lobster shacks and shops. Along the path there are superb vistas of the ocean and shoreline tidal pools.

With its cliffs, sandy beaches, and peaceful backdrop of rolling dunes, it is no surprise that Ogunquit and Perkins Cove became an attractive destination for artists at the turn of the century. A number of small

art galleries (along with a jumble of shops) can be found in the village.

The **Ogunquit Summer Playhouse**, ((207) 934-2091, the oldest in Maine, stages a different play each week during the tourist season. Started half a century ago in a local garage, it has become one of the premier summer stock theaters on the East Coast, with its drama school attracting students from around the country.

Where to Stay
The Cliff House (Bald Head Cliff; ((207) 361-1000; 94 rooms; moderate to ex-

The Kittery Point Lighthouse marks the entrance of the Piscataqua River to the harbor.

pensive) sits atop a bluff and most rooms have sea views. The **Sparhawk** (Shore Road; ((207) 646-5562; 82 rooms; expensive) also has excellent views and good service.

Eating Out

It is not unusual for diners to travel from nearby New Hampshire and Massachusetts to eat at **Whistling Oyster** (Perkins Cove; ((207) 646-9521; expensive).

For less expensive Maine seafood dinners, there are **Clay Hill Farm** (Agamenticus Road; ((207) 646-2272; moderate to expensive), which also serves prime rib, and **Old Village Inn** (30 Main Street; ((207) 646-7088; moderate).

THE KENNEBUNKS

Since the election of George Bush as president, the next set of villages along this picturesque coastline — Kennebunk, West Kennebunk, Kennebunk Beach, and Kennebunkport, collectively called The Kennebunks — have attracted even more attention than usual, although the area was already a vastly popular vacation spot in its own right. **Kennebunk**, settled in 1650, was once the shipbuilding capital of York County. But as the boatwright trade declined, the town became a fishing and tourism center. What remains of those affluent days when shipbuilders were king are some imposing homes, stately trees, and typical New England churches, including the 1772 **First Parish Church** (on Main Street) which has a bell cast by Paul Revere & Sons.

Perhaps the town's most beautiful and unusual building is the **Wedding Cake House**. It was apparently built by a sea captain who, about to marry, was suddenly called on duty. With little time to spare, the wedding took place but without a wedding cake. The captain promised his bride that when he returned he would build her a house frosted like the cake she had wanted. The ornate gingerbread trim on the spectacular two-story, 1826 house does indeed make it look like a lacy wedding cake. It is not open to public tours, but is one of the most photographed buildings in Maine.

For an inside look at Kennebunk's historic houses, some dating back to 1724, take

the **Brick Store Museum's** 90-minute architectural walking tour (117 Main Street; ((207) 985-4802), offered during summer only.

Kennebunkport, another picturesque town at the mouth of the Kennebunk River, is the summer hometown of President George Bush. In summer, Kennebunkport is transformed into a vacation boom town. It has the standard quota of quaint shops, old inns, and fancy private estates. Historical attractions include the **Seashore Trolley Museum** (on U.S. 1, just north of town; ((207) 967-2712; admission $5.50 for adults with reductions for children, families, and senior citizens; open daily 10 am to 5:30 pm, June 23 to September 4, or Saturday and Sunday, 12 to 5 pm in spring and fall). It displays 150 antique streetcars from the United States and abroad. There is good swimming at Arundel, Cleaves Cove, and Goose Rocks beaches.

Where to Stay

Since George Bush became President, prices have gone up and reservations are hard to come by. If you must stay here, the following are recommended: **The Captain Lord Mansion** (Pleasant and Green Streets; ((207) 967-3141; 18 rooms; expensive); **The Colony** (Ocean Avenue; ((207) 967-3331; 139 rooms; a deluxe resort); **Inn at Goose Rocks** (Dyke Road; ((207) 967-5425; expensive; near saltwater marshes and woods); a**Old Fort Inn** (Old Fort Avenue; ((207) 967-5353; 16 rooms; expensive); and **Village Cove Inn** (South Maine Street; ((207) 967-3993; 32 rooms; overlooks a private cove; expensive).

Eating Out

It is easier to get dinner reservations here than hotel accommodations, and there are several excellent restaurants.

The Kennebunk Inn (45 Main Street; ((207) 985-3351; moderate to expensive) is a classic seacoast inn, providing fine continental dining.

Olde Grist Mill (Mill Lane; ((207) 967-4781; moderate to expensive) serves traditional Maine seafood diners in its converted mill.

White Barn Inn (Beach Street; ((207) 967-2321; moderate to expensive) is popular for its sirloin steak *au poivre*.

OLD ORCHARD BEACH

Ten miles further north on U.S. 1, just east of Saco, is **Old Orchard Beach**, Maine's answer to Coney Island. Its seven-mile (11-km) strip of flat, sloping sand was once the departure strip for early attempts to fly across the Atlantic, and was long known for its stylish promenade and boisterous dance halls. Today its traditional boardwalk is lined with arcades and carnival rides. Perhaps because it is the first large saltwater beach south of Montreal, Old Orchard attracts large numbers of French Canadians. Many of the hotels and restaurants here employ bilingual staff to make these visitors feel at home.

Tourist Information

During the summer season, Old Orchard has many open air concerts and special events. The **Old Orchard Chamber of Commerce** (P.O. Box 600, Old Orchard Beach, ME 04064; ((207) 934-2091) has a complete schedule of events, maps, and other useful travel information.

Where to Stay

There are many hotels, good and bad, in Old Orchard Beach; the following are recommended: **Brunswick Inn** (West Grand Avenue; ((207) 934-2171; expensive); **Edgewater** (57 W. Grand Avenue; ((207) 934-2221; 35 rooms; moderate to expensive); and **Royal Anchor** (East Grand Avenue; ((207) 934-4521; 40 rooms; moderate to expensive).

Eating Out

For seafood and steaks, **Joseph's-by-the-Sea** (55 W. Grand Avenue; ((207) 934-5044; moderate to expensive) is a local favorite.

PORTLAND

Often called the San Francisco of the East, Portland dominates a long peninsula jutting into magnificent Casco Bay, with a panorama of the Bay's hundreds of islands. At both ends of the city, the land rises gently, forming excellent viewpoints, the Eastern and Western Promenades, from which to view the islands to the east and the hills and mountains to the west.

Background

First settled in 1631, Portland has been burned to the ground three times—by raiding Indians in 1676, by invading British troops in 1775, and by accident in 1866. Longfellow commented that the smoldering ruins of 1866 resembled the rubble of Pompeii.

Each time, Portland has rebuilt itself on its ashes, stronger than before. Today it is Maine's largest and most populous city (62,000 people), providing a center of culture and urbanity in a state best known for its back country and natural beauty.

From its very beginnings, the city was an important commercial and shipping center, its natural deep-water harbor being 100 miles (160 km) closer to Europe than any other port in the United States. From Portland's docks sailed many of the finest sailing vessels and clipper ships built in the United States; in the eighteenth and nineteenth centuries the city was a major center for lumber export, fisheries, and the West Indies sugar and molasses trade. Until the completion of the Saint Lawrence Seaway, much of Canada's wheat sold overseas was shipped from Portland; the city's large

Portland's famous Observatory, one of the nation's first.

oil depots supply a regional network of pipelines. The Bath Iron Works has established a ship repair facility in Portland which has a constant stream of U.S. Navy vessels in its drydocks.

Overfishing of Atlantic fisheries and lobster beds, however, has cut into Portland's trade, and many of the docks along the port have been turned to non-fishery uses. But the city continues to grow and diversify as many professionals from lower New England, New York, and the Atlantic states arrive each year in search of a more peaceful,

crime-free and pollution-free life. A not insignificant number still commute by plane to offices in New York and Boston; others find the technological revolution of telefaxes and computers has made it possible to live in Portland while keeping in daily contact with clients elsewhere.

Portland remains a lovely city with its historic waterfront district, a magnificent skyline and architecture, and many other fascinations for the traveler.

ABOVE LEFT: State Street in Portland.
ABOVE RIGHT: Relaxing in the shade of Portland's tree-lined streets. OPPOSITE: Portland's docks harbor fishing boats, tankers and cruise ships alike.

Tourist Information

The city's **Chamber of Commerce**, ((207) 772-2811, and **Visitors Bureau**, ((207) 772-4994, both at 142 Free Street, supply brochures outlining a self-guided **"Portland History Trail"** walking tour of nearly 40 historic buildings.

The History Trail

Parts of the waterfront district, now called the **Old Port Exchange** (Exchange and Pearl Streets), have been saved and resuscitated into a thriving commercial and tourist

center of historic buildings and brick sidewalks, with cafes, good restaurants, bookstores, clothing stores, and boutiques of all shapes and sizes amid lawyers' offices, ship chandlers, and seamen's bars.

Portland also contains some of the most exquisite historic homes of New England, including the 1785 boyhood **home** of the poet **Henry Wadsworth Longfellow**, which was also the first brick building in the city (admission $3.00 with reductions for children; open Tuesday to Saturday, 10 am to 4 pm, from June 1 to Columbus Day). The **Maine Historical Society**, a repository of information on four centuries of the city's life, is next door.

Also extraordinary is the **Victoria Mansion** (109 Danforth Street; ((207) 772-4841;

admission $3.00 with reductions for children; open Tuesday to Saturday, 10 am to 4pm, Sunday 1 to 4 pm, from June 1 to Labor Day, with shorter hours in September).

Both the Eastern and Western Promenades offer views of many large and impressive mansions; nearly any downtown street has its share of colonial or Victorian masterpieces.

The city is a major educational center as well, with both the **University of Maine**'s southern campus and **Westbrook College** — the nation's first coeducational college, dating from 1831. The latter, located on

Homer, Edward Hopper, and Andrew Wyeth. Another fine museum is Westbrook College's **Payson Gallery**, with its collection of impressionist and New England art.

The **Portland Civic Center** offers a variety of prominent sports events, conventions, and concerts staged by the **Portland Concert Society**. The Visitors Bureau has schedules and ticket information.

Where to Stay
EXPENSIVE
Portland Regency, in the Old Port (20 Milk

Stevens Avenue, is a lovely tree-shaded campus of brick buildings.

Outside Portland, near the airport, the **Tate House**, built in 1755, offers a detailed view of life in the eighteenth century (1270 Westbrook Street, off outer Congress Street at the airport turnoff; admission $2.50 with reductions for children; open Tuesday to Saturday, 11 am to 5 pm, Sunday, 1:30 to 5 pm, from June 15 to September 15).

Museums And Entertainment
The art scene is also well represented here. At the **Portland Museum of Art** (7 Congress Square; ((207) 773-2787), a new wing designed by I.M. Pei houses a fine selection of paintings by Maine artists like Winslow

Street; ((207) 774-4200), is superbly situated in the Old Port, with lovely rooms in a restored nineteenth-century armory. Outside the old town are the **Holiday Inn West** (81 Riverside Street; ((207) 774-5601; 205 rooms) and the **Ramada Inn** (1230 Congress Street; ((207) 774-5611; 149 rooms). Near the new Maine Mall is the **Sheraton Tara Hotel** (363 Maine Mall Road; ((207) 775-6161; 218 rooms).

MODERATE
Susse Chalet Motor Lodge has two locations, at 340 Park Avenue near the Maine Medical Center; ((207) 871-0611, and off the Maine Turnpike at Exit 8, Brighton Avenue; ((207) 774-6101. Both can also be reached at toll-free (800) 258-1980.

Eating Out

DiMillo's (121 Commercial Street; ((207) 772-2216; moderate) serves excellent food, including fresh lobster and other sea fare, amid pleasant decor and interesting views aboard a large docked cruise ship. Unfortunately it does not accept reservations, but is one of the very best restaurants in Portland.

Boone's (6 Custom House Wharf; ((207) 774-5725; moderate to expensive) and **Seamen's Club** (375 Fore Street; ((207) 772-7311; moderate) also serve fresh seafood meals.

The Village (112 Newbury Street; ((207) 772-5320; moderate) has fine seafood, New England and continental cuisine, with emphasis on the Italian.

The Good Egg (705 Congress Street near Longfellow Square; ((207) 773-0801; inexpensive) has excellent downeast cooking, homemade hearty breakfasts including blueberry pancakes, real maple syrup, and other delights.

No trip to Portland is complete without an Italian sandwich from **Amato's Sandwich Shop** (74 India Street; ((207) 773-1682 or 1379 Washington Avenue; ((207) 767-5916; delicatessen and take-out; inexpensive). Amato's is the original home of the Italian sandwich, made the way it used to be.

Another Portland tradition is **Three Dollar Dewey's** (446 Fore Street; ((207) 772-3310; inexpensive), a fine drinking emporium with many excellent Maine-brewed and other beers on tap, and famous chili, lunch and dinner specialities.

AROUND PORTLAND

CASCO BAY AND ISLANDS

A marvelous way to see Portland and its many beautiful neighboring islands is aboard a **Casco Bay Lines cruise** (Commercial and Franklin Streets; ((207) 774-7871). A variety of options is available, including a six-hour trip to **Bailey's Island**, a circumnavigation of the Bay stopping at all major islands including **Peaks, Great and Little Diamond**, and **Chebeague**, on the Mail Boat, and sunset and musical cruises. The

Sebago Lake and Sebago Lake State Park provide natural opportunities for fishing, swimming and boating.

Maine

islands are excellent for bicycling, strolling, and getting away fom the metropolis.

Portland is also the gateway to the Canadian province of Nova Scotia via the *Prince of Fundy* cruises, departing nearly every day from May through October, an 11-hour overnight voyage. High season (June to September) rates are $68, and half price for children, with an additional $93 to carry your car. A cabin for two people varies from $40 to $160 one way. In Portland call ((207) 775-5616, or within Maine toll-free (800) 482-0955, and outside Maine toll-free (800) 341-7540.

Finally, just south of the city is the historic **Portland Headlight**. This lighthouse dates from 1791, the first authorized by the United States, upon an order from George Washington.

SEBAGO LAKE

About 12 miles (19 km) north of Portland is lovely Sebago Lake. The 14-mile (23-km) lake, second largest in Maine, lies in rolling hills of birch, maple, oak, and pine, and offers swimming, boating, fine salmon and trout fishing.

Sebago Lake State Park, at the north end of the lake, is a prime summer swimming area with wide sandy beaches, although it tends to be very crowded on weekends and holidays.

Where to Stay

Migis Lodge (off Route 302; ((207) 655-4524; 30 rooms; moderate to expensive) is on the lake shore in South Casco. There are many motels and lakeside cabins for rent in the area.

FREEPORT AND L.L. BEAN

North of Portland on U.S. 1 is **Freeport**, once a sleepy village promoted to notoriety by **L.L. Bean**. For 365 days a year, 24 hours a day, L.L. Bean parking lots are crammed with the cars of shoppers who are confronted inside the building with an overwhelming array of fashions, camping gear, hunting and fishing goods, wilderness and outdoor clothing, and accessories.

It all started in 1912, when founder Leon L. Bean promoted a better boot for Maine hunters. His money-back guarantee earned him a lot of goodwill, and soon the store began to grow, reaching almost legendary status by the 1980's. Now, the outlet's "wilderness clothes" are much sought-after by the yuppie generation. With success comes imitators. L.L. Bean has drawn a rabble of fashionable designer outlets and retailers to Freeport, transforming what was once a lovely colonial town into a shopper's wasteland.

Tourist Information
The **Freeport Merchants Association** has prepared a free brochure that list outlet stores, restaurants, bed and breakfasts,

country inns, and campgrounds. It is available in all the stores in Freeport. For a copy, write to the Association (P.O. Box 452 DL, Freeport, ME 04032; ((207) 865-1212).

AUGUSTA

Inland, just off Interstate 95, about 30 miles (48 km) north of Brunswick, is **Augusta**, the state capital. A small city of less than 25,000, Augusta is situated on the banks of the Kennebec River in the heart of the Kennebec Valley. Primarily a residential community

---

ABOVE: The placid bay of Freeport provides docking for many of the town's inhabitants. OPPOSITE: Wild Mountain Man and his resume.

with little industry or manufacturing, Augusta is largely dependent for its livelihood on the many offices of the state government.

Well worth a visit is the **Maine State House** designed by Charles Bullfinch, who was also the architect of the Boston State House. Located at State and Capitol Streets, the Maine State House was completed in 1832, and is topped by an impressive cupola. Across from it is the **State Museum** (admission free; open Monday to Saturday, 9 am to 5 pm) which has dioramas that integrate live animals and plants and many interesting historical displays.

Fort Weston, on Bowman Street, is a restored eighteenth century, stockade. It is the site from which, in 1775, Benedict Arnold set out with his troops on the ill-fated march through the wilderness to attack Quebec.

From Augusta many scenic Kennebec Valley villages are an easy drive, including **Hallowell** and **Gardiner**. Further north is historic **Waterville**, home of prestigious Colby College.

WHERE TO STAY

There are many inexpensive to moderate motels in the Augusta area. One of the best is the **Best Western Senator Inn** (284 Western Avenue; ((207) 622-5804. 85 rooms; moderate). Also adequate is the **Holiday Inn** (Western Avenue and Interstate 95; ((207) 622-6371. 128 rooms; moderate).

EATING OUT

The **Best Western Senator Inn**, mentioned above, is also recommended for fine cuisine and "Downeast" food.

DOWNEAST MAINE

"Downeast" may be a confusing term to non-Mainers. It refers to the upper northern portion of the Maine coastline. But confused or not, once you travel north to Brunswick, you are down east. (The term was coined by sailors who were blown "down" the coast in their sailing ships by the region's prevailing winds.)

Lobster taken from the frigid waters off downeast Maine's rocky coastline has become a must for many travelers. Regional restaurants prepare the delicy in every possible fashion, but perfectly steamed lobster dipped in melted butter is hard to beat. Lobster, however, is far less consumed by Mainers than by tourists; the natives tend to find it too expensive, and are apt to prefer baked beans, corn bread, fish, and other traditional fare.

TOURIST INFORMATION

For more information, contact The **Down East Maine Association** (Box 662, Ellsworth, Maine 04605; ((207) 667-3615).

The town's most important landmark is **Bowdoin College**. A private college established in 1794, it is considered one of the best in the United States, and claims alumni such as writer Hawthorne, poet Longfellow, President Franklin Pierce and polar explorer Admiral Robert Peary. The school's **Walker Museum of Art** offers a fine collection of paintings, including a Gilbert Stuart portrait of Thomas Jefferson; its **Peary-MacMillan Arctic Museum** houses artifacts from historic Arctic expeditions.

BRUNSWICK

Brunswick is an attractive town best known for its wide avenues, tall trees shading Federal mansions, and the Bowdoin College campus. **Maine Street** is the state's widest at 198 ft (60 m). Locals explain that the wide street was built to give marauding Indians fewer places in which to hide.

The **Federal Street** area contains some of Brunswick's most impressive and historic homes, including the 1806 **Stowe House**, where Harriet Beecher Stowe wrote *Uncle Tom's Cabin*. Nearby, the **Pejepscot Historical Society Museum**, housed in an 1858 sea captain's home, has a display of local seafaring artifacts.

Where to Stay and Eating Out

Stowe House, an 1807 home, has been converted into a comfortable inn (63 Federal Street; ((207) 725-5543; 48 rooms; moderate to expensive).

For dining, **The Bowdoin Steak House** (115 Maine Street; ((207) 725-2314; moderate) is excellent.

BATH

In the last 200 years, more than 5,000 ships have been launched from Bath's historic shipyards at the mouth of the Kennebec River. Today, the **Bath Iron Works** continues the tradition. Since 1889, the company has made not only pleasure boats and freighters, but also destroyers, patrol boats, and battle-ships; it remains one of the busiest boatyards in the nation for U.S. Navy ships. While national security interests keep the boatyard closed to visitors, boat launchings are still festive events in the town.

Bath's shipbuilding legacy comes alive at the **Maine Maritime Museum** (Washington Street, just off U.S. 1; ((207) 443-1316). Several buildings exhibit models, gadgets, and other seafaring artifacts; a working apprentice boatyard demonstrates various stages of boatbuilding. In summer months

boat rides are scheduled to the mouth of the Kennebec River.

BOOTHBAY HARBOR

During the summer season, more than 60,000 visitors flock to Boothbay Harbor, a fishing town that lies at the end of a rugged peninsula between the Sheepscot and Damariscotta Rivers. Its streets are lined with small shops and seafood restaurants. At nearby wharves, fishermen unload catches of fish and lobster. In warm weather, dozens of ships and boats fill the harbor, creating an unmatched spectacle of masts, sails, and colors. Special celebrations in the self-proclaimed "boating capital of New England" include **Windjammer Days** and **Friendship Sloop Days**, both held in July.

Charter boats such as the *Maranbo II* and *Balmy Days* offer **harbor cruises** that include stop-over island clambakes, seal

Boothbay Harbor shops, crowded with trinkets, cater to summer's influx of tourists.

watching, lobster hauling, scenic sunsets, and more.

Back on dry land, the **Boothbay Railway Museum** (on Route 27, one mile or 1.6 km north of Boothbay Center; ((207) 633-4727) features a ride on a narrow gauge steam railway through a replica of an old New England village.

Where to Stay

There are many hotels in the Boothbay area, but in the summer they are in great demand and rooms can be difficult to find. Don't wait until dusk to begin looking.

The following provide good accommodations: **Brown Brothers Wharf Motel and Marina** (Atlantic Avenue; ((207) 633-5440; 70 rooms; moderate to expensive); **Fisherman's Wharf Inn** (40 Commercial Street; Z (207) 633-5090; 54 rooms; moderate to expensive); **Rocktide Inn** (45 Atlantic Avenue; ((800) 762-8433; 98 rooms; expensive); and **Spruce Point Inn** (Spruce Point on Route 27; ((207) 633-4152; 56 rooms; moderate to expensive).

Eating Out

For fresh lobster and local seafood, the **Brothers Wharf Restaurant** (Atlantic Avenue; ((207) 633-5440; moderate to expensive) is the best in town.

The Lawnmeer Inn Dining Room (Route 27, Southport; ((207) 633-2544; moderate) specializes in Downeast meals.

PEMAQUID POINT

The **Pemaquid Point Light**, built in 1827, might be the most painted, photographed and sketched lighthouse in the country. It sits on a bluff at the tip of Pemaquid Point, a ledge jutting into the sea.

The lighthouse's image is reflected in shallow pools of water left by the retreating surf. A small fishermen's museum is located in the lightkeeper's house.

The Point, south of Damariscotta on Route 130, is also home to colonial **Pemaquid**. In 1965 amateur archaeologists uncovered here the foundations of seventeenth-century houses and other artifacts which included a human skeleton outfitted in armor, believed to be a Viking. These discoveries are displayed at the tiny archaeological museum.

MONHEGAN ISLAND

Near **Port Clyde**, nine miles (15 km) off the coast, rise the dramatic cliffs of **Monhegan Island**, a ledge of rock and forest less than two miles (three kilometers) long and one mile (one and a half kilometers) wide. The ocean scenery and boulder-strewn coast are spectacular when viewed from atop **Lighthouse Hill**. There are 17 miles (27 km) of **hiking trails** along the 150-ft (46-m) cliffs. The open meadows are blanketed with wildflowers, and **Cathedral Woods** display majestic pines and firs.

Leif Ericsson is said to have walked this island more than 1,000 years ago. English explorer John Cabot referred to it on his journeys. Its headlands were reputed to be hideaways for pirates, who plundered ships off the Maine coast.

The easiest way to get to Monhegan is aboard the *Laura B.*, a converted trawler which ferries passengers from Port Clyde (at the bottom of Route 131). Along the way, the captain of the *Laura B.* will stop to let his passengers watch dolphins and whales. From a distance, the island itself resembles a huge floating whale. No cars are permitted on the island.

PENOBSCOT BAY

Rockland

Continuing north on U.S. 1, travelers pass through Rockland (north of Owls Head on the western edge of Penobscot Bay), a modern-day seaport that is the leading lobster distribution center in Maine. It is perhaps best noted for its **Maine Seafood Festival**, a three-day-long event held annually during the first weekend in August. Everything revolves around the catch — there are lobster boils, harvesting excursions, and even displays of lobster trap building.

A windjammer fleet, ((207) 596-0376, offers week-long cruises along the coast, and handsome schooners ply the waters on three- to six-day island cruises from May to October. **Owls Head Lighthouse**, four miles (six and a half kilometers) south of Rock-

land, sits atop a 100-ft (30-m) cliff, and for lighthouse fans it is worth the short drive.

Camden

Camden, at the base of the Camden Hills with a long view of Penobscot Bay and its picturesque harbor, is a Maine classic. It is a yachting center and one of the loveliest towns in New England, it is also in its quiet, undemonstrative way an oasis of downeast wealth and glamour.

For a majestic panorama, head to **Camden Hills State Park** (two miles or just over three kilometers north of Camden on U.S. 1) where Mt Battie (800 ft or 244 m high) stands sentinel over the town; a stone viewing tower on top of the mount provides a spectacular view of the coast.

Camden is also a Maine publishing center, home to periodicals such as the *Down East Magazine*. It is also a renowned summer resort, attracting businessmen, Hollywood celebrities, and tourists.

Sailing is the primary attraction. In summer the harbor is filled with graceful yachts, sailboats with colorful canvases, and every other kind of floating vessel imaginable.

Sightseeing cruises and sailing trips on old schooners depart from the **Town and Public landings** (for schedules call ((207) 236-4404), offering tours of Penobscot Bay and views of Mounts Battie and Megunticook.

In winter, bitter winds laden with moisture sweep in from Penobscot Bay, which means plenty of snow for the **Camden Snow Bowl**, ((207) 236-3438, offering both downhill and cross-country runs. You can also ice skate on the vast **Lake Megunticook**. (If you are in Camden during early spring, you can enter a local gambling pool, centered on the day that the ice will break on the lake.)

At any time of year, you can browse through the expensive shops that cater to Camden's decidedly upscale clientele and to unwary tourists.

For those city and suburb dwellers anxious to prove themselves outdoorsmen, there is always the **Outward Bound School** on **Hurricane Island** in Penobscot Bay. This training school for wilderness survival skills claims that students should be prepared for the "most miserable, most wonderful days of your life." Two weeks of backpacking, rock climbing, or maneuvering tiny boats past bay islets is standard curriculum.

Where to Stay
Camden Harbor Inn (83 Bayview Street; ((207) 236-4200; 22 rooms; expensive) and the old colonial **Whitehall Inn** (52 High Street; ((207) 236-3391; 54 rooms; expensive), are the best accommodations in Camden.

Eating Out
Dinners at the **Whitehall Inn** (expensive) are unforgettably good and **Aubergine** (6

"Mount Desert" is certainly a misnomer. Sixteenth-century French explorer Champlain noticed its treeless mountain peaks, and gave the island its name. However, it is a place of dense forests, quiet bays and inlets, and has the highest mountains on the Atlantic coast.

BAR HARBOR
Bar Harbor is the gateway to the Acadia National Park, and a good base for visiting the only national park in New England. It is

Belmont Avenue; ((207) 236-8053; moderate to expensive) serves excellent French-style meals.

Rockport
Located on U.S. 1 between Rockland and Camden, **Rockport** is a fishing town with carefully landscaped grounds along its waterfront.

MOUNT DESERT ISLAND

Even in Maine, a land of intense natural beauty, Mount Desert Island and its largest town, Bar Harbor, are unusual. The name

a town which once rivaled Newport, Rhode Island, for its wealth and extravagance.

In the late nineteenth-century the island attracted artists who came to paint its incredible beauty. They were soon followed by rich East Coast families, such as the Rockefellers and Vanderbilts, who built mansions and elegant summer "cottages," transforming Mount Desert, and more specifically Bar Harbor, into their own personal playground. (One mansion featured a massive banquet table that would descend from a retractable hole in a dining room ceiling — completely set for the meal, including food and drinks!)

In 1947, a great forest fire burning out of control for nearly a month destroyed much of the island, including most of the man-

Dining at one of Bar Harbor's colonial mansions.

sions. They were replaced by more modest motels and hotels, and the island opened up to accommodate tourists of all means.

The few mansions that survived have been transformed into elegant inns, such as Cleftstone Manor in Bar Harbor, a 33-room house built in the late nineteenth century by the Blairs of Washington, D.C. (the same family that built the Washington landmark house across the street from the White House where dignitaries stay when visiting the capital).

Today, almost three million people visit Mount Desert Island (pronounced "des-SERT") annually. They come primarily to see Acadia National Park, for the yachting, and for the sightseeing cruises that leave from Municipal Pier at West Street for the Bar's scenic bays and inlets.

Tourist Information
With year round outdoor recreation opportunities in the area, the **Bar Harbor Chamber of Commerce** (Bar Harbor, ME 04609; ((207) 288-5103) has prepared several free brochures and maps for vacation planning.

Where to Stay
There is no lack of good accommodations here, although they do tend to fill up during peak summer months: **Atlantic Eyrie Lodge** (Highbrook Road; ((207) 288-9786; 57 rooms; expensive); **Bar Harbor Inn** (Newport Drive; toll free ((800) 248-3351; 115 rooms; expensive); **Bay View Inn** (111 Eden Street; ((207) 288-3173; 32 rooms; expensive); **Cleftstone Manor** (92 Eden Street; ((207) 288-4951; 16 rooms; expensive); **The Ledgelawn Inn** (66 Mount Desert Street; ((207) 288-4596; 34 rooms; expensive); **Stratford House Inn** (45 Mount Desert Street; ((207) 288-5189; 10 rooms; moderate to expensive); and **Wonder View Motor Lodge** (Eden Street; ((207) 288-3831; 82 rooms; moderate to expensive).

EATING OUT
Lorenzo Creamer's Lobster Pound (West Street; ((207) 288-5033; expensive) is a cut above the other seafood restaurants in town.

ACADIA NATIONAL PARK

33,000-acre (13,350-hectare) Acadia National Park occupies most of Mount Desert Island

and is certainly one of the nation's unique national parks. Small by comparison with Yellowstone or Yosemite, it has nonetheless an equally grand diversity of landscapes, colors, geology, flora, and fauna. It is the home of 250 different bird species and over 500 varieties of wildflowers. In ecological zones it varies from sandy and rock-strewn beaches to coastal coniferous forests to montane rock and lichen. Miles of Park Service trails crisscross the island from beach to peak, through pine forest and meadows. Dominating Mount Desert Island above the bare granite of lesser peaks is majestic Cadillac Mountain, at 1,530 ft (466 m), the highest mountain on the East coast.

Much of the land comprising the park, which was established in 1916, was given by a wealthy Bostonian, George B. Dorr, and by John D. Rockefeller, Jr., who also paid for construction of many of the Park's roads. A good place to begin a tour of the Park is at the **Visitor Center** (Hull's Cove, Route 3; ((207) 288-3338; open June to November).

Seeing the Park
Park rangers can help in planning tours, including **naturalist-led hiking treks** or self-guided 56-mile (90-km) auto tours, enhanced by prerecorded cassette tapes which describe points of interest, history, and geography. **Guided bus tours** motor through the park (depart from Main Street, Bar Harbor; ((207) 288-5218). You can also hop aboard a **sightseeing plane** of Air Acadia, Inc. (along Route 3). Another option is to hike or bike the nearly 200 miles (322 km) of footpaths and trails. Unfortunately, Park Service budget cuts by the Reagan and Bush administrations have closed many of the Park's trails, so check with Rangers for the latest details.

The 30-mile (48-km) **Loop Road** tour of the park offers memorable views. The Loop's Ocean Drive section is one-way for 11 miles (18 km) along the Park's eastern perimeter with the Champlain Mountain's pink cliffs ahead. A hike up the **Precipice Trail**, using ladders and handrails, is rewarded by a summit-top mountain vista. On the Loop's southeastern section, **Otter Cliffs** rise precipitously more than 100 ft (30 m) above the ocean.

The Park's most spectacular site is **Cadillac Mountain**, with its unparalleled views of breathtaking ocean views and rugged island interiors, including Mt Katahdin, Maine's highest peak. For those who prefer not to walk there is an automobile road to the top.

EASTERNMOST UNITED STATES

LUBEC

Visitors often travel no further up the Maine coast than Bar Harbor. However, if they continue up U.S. 1, then detour at Route 189 toward Lubec, and **Quoddy Head State Park** (just south of Lubec), the easternmost patch of land in the United States. "Sunrise County," as it likes to be called, receives the warming rays of the sun earlier than any other point in the nation. The country's greatest variation in tides is found here, with differences ranging to almost 30 ft (nine meters).

CAMPOBELLO ISLAND

Lubec is also the gateway to **Campobello Island**, New Brunswick (Canada). Linked to the mainland by a bridge stretching over Lubec Narrows, Campobello is the location of President Franklin D. Roosevelt's family summer home. There is an 11-acre (four hectare) estate surrounding the house, which is furnished with family memorabilia, ((207) 752-2922.

WAY UP NORTH

There are entire sections of Maine, basically the larger top half of the state, that most travelers never see. It is a vast wilderness of pines, balsam firs, spruce swamps, and birch, pocketed with sandy-bottomed lakes and drained by countless trout-filled streams.

BANGOR

On route to these northern wilds via the seacoast and Interstate 95, Bangor is the first stop, and the last urban center south of Canada. This city on the west bank of the Penobscot River, once the "lumber capital of

the world," was the brawling center of a young logging industry back in the days when Maine still had tall trees. In those boisterous times, lumbermen would come in after weeks in the woods, sailors would sail upriver after weeks or years at sea, and a wild and often bruising time was had in "Devil's Half-acre," the city's bar and brothel district.

Now, in more temperate times, the city maintains a giant statue of mythical lumberjack Paul Bunyan on Main Street opposite the Civic Center. Bangor still relies on the wood industries and pulp processing as the mainstay of its economy, although it is now diversifying rapidly. A Bangor Victorian mansion is the home of "horror" novelist Stephen King.

Above Bangor, the roads fan out northeast to **Moosehead Lake**, north to **Millinocket** and **Baxter State Park**, beyond to **Aroostook County**, and west to Maine's major ski areas, **Sugarloaf** and **Saddleback Mountain** near Lake Mooselookmeguntic.

Where to Stay
Holiday Inn-Main Street (500 Main Street; ((207) 947-8651; 125 rooms; moderate to expensive), and **Ramada Inn** (357 Odlin Road; ((207) 947-6961; 116 rooms; moderate to expensive).

MOOSEHEAD LAKE

Moosehead, the largest lake in Maine, lies some 90 miles (145 km) beyond Bangor. It covers more than 120 sq miles (310 sq km), with a shoreline of 420 miles (677 km). Much of the shore is inaccessible except by canoe or float plane, both of which are available for hire or charter at **Greenville** at the south end of the lake. The region remains rich in wildlife, including, deer, bear, and moose; the lake's waters abound with lake salmon and trout. For the hunter and fisherman, there are many lodges and hunting camps.

The less adventurous can get a panoramic view of the north woods from the scenic chair lift at **Big Squaw Mountain Ski Area**, ((207) 695-2272, about five miles (eight kilometers) northwest of town, off Route 15; the view in the fall is spectacular.

The craggy shores of Acadia National Park.

Tourist Information

The **Moosehead Lake Region Chamber of Commerce** (P.O. Box 581D, Greenville 04441; ((207) 695-2702) claims no visitor will be dissappointed with facilities in the area and provides free maps and brochures.

ALLAGASH WILDERNESS WATERWAY

Not for the average traveler, this wonderland of lakes, rivers, and forest is a remnant of the north woods as they used to be. Accessible by canoe, it is best known for the 98-mile (158-km) **Allagash Wilderness Waterway**, a superlative chain of lakes, some up to 20 miles long, linked by the thundering rapids and slick current of the Allagash River. Here the traveler goes at his or her own pace, paddling the long lakes and riding down the fast-moving river, camping at night with the song of loons and the Northern Lights for company. Hundreds of miles of rivers and lakes can be traveled this way, like the voyagers of old, portaging one's canoe between watersheds. Many canoeists put in on the Penobscot River just east of Moosehead Lake, cross over into the Allagash drainage at Mud Pond, and paddle all the way to the St John River, or even down to **Calais** and the Atlantic.

Again, this is only for experienced canoeists, and not to be done alone. Parts are definitely Class V whitewater and difficult even for the most experienced; the worst of Allagash Rapids and Falls is portaged even by the best. But if you think you'd some day like to try it, spend part of this visit canoeing, and plan to try the Allagash later, when you've gained the necessary skills.

An even longer voyage can be made down the **St John River**. This tends to become shallow by late summer, and is even wilder than the Allagash in early summer. Trips on the Penobscot and Kennebec Rivers can also begin here. Canoe tours are available for those not sufficiently experienced to try it on their own. For those who are, canoes can be rented at Greenville, and then carried by car back to Greenville when you leave the River. Two cars are an advantage: one to leave at your destination, and the other to bring back to Greenville or wherever you begin, or "put in," as Mainers say. As with any trip to the North Woods, black flies are a major problem in May and June, and mosquitoes in June through September. For further information, contact the **Moosehead Lake Vacation and Sportsmen's Association** (Rockwood, Maine 04478; ((207) 534-7300).

BAXTER STATE PARK

Percival Proctor Baxter, Governor of the State of Maine, was an early environmentalist. Knowing that civilization would one day doom the wilderness, he dreamed to set aside great tracts of land in central Maine as a nature preserve in order that generations to come might enjoy the land as it once had been.

Unable, during his two terms as governor, to persuade the Legislature to support his intent, Baxter undertook, nonetheless, to make his dream a reality. A man of considerable wealth, he devoted his life to the purchase and consolidation of 200,000 acres (81,000 hectares) of wild land which he then deeded to Maine as a state park on condition that the land remain "forever wild."

The state park that bears this extraordinary man's name is located 18 miles (29 km) north of **Millinocket**, and 75 miles (121 km) north of Bangor. It is an area of dense forests, pristine streams, lakes, and mountains, and shelters abundant wildlife. Apart from a few narrow unpaved roads, access to its interior is chiefly by the many hiking trails across it.

Mt Katahdin

Baxter State Park is dominated by Mt Katahdin, at 5,267 ft (1,605 m) the highest peak in the state, second highest in New England, and one of the highest points east of the Rockies. The Abenaki Indians' god Pamola lived on the summit, hurling thunderbolts and conjuring up fierce storms in times of anger. You can cross Pamola Peak by trekking the **Hunt Trail**, an 11-mile (18-km) path leading to the top of Katahdin. It is an

Northern Maine is spotted with pristine lakes which offer a haven from the civilization of the south.

all-day, very demanding hike; beware of high winds and treacherous weather.

Most of Baxter's wilderness attractions require hiking to reach them, but the park's 162-mile (261-km) trail system guarantees access. One of the Park's loveliest sights, **Chimney Pond**, is accessible by a three-hour moderate hike from the Chimney Pond parking lot. There is a campground at the Pond (reservations normally necessary in summer), and the view of Katahdin's sheer, massive granite walls towering straight up from the far side of the Pond cannot be described.

On **Sandy Stream Pond Trail** there are often moose lingering at the pond; **Cathedral Trail** demands serious rock climbing techniques to reach the Katahdin summit; and the northern portion of the **Appalachian Trail** leads to both **Big** and **Little Niagara Falls**.

Baxter Peak is one of four Katahdin summits, the others being Hamlin, Pamola, and South. The latter two are connected by one of the park's most extraordinary geologic features: the **Knife Edge**, an extremely narrow, serrated wall of granite 4,000 ft (1,219 m) high.

Park Information

For more park information, contact the Reservation Clerk, **Baxter Park Headquarters** (64 Balsam Drive, Millinocket, Maine 04462.)

AROOSTOOK COUNTY

Still farther northeast (from the Baxter Park access road, hook up with Interstate 95, go north to U.S. 1, and continue north) is **Presque Isle**, the commercial center of Aroostook County, Maine's prime potato-growing country. Just south of town is **Aroostook Farm — Maine Agricultural Station**, 375 acres (152 hectares) devoted to potato growing research. By calling ((207) 768-8341, one can arrange a free tour.

Potato Blossom Festival

Fort Fairfield, eight miles (13 km) north of Presque Isle on U.S. 1, just a stone's throw from New Brunswick, Canada, holds its annual Potato Blossom Festival in July. This is the height of the potato blossom season, and

Aroostook is awash with pink, white, and lavender blooms.

SKIING IN MAINE

Two of Maine's major ski areas, Sugarloaf and Saddleback Mountains, lie 80 miles (128 km) west of Bangor, near Lake Mooselookmeguntic.

SUGARLOAF MOUNTAIN

Sugarloaf is one of the highest peaks in the east with a summit of 4,237 ft (1,291 m). With an annual snowfall of 14 ft (4.3 m), it seems, as skiers say, "to have been created especially for skiing." A lattice-work of 50 ski

trails totaling more than 30 miles (48 km), with a vertical drop of 2.637 ft (804 m), offer something for every skier.

Novice runs drop off the hills into the center of the ski village, which is filled with shops, restaurants, and watering holes. Along the mountain's western edge, the intermediate Tote Road run stretches an incredible three miles (4.8 km), and the Narrow Gauge, a famous World Cup run, offers the ultimate skiing experience for the expert.

Sugarloaf USA, ((207) 237-2861, is Maine's premier ski resort, and among the most popular in New England. It is a blend of old-time Yankee, deep-woods wilderness, refined hospitality, and superb skiing guaranteed to make any skier feel at home.

SADDLEBACK MOUNTAIN

Saddleback Mountain, ((207) 864-5364, Maine's second-largest ski resort, is about a one-hour drive south from Sugarloaf. Its summit rises to 4,116 ft (1,255 m), with a vertical drop of 1,826 ft (557 m). There are more than 40 runs, including Rustler's Range and Bronco Buster — both steep, mogul-filled slopes. Saddleback sponsors an annual ski contest here in March — anyone who can cruise Bronco from top to bottom without falling or stopping earns free ski passes.

Sunset at Acadia

New Hampshire

IN HIS poem "New Hampshire," Robert Frost wrote,

Just specimens is all New Hampshire has,
One each of everything as in a show case,
Which naturally she doesn't care to sell.

Travelers to this state quickly discover what the poet meant. Despite its small size (180 miles, or 290 km, from north to south, and 100 miles, or 160 km, at its widest point), New Hampshire has a variety of geographical and scenic features.

SEVEN DISTINCTIVE AREAS

The **Hampshire seacoast**, less than an hour's drive from Boston, follows the Atlantic Ocean for 18 miles (29 km) between Maine on the north and Massachusetts to the south.

The **Merrimack River Valley** has a colorful history but is often now referred to as "The Golden Corridor" because of the many financial institutions and high-tech industrial firms which have located there.

The **Monadnock** region, on the other hand, is reminiscent of Currier and Ives prints: a rolling countryside of small villages, the land crisscrossed with hiking paths and ski trails.

Along the western border of the state, the **Hanover and Lake Sunapee** region is the home of venerable Dartmouth College and the locale, as well, of popular winter resorts that attract skiers from all over the East.

In the **Lakes region**, Lake Winnipesaukee draws many of the state's summer visitors. Its broad expanse, wooded shores, and 274 islands offer a variety of summer pleasures for the vacationer.

The **White Mountains**, tallest in the East, tower over the Maine border and extend southwest through the center of the state. The scenery here is rugged and dramatic, with the mountains' granite faces staring down at the valley towns far below. It is a region of forests and whitewater streams that, with the changing colors of the autumn leaves, takes on a particular beauty.

The **Far North** area near the Canadian border is almost totally unspoilt and contains one of the most scenic waterways in the State.

These regions, each distinctive, can be found within the confines of a state that can be traversed from south to north in little more than three hours.

TOURIST INFORMATION

The **State of New Hampshire, Office of Vacation Travel** (P.O. Box 856-RC, Concord, NH 03301; ((603) 271-2666) has free maps and information, which it will mail to you upon request. For travel information, call toll-free (800) 258-3608.

"LIVE FREE OR DIE"

Somewhat isolated geographically from the other New England states, New Hampshire was the only one of the thirteen colonies not invaded by British troops during the Revolution. The people of the state had then, and still retain, a determined sense of independence, and have embraced conservative democracy with a particular fervor. One of New Hampshire's major newspapers, *The Manchester Union-Leader*, has in its editorial policies and news coverage embraced one

ABOVE: A commemoration of emancipation from tyranny. OPPOSITE: A New Hampshire country hotel and its tranquil setting.

of the most ferocious right-wing stances in the nation. Although many New Hampshire residents would disagree, such attitudes seem to have filtered down into the daily attitudes of the population.

New Hampshire's strong-willed, independent attitudes manifest themselves in other substantive ways. New Hampshire has no state income tax or sales tax. State revenues are generated through so-called "sin" taxes on lottery tickets and liquor and cigarette sales. Most notably, the state's Bill of Rights recognizes "revolution" as a legit-

imate means of carrying out the will of the people, hence the state motto: "Live Free or Die" found also on its license plates.

Political awareness and self-determination are also evident in New Hampshire's form of local government, the town meeting. Established early in New England's history, the town meeting was, in a sense, the genesis of American democracy, giving each man and woman in the community an equal voice in local affairs. Town Meeting Day remains an important element of that process throughout New Hampshire. In the state government, more than 420 legislators constitute one of the largest legislative assemblies in the world.

PRESIDENTIAL PRIMARIES

New Hampshire's Presidential primary, the nation's first in a presidential election year, has become the forecast of success or failure

A New Hampshire license plate, the state's motto rooted in American Revolution history, and a friendly invitation.

for candidates for that office, a mega-media event that has somehow achieved "make or break" status on the political scene. Candidates who might otherwise have difficulty pointing out New Hampshire on a map of the United States descend quadrennially upon the state to offer political platitudes to this independent people.

But platitudes do not seem to work in New Hampshire. Its residents are straightforward, unpretentious Yankees who cut to the political quick of issues. They also have an uncanny record of reflecting the national mood. Around 75 percent of the time, New Hampshire Primary winners have become presidential candidates of both the Republican and Democratic parties. Witness 1988, when both former Vice President George Bush and former Massachusetts governor Michael Dukakis gained victories.

BACKGROUND

It is not surprising that New Hampshire residents relish their tough streak of independence. Ever since Englishman David Thomsom and a small group of fishermen made the dangerous journey across the Atlantic, landing at Odiornes's Point (the town of Rye) in 1623 to establish a fledgling fishing industry, independence and self-reliance have been traits vital to survival.

Early settlers experienced severe hardships: the land had only a thin layer of topsoil, with a profusion of rocks and boulders (that's why you see so many old stone walls in the region); it was also heavily forested, requiring much hard labor to clear it before food crops could be planted; and winters were bitter, with sub-zero temperatures and mounds of snow.

Apart from subsistence farming, there were two basic means of support for the new settlement. Fishing fleets set sail from the state's only deep water port, now Portsmouth, to seek cod on the west Atlantic, while loggers cut down New Hampshire's 1,000-year-old pines for use as masts and shipbuilding timber.

By 1641, the struggling settlements had agreed to consolidate with the flourishing Massachusetts Bay Colony to the south. But the year-long King Phillip's War (named for

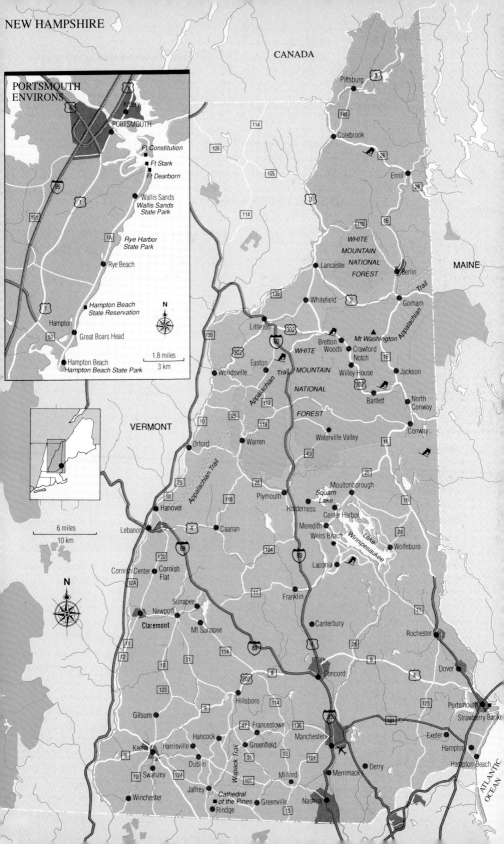

a Wampanoag Indian chief) caused much disruption when it began in 1675, and the settlements did not recover until just before the American Revolution.

INDEPENDENCE

New Hampshire received its "independence" from Massachusetts in 1679, when King Charles II declared it a royal province. John Wentworth, a successful merchant, was appointed to govern the colony in 1717; it prospered for a time, with Portsmouth taking on an English elegance that is still apparent today.

Later, the colony became caught up in the fervor for independence and Wentworth was forced to leave Portsmouth in 1775. One year later, on January 5, 1776, New Hampshire drew up its own constitution, and declared its independence from England six months before the Declaration of Independence of July 4, 1776.

ECONOMIC DIVERSIFICATION

In the 1800's, New Hampshire changed gradually from a logging, fishing, and farming economy into a manufacturing center for cotton and wool.

Manufacturing continued to grow well into the twentieth century, attracting thousands of French Canadians from poor farms across the border. Many factories, including the Amoskeag Manufacturing Company, then one of the largest mills in the country, drew immigrant workers from around the world who toiled long, grueling hours. The mills are said to have produced more than one mile (1.6 km) of cloth every working minute. However, the Great Depression, labor strikes, and the changing economy combined to deal New Hampshire's economy a serious blow.

Today, a revitalized (and diversified) manufacturing industry combines with tourism, a relaxed lifestyle, and a favorable tax climate to make New Hampshire an attractive place in which to live and work.

ABOVE Portsmouth's historic churches and expansive mansions OPPOSITE were built when the town was a flourishing seaport during the eighteenth century.

THE NEW HAMPSHIRE SEACOAST

PORTSMOUTH

New Hampshire's only seaport, Portsmouth was once the capital of the state and home port to a long-lived dynasty of merchant seamen. Great riches were amassed from their trade, which then were used to build handsome houses befitting their status, bringing to the settlement a veneer of refinement and culture. The city has since

experienced wildly changing fortunes and its "Golden Age" has long passed.

Tourist Information
Travelers can still sample a bit of Portsmouth's colonial past by following the **Portsmouth Trail**, which tours six of the city's finest seventeenth- and eighteenth-century homes. Tour guides (wearing period costumes) relate the history of the houses and tell anecdotes of their original owners. The city's **Historic Associates**, ((603) 436-1118, offers combination tickets (sold at any of the houses) and tour maps. For more information contact the **Portsmouth Chamber of Commerce** at 500 Market Street, Portsmouth, NH 03801.

The **Seacoast Council on Tourism** (Box 4669, Portsmouth, NH 03801; ((603) 436-7678) is actively promoting tourism to the coast.

Portsmouth Trail

On Market Street, is the **Moffatt-Ladd House**, built in 1763 by Captain John Moffatt as a wedding gift for his son, Samuel, and noted for its elegant furnishings and eighteenth-century architectural style. Visitors are also welcome in the formal gardens, where peonies blossom in colorful splendor each June.

Pleasant Street, "the handsomest house in Portsmouth." Built in 1784 for a prominent Revolutionary War political leader who has twice governor of New Hampshire, and first president *pro tempore* of the U.S. Senate, this elegant Georgian mansion remains one of the finest eighteenth-century homes in New England. The exterior proportions are enormous, while the gracious interiors contain some of the finest hand carving in the city. The gardens have been restored to their original state, with rose and grape arbors, perennial garden beds, and a handsome

The **Warner House** (next to the Town Hall on Daniel Street), built in 1715 by another wealthy sea captain, was occupied by the old salt's descendants as late as 1930. It has been called "one of the finest urban brick residences of the first quarter of the eighteenth century" in America today. It is one of New England's most beautiful Georgian houses, with several historic murals hanging in their original positions along the staircase. Especially noteworthy is the lightning rod on the west wall, said to have been installed by Benjamin Franklin in 1762. There are also several portraits by Blackburn, including one of Polly Warner.

No less than George Washington called the **Governor John Langdon House**, on

gazebo. Washington, Lafayette, and other statesmen of the time were entertained here.

Other houses on the tour include the 1758 residence of famed American naval leader **John Paul Jones** (who, when beckoned by the British to surrender during one high-seas battle, uttered the renowned line, "We have just begun to fight"); the grand 1807 Federal mansion called the **Rundlet-May House**; and the **Wentworth Gardner House**, whose grand woodcarvings are said to have kept a master craftsman busy for more than a year.

A different way to see all six houses is on the evening candlelight tour, held once a year, which features special trolley car transportation and accompanying guides in period costume.

Strawberry Banke

Named for the wild strawberries that grew here in abundance when early settlers arrived, Strawberry Banke is a 10-acre (four-hectare) outdoor museum preserving the historic waterfront neighborhood that was the site of the original Portsmouth settlement. About 35 historic buildings, dating from 1695 to 1940, are being restored. Seven are completed (including the 1780 Captain John Wheelwright House) and are furnished with period antiques. The restoration is so well done it appears as though people still

live and work here, but are momentarily absent. Also undergoing restoration is the 1766 William Pitt Tavern, a former stagecoach stop and hotbed of Revolutionary politics. George Washington often came here when visiting local state officials.

Not only can you stroll among the historic structures (in many cases watching actual restoration taking place), but you can also participate in a number of interesting activities. Several of the historic homes have been transformed into workshops, where programs geared to the family offer educational seminars on colonial crafts (including hands-on demonstrations), lectures, and special events such as the December candlelight tour through the "village." Other

houses contain craft shops of working artisans who display their handiwork. Even historic landscapes have been recreated, including eighteenth-century herb and vegetable gardens. Set your own pace; all tours are self-guided. Strawberry Banke is at Hancock and Marcy streets (((603) 433-1100; open daily May to October).

Old Harbor

The Portsmouth area has several other historical attractions, including **Fort Constitution**, the 1632 site of a British fort captured by the Sons of Liberty in 1774 (the gunpowder seized here was used in the battle of Bunker Hill); **Fort Stark State Historic Site**, the remains of a seacoast defense system dating from 1746; and the **Old Harbour Area**, located on the waterfront, now filled with crafts and antique shops and restaurants.

Both **"Viking"** and **"Heritage"** Portsmouth Harbor cruises offer narrated boat tours down the **Piscataqua River**, where 90 sawmills once cut the virgin pine trees used for masts in the Royal Navy, and out into the Atlantic, bound for the historic **Isles of Shoals**. Contact **Star Island Cruises** (P.O Box 311, Portsmouth, NH 03810; ((603) 431-4620) and **Portsmouth Harbor Cruises** (64 Ceres Street; ((603) 436-8084).

Summer Festivals

Portsmouth also attracts the **Tall Ships Festival** in summer, when visitors are welcome to climb aboard these historic vessels. The **Prescott Park Arts Festival** is another major summertime attraction, with its all-day, all-night free entertainment.

Where to Stay

EXPENSIVE

Anchorage Motor Inn (Portsmouth Traffic Circle, Portsmouth; ((603) 431-8111; 46 rooms); there are also several fine hotels located in nearby Hampton Beach.

MODERATE

There is a wide variety of accommodations in this category. In the summer, they are frequently booked; reservations are recommended.

A few recommendations are: **Holiday Inn** (300 Woodbury Avenue, Portsmouth; ((603)

431-8000;130rooms);**Howard Johnson Hotel** (Interstate 95, exit 5, Portsmouth; ((603) 436-7600; 135 rooms); **Inn at Christian Shore** (335 Maplewood Avenue, Portsmouth; ((603) 431-6770; six rooms); **The Port Motor Inn** (Portsmouth Traffic Circle, Portsmouth; ((603) 436-4378; 56 rooms); and **Sheraton Portsmouth Hotel** (Interstate 95, exit 7, 256 Market Street, Portsmouth; ((603) 431-2300; 148 rooms).

Eating Out

EXPENSIVE

Ashworth By The Sea (295 Ocean Boule-

HAMPTON BEACH

Hampton Beach is located about eight miles (13 km) south of Portsmouth. This long, sandy beach provides excellent swimming, with arcades and rides for children and the **Hampton Beach Casino,** which features top-name entertainment.

Where to Stay

EXPENSIVE

The following inns with access to the ocean

vard; ((603) 926-6762) is the state's premier seacoast restaurant featuring lobster, seafood, and steaks. **Blue Strawberry Restaurant** (29 Ceres Street, Portsmouth; ((603) 431-6420) serves six-course gourmet fixed-price dinners.

On the waterfront in Portsmouth are two fine restaurants: **The Oar House** (55 Ceres Street, Portsmouth; ((603) 436-4025) and **Pier II** (next to Memorial Bridge, Portsmouth; ((603) 426-0669).

MODERATE

Located in the Old Harbour area next to the tugboat docks in Portsmouth, **The Dolphin Striker** (15 Bow Street, Portsmouth; ((603) 431-5222) has a good ambiance and excellent food.

are recommended: **Hampton Beach Regal Inn** (162 Ashworth Avenue, Hampton Beach; ((603) 926-7758; 36 rooms); and **Kentville on the Ocean** (315 Ocean Boulevard, Hampton Beach; ((603) 926-3950; 37 rooms).

MODERATE

Some recommendations: **Ashworth By The Sea** (295 Ocean Boulevard, Hampton Beach; ((603) 926-6762; 100 rooms); **Best Western Seabrook** (Route 107, Hampton Beach; ((603) 474-3078; 107 rooms); **Hampton House** (333 Ocean Boulevard, Hampton Beach; ((603) 926-1033; 51 rooms); and

Strawberry Banke, an outdoor museum and restored neighborhood, OPPOSITE preserves Portsmouth's past. ABOVE: Portsmouth's harbor.

Lamie's Inn and Tavern (490 Lafayette Road, Hampton Beach; ((603) 926-0330; 30 rooms).

Eating Out
Lamie's Tavern (Hampton Beach; ((603) 926-0330) specializes in New England dishes, and **Lincoln House** (95 Ocean Boulevard, Hampton Beach; ((603) 926-6069) where one can enjoy spectacular ocean views and excellent meals.

For seafood, the **Galley Hatch** (Route 1, Hampton Beach; ((603) 926-6152) is the best in the area.

THE MERRIMACK RIVER VALLEY

More than half of New Hampshire's population resides in the Merrimack Valley, which offers the traveler everything from high-tech industry to superb colonial architecture, clear streams, and forests.

NASHUA

Just a short distance from either Portsmouth Boston is Nashua, home of the University of New Hampshire. There are many hotels and restaurants in the area, including **Best Western Hallmark Motor Inn** (Route 3, exit 1; ((603) 888-1200; 81 rooms; expensive); **Sheraton Tara Hotel** (Route 3, exit 1; ((800) 325-3535; 345 rooms; expensive); **Comfort Inn** (Route 3, exit 7E; ((800) 228-5150; 104 rooms; moderate); and **Howard Johnson Lodge & Restaurant** (Everett Turnpike, exit 5E; ((603) 889-0173; 72 rooms; moderate).

Green Ridge Turkey Farm Restaurant (Daniel Webster Highway; ((603) 888-7020)

serves traditional Thanksgiving roast turkey dinners year-round for a moderate price.

MYSTERY HILL

Of more interest is Mystery Hill, which unashamedly compares itself to the massive stone structures found at England's Stonehenge. Located east of Nausha on Route 111, less than three miles (five kilometers) east of Interstate 93, it is proclaimed to be one of the oldest building sites in North America. Radiocarbon testing pinpoints the origin of these eerie stone buildings, walls, chambers, and carvings at 4,000 years ago; numerous ancient hieroglyphics have been found, but few have been deciphered.

The question of who built them has sparked heated debate. Some argue for North American Indians, and others for ancient seafarers such as the Phoenicians, or the Celts from the Iberian Peninsula. Whoever was responsible for constructing this awesome complex, they were masters of astronomy. Scientists have determined that the rings of carefully arranged stones pinpoint solstices, equinoxes, and other astronomical phenomena. Trails to the astronomical stones, viewing ramp, and self-guided tour map (allow at least one hour) are available at the site headquarters, ((603) 883-8300. Guided tours are offered in summer, and on weekends during spring and fall.

MANCHESTER

Manchester, 16 miles (26 km) south on the Everett Turnpike, is worth the drive if only for the **Currier Gallery of Art** (192 Orange Street; ((603) 669-6144; open daily except Mondays and holidays). It is a fine small art museum with a choice collection of American and European paintings.

The city — one of the state's textile centers — has attracted large numbers of French Canadians, who crossed the border to work in the mills here. A large proportion of the city's population is bilingual.

Nine miles (15 km) further south down the turnpike is the **Budweiser Brewery** in Merrimack, with its famous Clydesdale horses. (Tours can be arranged by calling ((603) 889-6631.)

Where to Stay

With the exception of **Howard Johnson Hotel** (Interstate 293, exit 4, Queen City Avenue; ℂ (603) 668-2600; 104 rooms; moderate), accommodations in this area are expensive: **Holiday Inn Center of New Hampshire** (700 Elm Street; ℂ (603) 625-1000; 251 rooms); **Holiday Inn West** (Amoskeag Bridge; ℂ (800) 465-4329; 120 rooms); and **Koala Inn** (Interstate 293, exit 1; ℂ (603) 668-6110; 125 rooms).

Eating Out

The most elegant restaurant in the city is the **Renaissance** (1087 Elm Street; ℂ (603) 669-8130; moderate to expensive) serving Greek and Italian specialties.

CONCORD

Concord (40 miles or 65 km west of Portsmouth along U.S. 4), in the center of the valley region, is the state capital. It is a rather sleepy town, founded as a trading post in 1659, then later granted a royal charter in 1725, when its name was changed to the Plantation of Penacook. Today, its most notable landmark is the golden dome of the **State Capital** (on Main Street; ℂ (603) 271-2154), with its hall of historic New Hampshire battle flags, and statues of political favorite sons such as Daniel Webster and former president Franklin Pierce.

The **New Hampshire Historical Society** has an interesting collection of Concord Coaches dating from 1827. Many of the wagons that helped to open the American West were manufactured here.

South and west of Concord are the villages of **Hopkinton**, with its placid streets, and **Henniker**, with its double-arched stone bridge — both are pleasant towns with handsome colonial homes.

Where to Stay

The **Ramada Inn** (Interstate 93, exit 14; ℂ (603) 224-9534; 99 rooms) is the most expensive of the hotels in Concord.

Moderately priced are **Concord Coach Motor Inn** (Interstate 93, exit 12S; ℂ (603) 224-2511; 40 rooms) and **New Hampshire Highway Hotel & Convention Center** (Crossroads of Route 14, Interstate 93 and Route 9; ℂ (603) 225-6687; 140 rooms).

Eating Out

Land 'N Sea Restaurant (across from State Capitol; ℂ (603) 224-7420; moderate) is called "Concord's seafood experience."

The **Red Blazer Restaurant & Pub** (72 Manchester Street; ℂ (603) 224-7779; moderate) serves a continental menu in a rustic atmosphere.

For those with a sweet tooth, there is **Thursday's Restaurant** (6 Pleasant Street; ℂ (603) 224-2626; moderate) where the meals are like homemade and the desserts excellent.

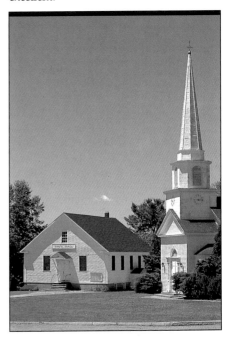

CANTERBURY SHAKER VILLAGE

Located about 17 miles (27 km) north of Concord off Interstate 93, Canterbury Shaker Village (ℂ (603) 783-9511; open May to October, Tuesday through Saturday) was once home to 300 farmers and craftspeople who led a simple life governed by their belief in God, a communal lifestyle, and a "Hands to Work and Hearts to God" philosophy.

The Shakers, a religious sect founded in eighteenth-century England, shunned contact with the outside world, and demanded

ABOVE: New Hampshire's Mystery Hill is one of the oldest building sites in North America. OPPOSITE: The Canterbury Shaker Village.

celibacy of their followers. As a result, they have all but disappeared from the modern American scene, but settlements such as Canterbury convey the eloquent simplicity of their world — a world that has become much-admired for ingenious solutions to complicated problems.

The Canterbury Shakers' two surviving members offer walking tours of the 22 historic Shaker buildings which date back to the 1780's. Tours last about 90 minutes. A museum displays Shaker crafts (famed for woodworking, basket making, and sewing), and offers workshops. The Creamery Restaurant offers Shaker food specialties.

THE VALLEY'S HISTORIC HOMES

Daniel Webster's birthplace is off Route 127, just south of Franklin. The small frame house where this noted political leader was born in 1782 is filled with family artifacts. Other historic Merrimack Valley homes open to tourists include **President Franklin Pierce's manse** in Concord, the **Pierce Homestead** in Hillsboro, and poet **Robert Frost's** 1880s white-clapboard **farmhouse** in Derry.

THE MONADNOCK

This small region in southwest New Hampshire shares its border with Massachusetts to the south and the Connecticut River with Vermont to the west. Many of New Hampshire's 54 covered bridges can be found here, and eighteenth-century villages are showcased against the backdrop of majestic Mt Monadnock. When it snows, these towns literally glow with the "Currier & Ives" imaginary romantic quality of colonial America.

KEENE

The region's finest museum is located in Keene, which also has a 172-ft (52-m)-wide, oak tree-lined Main Street, believed to be the widest paved street in the world. **Colony House Museum**, the 1819 home of Keene's first mayor (104 West Street Keene, NH 03431; ((603) 357-0889), contains a fine collection of nineteenth-century Stoddard glass and Staffordshire pewter.

Where to Stay
The Coach & Four Motor Inn (Route 12, Keene; ((603) 357-3705; 22 rooms; moderate) is a well-run small motel, providing good service and clean rooms, as do the larger **Ramada Inn** (401 Winchester Street, Keene; ((603) 357-3038; 130 rooms; moderate to expensive) and **Winding Brook Lodge** (Park Avenue, Keene; ((603) 352-3111; 90 rooms; moderate).

Eating Out
Millside Cafe (Colony Mill Marketplace on West Street, Keene; ((603) 357-4353;

moderate) is set in the warehouse of a restored woolen mill and serves continental cuisine.

For something more American, there is the **Black Lantern** (Route 12, Keene; ((603) 357-1064; moderate) whose speciality is fried chicken.

AROUND KEENE

Other Attractions
Other attractions in the region include **Francestown**, with its old colonial houses dating back to the town's 1772 beginnings; **Gilsum**, which has a stone arch bridge, and offers maps of 56 local abandoned mines; **Jaffrey Center's Old Town Burying Yard**, where novelist

Willa Cather is buried; and **Hancock**, with its Revolutionary War graves in Pine Ridge Cemetery and a splendid covered bridge spanning the Contoocook River. In **Milford**, an 1802 Paul Revere bell in the town hall tower tolls every hour. **Dublin** is a resort colony that once attracted Mark Twain and other literary figures. It is the highest town in New England, at 1,439 ft (439 m) above sea level. **Swanzey** has four covered bridges, and its theater continues to perform the 100-year-old play *Old Homestead* annually. Nearby **Winchester** has two covered bridges. And **Har-**

risville has been called the "most paintable, photogenic mill town in the United States."

On Route 119 in **Rindge**, you will find the **Cathedral of the Pines**; thousands of visitors annually visit this pine forest memorial dedicated to a son lost in World War II.

Hiking and Biking

The area provides some of New Hampshire's best hiking country, with trails through a variety of picturesque landscapes. The best is the **Wapack Trail**, which offers spectacular vistas along a 21-mile (34-km) marked path (look for yellow paint on the trees) following a high ridge from Mt Watatic in Massachusetts to the 2,280-ft (695-m) North Pack Monadnock near Greenfield.

Using Keene as a hub, the Monadnock has several scenic bicycle trails on roads with little or no traffic. One of the best follows the **Ashuelot River**, and crosses many covered bridges. The **Keene Chamber of Commerce** (c/o NEG, 8 Central Square, Keene, NH 03431; ((603) 352-1301) has regional biking trail maps.

A warning to European cyclists: American drivers tend to be far less courteous to bicycles than European drivers, so be cautious, wear a helmet, and by all means avoid well-traveled roads!

Monadnock State Park

Monadnock State Park (off Route 124, west of Jaffrey, then follow the signs) offers several trails leading to the summit of **Mt Monadnock**, one of the most-climbed mountains in the world. It is about a three- to four-hour round trip to the 3,165-ft (965-m) summit, but you will be rewarded by a commanding vista of the surrounding region. Among those who have climbed Monadnock are Emerson and Thoreau. The summit is quite barren, the trees and bush having been burned off in the 1820's by farmers. **New Hampshire Division of Parks and Recreation** (Box 856, Concord, NH 03301; ((603) 271-3254) has maps of the parks.

HANOVER AND LAKE SUNAPEE

DartmouthLake Sunapee is a region of lakes, picturesque villages lining the Connecticut River, and gentle mountains and hills.

HANOVER

Dartmouth College, founded in 1769, dominates every phase of life in Hanover, and is the cultural anchor for the entire region. Originally founded by Reverend Eleazar Wheelock "for the instruction of the Youth of Indian tribes," it now attracts well-heeled "youths" of every persuasion from all over the country.

Its handsome campus retains much colonial flavor, with stately Federal and Georgian buildings and an attractive village

ABOVE: Dartmouth College, at Hanover.
OPPOSITE: Robert Frost's mailbox and his home.

green. **Dartmouth Row**, located on the east side of the Green, has several white brick buildings dating from 1784, and the **Baker Memorial Library** displays frescoes by the famed Mexican artist Orozco. Guided campus tours are offered during summer only.

In town, the **Webster Cottage** on North Main Street was the residence of Daniel Webster during his final year at Dartmouth. **Lebanon Street** offers handiwork by the League of New Hampshire craftsmen. Hanover's streets are lined with bookstores, restaurants, and shops.

Where to Stay

The best accommodations in Hanover are at the 200-year-old **Hanover Inn** (Main and Wheelock Streets; ((603) 643-4300; expensive).

Eating Out

There are many good restaurants in the Hanover area. Recommended are **Bentley's** (11 S. Main Street; ((603) 643-4075; moderate to expensive) and **Jesse's** (Route 120; ((603) 643-4111; expensive).

Tourist Information

For maps of the area contact the **Hanover Chamber of Commerce** (Box 930, Hanover, NH 03755; ((603) 643-3115).

AROUND HANOVER

Orford

The hamlet of Orford, about 17 miles (27 km) north of Hanover, has an interesting area called "The Ridge," with a half-dozen stately homes dating from the 1770's to the 1830's.

Cornish

South of Hanover is the **Saint-Gaudens National Historic Site**, ((603) 675-2175, located on Route 12A north of the Cornish-Windsor covered bridge. Here are the summer home, gardens, and studio of American classical sculptor Augustus Saint-Gaudens, and many examples of his work.

The town of **Cornish** was home to the famed **Cornish Colony** for artists and writers; set up in 1885, it "officially" lasted for 50 years. Reclusive J.D. Salinger, author of *The Catcher in the Rye*, still lives in this town. Cornish also has the longest remaining

covered bridge in the United States. Built in 1866, it stretches 466 ft (142 m) over the Connecticut River to Vermont.

Still farther south is the **Fort at No. Four**; ((603) 826-7751, a reconstruction of an original 1746 fortified settlement which defended the region during the French and Indian Wars. Its buildings appear much as they did in the eighteenth century. Colonial craft demonstrations (candle making, weaving, etc.), and reenactments of a soldier's life in the colonial militia are part of the "living history" show.

Mt Sunapee State Park, outside **Newbury** (on Route 103), offers gondola rides up to the mountain's 2,700-ft (823-m) summit, with panoramic views of Lake Sunapee, known for its fine salmon and lake trout fishing, the Green Mountains in the distance to the west, and the White Mountains to the northeast.

THE LAKES REGION

With its more than 600 lakes and ponds, east-central New Hampshire is justifiably termed The Lakes Region. With their romantic Indian names, deep fish-filled waters, and good harbors, the lakes invite a leisurely, unhurried pace of life. **Lakes Region Association** (Box 300, Wolfeboro, NH 03894; ((603) 569-1117) has brochures about recreation in the area.

OPPOSITE and ABOVE: New Hampshire's larger lakes are well-used by pleasure boaters and fishermen in summer.

and **Wolfeboro Inn** (44 N Main Street, Wolfeboro; ℂ (603) 569-3016; 43 rooms; moderate)

In Laconia, the largest town in the area, there are several good establishments: **The Anchorage on Lake Winnisquam** (RFD#1, Laconia; ℂ (603) 524-3248; 32 rooms; moderate); **Christmas Island Resort** (Route 3, Laconia; ℂ (603) 366-4378; 27 rooms; moderate to expensive); **The Margate at Winnipesaukee** (Route 3, Laconia; ℂ (800) 258-0304; 146 rooms; expensive);and **Shalimar**

WOLFEBORO

Wolfeboro, on Route 28 between Lakes Winnipesaukee and Wentworth, is the heart of the lake region, although Laconia, on Route 3 to the southwest of Lake Winnipesaukee, is the region's largest town.

Wolfeboro claims to be the country's oldest summer resort. Governor John Wentworth built a summer mansion here on **Lake Wentworth** in 1771. The **Wolfeboro Railroad** offers 24-mile (39-km) two-hour round-trip tours, with antique steam engines, along Lake Winnipesaukee's southeastern shore. These trips are especially rewarding during the fall foliage season.

WHERE TO STAY IN THE LAKES REGION

The Pick Point Lodge (on Lake Winnipesaukee, Route 109 Wolfeboro; ℂ (603) 569-1338; 12 rooms; expensive) has individual cottages.

Winnipesaukee (Route 11D, Wolfeboro; ℂ (603) 875-5005; 24 rooms; moderate); **Lakeview Inn & Motor Lodge** (Route 109, Wolfeboro; ℂ (603) 569-1335; 17 rooms; moderate);

Faces of New Hampshire.

Resort Motel and Spa (Route 3, Laconia; ℂ (800) 742-5427; expensive).

EATING OUT IN THE LAKES REGION

Wolfeboro Inn (Route 109; ℂ (603) 569-3016; expensive) serves excellent New England dinners, as does **Blackstone's, At the Margate** (76 Lake Street, Laconia; ℂ (603) 524-7060; moderate to expensive) in nearby Laconia. **Hickory Stick Farm** (Southeast of Laconia; ℂ (603) 524-3333; moderate) is a three-star restaurant renowned for its roast duckling.

LAKE WINNIPESAUKEE

Lake Winnipesaukee covers 72 sq miles (186 sq km), with 283 miles (456 km) of shoreline and coves, 274 habitable islands, and eight towns on its shores. Winnipesaukee is an Indian word meaning "smile of the great spirit."

Perhaps the most active lakeside town is tacky, overbuilt **Weirs Beach**, on the western shore, a taste of Atlantic City in New Hampshire. In addition to visual pollution, it also offers the jaded traveler an assortment of band concerts, fireworks, boat races, seaplane rides, water skiing shows, arcades, miniature golf links, slot cars, a surfcoaster water park, and a 325-ft (99-m) water slide where revelers plummet down flumes to the pool below.

This is, however, great boating country, whether you own, charter, rent, or take public cruises. The largest boat on the lake is the 230-ft (70-m) *Mt Washington*, which offers narrated 50-mile (81-km) **cruises** departing

fishing can also be found here, but you will need a boat to escape the crowded and noisy docks.

Another way to get away from the crush of summer visitors is by biking around Lake Winnipesaukee along a series of back roads and uncrowded highways.

Summer Music

Professional musicians have gathered at Center Harbor on the northern end of Lake Winnipesaukee for six weeks each summer since 1952 to perform orchestral concerts, chamber music, and original commissioned pieces at the **New Hampshire Music Festival** (c/o NEG, P.O. Box 147, Center Harbor, NH 03226; ☎ (603) 253-4331).

SQUAM LAKE

Squam Lake (just northwest of Winnipesaukee) — the filming location for the Henry/Jane Fonda melodrama *On Golden Pond* — is the second largest lake in the state. The Manor in **Holderness** (northeast shore of Squam Lake; ☎ (603) 968-3348) offers two-hour cruises that take you to *"On Golden Pond"* film locations and provide commentary on the lake's loon population. Hiking trails in the area lead to the summit of the Squam Mountain.

from **Weirs Beach** and ending at nearby Wolfeboro. There are also breakfast, lunch, dinner, and moonlight cruises, and several so-called theme trips — Fabulous 50's, Hawaiian Luau, Buccaneers Ball and Irish Fling. For information and booking, call ☎ (603) 366-5531.

Another Weirs Beach option is a cruise on the *SS Mail Boat*, which makes two-hour mail trips to islands on the western side of the lake. Excellent lake trout and salmon

OTHER LAKE REGION ATTRACTIONS

Moultonborough

Just north of Center Harbor on Route 25 is Moultonborough, known for the **Castle in the Clouds**, a 6,000-acre (2,430-hectare) mountaintop country estate built in 1910 by eccentric millionaire Thomas Gustav Plant at a cost of $7 million. It provides a 75-mile (121-km) panorama of Lake Winnipesaukee.

Plymouth

North of Laconia just off Interstate 93 in Plymouth are the **Polar Caves**, glacial caverns that are said to have been a last refuge for the Pemigewasset Indians when they were attacked by settlers in colonial times.

WHITE MOUNTAINS

No visitor to New Hampshire should miss its breathtaking White Mountains. Long a wild, forbidding region almost inaccessible from the rest of the state, these grand mountains are now one of New England's prime natural vacation areas, with year-round attractions.

WHITE MOUNTAIN NATIONAL FOREST

The White Mountain National Forest, which covers much of the White Mountain region, extends over 760,000 acres (307,700 hectares). Access is facilitated by more than 100 miles (160 km) of roads, which cut across whitewater rivers (totaling 650 miles or 1,048 km of fishing streams), dense forests with mountain lakes, ponds, and deep valleys. It is also a hiker's paradise, with nearly 1,200 miles (1,935 km) of foot trails.

And the standard United States Forest Service policy of clearcutting huge patches out of the forest to prevent their being designated as Wilderness Areas seems less active here, with the logging generally in smaller areas, and even European-style selective cutting being practiced.

Here the **Appalachian Trail** snakes across some of its most spectacular scenery, including several of the tallest peaks in the

Fall in the White Mountains.

East. The Appalachian Mountain Club (Pinkham Notch, Gorham, NH 03581; ((603) 466-2727) provides information about hikes and lodging along the Trail; the **Mt Washington Valley Chamber of Commerce** (Box 385S, North Conway, NH 03860; ((603) 356-3171) has more general information about the area.

MT WASHINGTON

Mt Washington, the tallest peak in the White Mountain chain, is 6,288 ft (1,916 m) high; seven other peaks rise to more than a mile (1,609 m) high; and 22 others reach more than 4,000 ft (1,219 m). But despite such imposing statistics, the White Mountains are not that difficult for the traveler to negotiate. Most highways are well-maintained, including the 90-minute round-trip road leading to the summit of Mt Washington (but eight miles, or 13 km, of braking can be tough on some cars). If you have any doubts, leave your car at the foot of the mountain and take a shuttle (chauffeured van service) to the top.

While several hiking trails accommodate even the casual stroller, some leading to the Mt Washington summit may require more than a few hours of moderate to tough hiking. The climb to the summit is not a casual climb. Although the terrain is neither too rough nor too steep, the mountain peak is susceptible to sudden weather changes that bring in sudden blizzard conditions that have resulted in the death of unprepared hikers. Rewards include spectacular views of waterfalls, deep gorges, rushing streams, and peaceful valleys.

However, mountain weather can be treacherous. Even in the middle of summer, violent blizzards and freezing temperatures do occur; winds of 231 mph (372 kph), the highest ever measured in the world, have been recorded at the summit. Unless you are an experienced, well-supplied hiker, it is advisable to keep to the short, heavily-used trails. The White Mountain National Forest, Forest Supervisor's OfficeForest Supervisor's Office (719 Main Street, P.O. Box 638, Laconia, NH 03247; ((603) 524-6450) will gladly advise hikers on trail conditions and assist in selecting the best routes for day outings or longer treks.

Mount Washington Cog Railway

Another option for a visit to the White Mountains is a ride on the Mt Washington Cog Railway. (✆ (603) 846-5404, toll-free (800) 922-8825m, fare $27). It operates April to mid-October and leaves from the Base Station, one mile (1.6 km) north of Crawford Notch on U.S. 302. Since the mid-nineteenth century, the train has hauled tourists to the summit of the White Mountains' tallest peak — the highest north of the Carolinas and east of the Rockies.

Hailed in 1869 as a marvel of "modern" technology, this was the world's first moun-

tain climbing cog railway. The "cog" is a toothed or notched wheel that latches on to a center track, pulling and lowering the train up and down the mountain.

Today the train, powered by steam locomotives, climbs a three-mile (five-kilometer) route to the summit on the second steepest railway track in the world. (Only a track in the Swiss Alps beats it.) One trestle, "Jacob's Ladder," registers an incredible 37 percent grade. Each locomotive consumes a ton of coal and 1,000 gallons (3,785 liters) of water while making the one-hour climb to the top.

On clear days the view from the summit's observation center spans four states. Often, however, the mountain is shrouded in gray clouds and thick mist, and the train literally climbs through the fog.

CRAWFORD NOTCH

Crawford Notch, a narrow, rugged mountain pass off U.S. 302 (north of Bartlett), offers some incomparable views of the Presidential

Range, including the 4,052-ft (1,235-m) Jackson Mountain. The Saco River also runs through the Notch, creating some of the tallest and most spectacular waterfalls and cascades in New Hampshire. **Arethusa Falls**, the state's highest, a is 50-minute walk from the parking area; **Silver Cascade**, a 1,000-ft (305-m) cataract, is visible from the highway.

A plaque marks the site of **Willey House**, an historic stopover for wagon teams traveling between northern New Hampshire and the seacoast. The Willey family was killed here in 1826 when they fled their home during a rockslide; ironically, the home was untouched.

Crawford Notch is also the site of the White Mountains, first attempt at a tourist industry. It is named for Abel and Ethan Crawford, who in 1819 blazed the first footpath to the summit of Mt Washington, then advertised their services as tour guides and arranged for visitor lodging.

NORTH CONWAY

There are few interstate or major highways in New Hampshire, so travelers wishing to explore the heart of the White Mountains region must abandon the four-lane roads and continue their journey on country back roads. This is actually more a bonus than an inconvenience, since "Sunday driving" is one of the most enjoyable ways to explore the state's natural wonders.

North Conway is the heart of the Mt Washington Valley region, with several touring options available. Go north from Manchester on I 93, then east on one of several roads until you reach Route 16, and turn north to North Conway.

Perhaps the easiest way to get a quick overview of the region is by boarding the **Conway Scenic Railroad** (open May to October; ✆ (603) 356-5251) at the Main Street depot, a canary yellow building built in the 1870s. Steam locomotives puffing billows of black smoke pull restored turn-of-the-century coach cars through the **Saco River Valley** on one-hour train rides. The 11-mile (18-km) round trip also offers first-class service on an 1898 Pullman observation car.

Another option is to take a short drive to **Mt Cranmore** and board the *skimobile*

(Routes 16 and 302; ((603) 356-5543). In operation for more than 50 years, it is the oldest operating ski lift in the country. Its colorful cars glide smoothly up a trestle to the summit of Mt Cranmore, which also provides fine winter skiing.

Those with more time might consider a guided whitewater or a calmer canoe tour on the **Saco River**, which winds through the splendid wilderness scenery of Mt Washington Valley. The Saco Bound Northern Waters, two miles (three kilometers) east of Conway Center on U.S. 302, (P.O. Box 113,

Yet another way to experience the region is from the air. Scenic flights aboard a jet helicopter operate out of North Conway's **White Mountain Heliport** (P.O. Box 679, North Conway, NH 03860; ((603) 356-2930 or 356-2946).

Autumn Foliage

In addition to its other attractions, the region offers a dramatic display of fall foliage. While the weather can play havoc with the change of seasons, the most colorful time is traditionally the first two weeks in October. More than a half-million people jam New Hampshire's

Conway Center, NH 03813; ((603) 447-2177) provides guide services.

Several stables in the region offer guided trail rides through the mountains. For example, **The Riding Place** in Bretton Woods, ((603) 278-1836, tours the 75 miles (121 km) of scenic bridle paths belonging to the venerable Mount Washington Hotel. And the **Nestlenook Inn and Equestrian Center** in Jackson, ((603) 383-9443, offers all-day trail rides over Black Mountain and through local farmlands.

If mountain biking from country inn to country inn is more your style, consider one of the special weekend tours put together by **New Hampshire Bicycle Touring** (10 Maple Street, Henniker, NH 03242; ((603) 428-3147).

roads each year to have a glimpse of nature's annual color extravaganza, so it is advisable to take the back roads to avoid the crowds.

But before you leave North Conway itself, make certain to catch the view of Mt Washington from the middle of Main Street; it has been called "one of the great views in the East."

Where to Stay
EXPENSIVE
Attitash Mountain Village & Conference Center (Route 302 at Attitash Mountain; toll-free (800) 862-1600; 225 rooms) origi-

ABOVE: Indian summer in New Hampshire. OPPOSITE: An engineer for the Mount Washington Cog Railroad.

nally built for the ski season now stays open year-round. Of a similar style is **Red Jacket Mountain View Motor Inn** (Route 16; ((603) 356-5411, toll-free (800) 752-2538; 152 rooms). Ask about package deals at both of these resorts.

Peacock Inn (Kearsarge Road; ((603) 356-9041; 18 rooms) and **Stonehurst Manor** (Route 16; ((603) 356-3271; 24 rooms) are traditional New England country inns. A mile and a half (2 km) from the center of town is **Cranmore Mountain Lodge** (Kearsarge Road; ((603) 356-2044; 17 rooms). The

10 rooms in the old lodge have shared baths and are less expensive. The remaining seven are in the recently renovated loft of the barn.

MODERATE

Eastern Slope Inn Resort & Conference Center (Routes 16 and 302; ((603) 356-632, toll-free (800) 258-47091; 125 rooms) is next door to the summer theater and has clay tennis courts. Children stay free here.

The Riverside (Route 16A; ((603) 356-9060) is a small country inn with only seven rooms (four have shared baths). Rates include breakfast.

In nearby Gorham is the **Tourist Village Motel** (130 Main Street; ((603) 466-3312; 68 rooms).

INEXPENSIVE

With only seven rooms, it is more like staying at home than a hotel at the **Old Red Inn** (Main Street; ((603) 356-2642).

Eating Out

The inns all have their own dining rooms which also serve non-residents. **Stonehurst Manor** is noted for its Beef Wellington, but there are other fine restaurants in the area.

As its name would indicate, the **Scottish Lion** (Route 16; ((603) 356-6381; moderate) serves Scottish-American cuisine. **Welsh's Restaurant** (88 Main Street, Gorham; ((603) 466-2500; inexpensive to moderate) is New Hampshire's oldest family-owned restaurant.

FRANCONIA NOTCH STATE PARK

Franconia Notch State Park is another New England tourist shrine, but well worth a visit nonetheless. The Notch is a deep valley cut between the towering peaks of the Franconia and Kinsman mountain ranges, with the granite-walled, 4,200-ft (1,280-m)-high **Cannon Mountain** on the east, and the twin 5,000-ft (1,524-m) peaks of **Mounts Lafayette and Lincoln** to the west. It also contains some of the region's most familiar landmarks.

Flume Gorge

The spectacular Flume Gorge extends for 800 ft (244 m) at the base of **Mt Liberty**, down which cascades the **Pemigewasset River**, flanked by 90-ft (27-m) granite walls. Close up views (accessible by stairs and walkways) yield glimpses of rare mountain flowers and luxuriant mosses that cling to the moist walls. Nearly a half-million travelers visit the gorge annually.

Great Stone Face

Old Man of the Mountain (also known as the Great Stone Face) is a natural granite profile of a man's finely detailed face jutting from a sheer cliff 1,200 ft (366 m) above **Profile Lake**. Carved by nature over millions of years, it is formed by five separate ledges of granite, and measures 40 ft (12 m) from jutting brow to bearded chin.

Other Park Features

Panoramic views of the mountains and distant valleys are provided by the **Aerial Tramway**, which carries tram cars more than a mile (1.6 km) at an average height of 2,022 ft (616 m) to the summit of Cannon Mountain at 4,180 ft or 1,263 m.

South of the Notch are three other natural phenomena. **The Basin** has a deep glacial pothole 20 ft (six meters) in diameter at the foot of a waterfall. **Indian Head** is a 98-ft (30-m)-high profile carved by the elements in granite; its scowling visage is likened to

that of an Abenaki chief. **Lost River** and the **glacial caves**, both west of Lincoln, owe their existence to the passage of glaciers which gouged out depressions and then receded north, leaving unique boulder-strewn ravines and tunnel-like caves.

American Indian Crafts

Today, in a kind of legacy from New Hampshire's native Algonquin Indians, who crafted birch bark canoes, split ash baskets, and snowshoes, the White Mountain region offers works by some of the state's finest craftspeople. At the **Franconia League of New Hampshire Craftsmen** (on Access Road, off U.S. 3; ((603) 823-9521) one can find fine displays of their handiwork.

Where to Stay

EXPENSIVE

At the top of the line in Franconia is the **Franconia Inn** (Easton Road; ((603) 823-5542; 32 rooms) and **Sugar Hill Inn** (Route 117; ((603) 823-5621; 16 rooms) where rates drop to moderate in the off-season. Guest are required to take dinner at the inn.

MODERATE

In this category the traveler can find the following: **Gale River Motel** (Route 18; toll-free (800) 255-7989; 13 rooms); **Ledgeland**

(Route 117; ((603) 823-5341; 21 rooms); **Lovett's by Lafayette Brook** (Routes 18 and 141; ((603) 823-7761, toll-free (800) 346-3806; 32 rooms); **Stonybrook Motor Lodge** (Route 18N; ((603) 823-8192; 24 rooms); and **Sunset Hill House** (Route 117; ((603) 823-5522; 35 rooms).

INEXPENSIVE

Pinestead Farm Lodge (Route 116; ((603) 823-8121; nine rooms) is the best buy in the area and is often fully booked for the summer.

OPPOSITE: Steam engine on display at Clark Trading Post in Franconia. The Old Man of the Mountains ABOVE LEFT and Flume Gorge RIGHT in the White Mountains.

Eating Out

For a river view and good seafood meals, the **Rivagale Inn** (Main Street; ((603) 823-7044; moderate) is recommended.

The **Horse and Hound Inn** (off Route 18; ((603) 823-5501; expensive) has an excellent wine list to complement its continental cuisine.

The **Franconia Inn** (Route 116; ((603) 823-5542; expensive) serves local veal and excellent desserts, and **Lovett's Inn** (Routes 18 and 141; ((603) 823-7761; expensive) also has an excellent dining room.

SKI THE WHITE MOUNTAINS

The White Mountains provide the best skiing, both alpine and nordic, in the state. Ten full-service "Ski the White Mountains" resorts offer a panorama of slopes and cross-country ski trails against a backdrop of snowcapped peaks and serene New England scenery. **Attitash**, in Bartlett, offers some of the most consistently fine skiing in the state and is one of six nationwide United States Ski Team training centers. In **Bretton Woods** (in the shadow of Mount Washington), snow squalls known as "Bretton Woods flurries" blanket a landscape that offers some of the best views in the east. **Waterville Valley**, after a new $30 million expansion, even has its own snowboarding park — the newest rage in American winter sports. Then there's **Tuckerman Ravine**, about 12 miles (19 km) north of Jackson, a huge, precipitous, steep-walled bowl that is regarded as the only authentic Swiss-style alpine ski area in the east.

Tourist Information

Package plans include lift tickets and lodging, with several midweek specials. For more ski information, contact the **Mount Washington Valley Chamber of Commerce** (Main Street, P.O. Box 385, North Conway, NH 03860; ((603) 356-3171).

Where to Stay

In a class by itself is **Mount Washington Hotel** (Route 302, Bretton Woods; ((603) 278-1000; 185 rooms; luxury). In 1944 the Bretton Woods conference that established an international monetary system for the post-war era was held here. The same company operates the Victorian **Bretton Arms** (Route 302, Bretton Woods; ((800) 258-0330; 34 rooms; expensive) and **The Lodge at Bretton Woods** (Route 302, Bretton Woods; ((800) 258-0330; 50 rooms; moderate), and guests can use Mount Washington Hotel facilities.

Waterville Valley is a four-season vacation resort with inns, luxurious condominiums, spa and fitness programs, free lodging for kids 12 years and under, and other facilities. The Lodging Bureau (Box LD, Water-

ville Valley, NH 03215; ((603) 236-8371) has many listings and can help make reservations for short or long visits.

In addition to the resorts there are the following:

EXPENSIVE

The Valley Inn and Tavern (Tecumseh Road, Waterville Valley; ((603) 236-8336; 50 rooms); **Christmas Farm Inn** (Route 16B, Jackson; ((603) 383-4313; 38 rooms); and **Wentworth Resort Hotel** (Route 16A, Jackson; ((603) 383-9700; 65 rooms).

The Mount Washington Hotel OPPOSITE, one of New Hampshire's most stylish hotels.
ABOVE: The quietly simple style of North Woodstock.

MODERATE

Covered Bridge Motel (Route 16, Jackson; ((603) 383-9151; 28 rooms); **Dana Place Inn** (Route 16, Jackson; ((603) 383-6822; 14 rooms); **Eagle Mountain House**, a historic 1897 resort, Carter Notch Road, Jackson; ((603) 383-9111, toll-free (800) 527-5022; 94 rooms; **The Inn at Thorn Hill** (Thorn Hill Road; ((603) 383-4242; 20 rooms); **Nestlenook Inn** (Dinsmore Road, Jackson; ((603) 383-9443); and **Wildcat Inn & Tavern** Main Street, Jackson; ((603) 383-4245; 18 rooms).

Eating Out

The **Mount Washington Hotel** has the best dining room (expensive) in the area, serving traditional American cuisine.

Darby's in the Lodge at Bretton Woods is fine dining at a moderate to expensive price.

Fabyan's Station (Route 302 Bretton Woods; ((603) 846-2222; moderate) is a restored train depot that serves seafood and steaks.

For excellent prime rib, there is **O'Keefe's Restaurant and Speakeasy Lounge** (Waterville Valley, Interstate 93, exit 28, then to Route 49; ((603) 236-8331; moderate).

THE FAR NORTH

Pittsburg, only six miles (10 km) from the Canadian border, is the heart of New Hampshire's northernmost wilderness. The township comprises 300,000 acres (121,500 hectares) of timberlands, mountains, streams, and the Connecticut Lakes (headwaters of the Connecticut River), making it easily the largest township in the United States, as well as one of the most isolated.

This is largely uninhabited country. The roads through this remote area border sections of the **Androscoggin River**, one of the most scenic waterways in the state. You may even catch glimpses of moose grazing in the meadows and swamplands. Waterfalls sparkle down granite cliffs, the stars are bright in the unpolluted night, and the hunting and fishing are among the best in the state.

Where to Stay

Near Pittsburg on U.S. 3 toward the Canadian border is **The Glen** (First Connecticut Lake; ((603) 538-6500; 18 rooms; moderate to expensive), a fine New Hampshire country inn.

In New Hampshire, fly-fishing purists ABOVE enjoy luxurious accomodations as well as the state's rivers and streams. OPPOSITE: A meeting house in the town of Sugar Hill.

Vermont

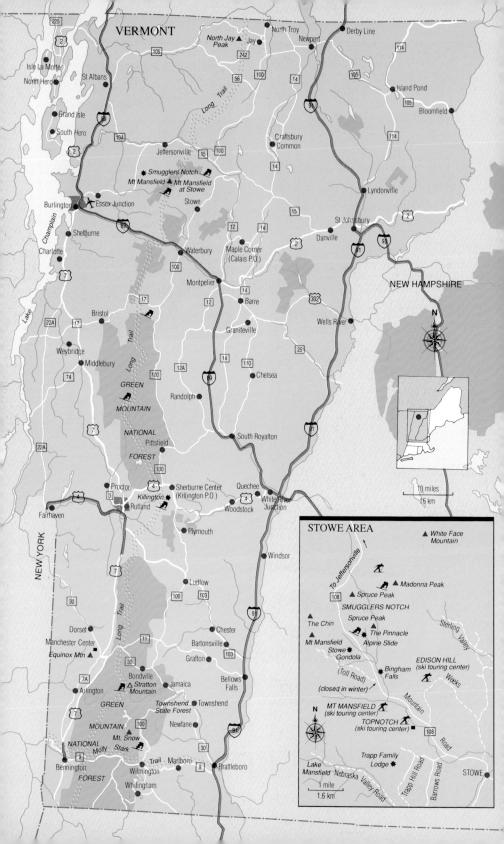

VERMONT is a rural state of farms, gentle hills, and mountains with picturesque towns that look as if they were illustrations for storybooks. Its pastoral landscapes are relatively free of sizable cities or centers of industry; Burlington, Vermont's largest community, has a population of less than 40,000.

White steeples dominate the colonial villages, and forests and pastures rise above country roads. More than 200 covered bridges add a charm to the countryside as do the maple groves which give rise to the state's claim to be the maple syrup capitol of the world.

Vermont's Green Mountains are the ski center of New England, offering a variety of downhill and cross-country trails at places like the modern complex at Killington or the traditional Stowe. Hikers, as well, can follow the 260-mile (419-km) Long Trail that tops the Green Mountain ridge all the way from Massachusetts to Canada and intersects with the Appalachian Trail near Killington.

Vermont's size only 151 miles (243 km) long and 40 to 90 miles (64 to 145 km) wide makes it a perfect place to enjoy classic New England at your own pace.

The state is bicycle-rider's dream with long stretches of back roads dotted with historic inns and lodges. Vermont's fall color extravaganza is a major attraction.

Abraham Lincoln and his family, in the mid-nineteenth century, discovered the state's special qualities. They often vacationed in the Green Mountain resort town of Manchester, in southern Vermont. (In fact Lincoln had reservations at Manchester's historic Equinox Hotel when he was assassinated in 1865.) Noted British historian Lord Bryce was also smitten with Vermont's charm when he called it the "Switzerland of North America."

Vermonters are keen to keep their state's unspoiled, serene image. The state legislature has enacted some of the toughest land use, zoning, and environmental protection laws in the nation. Even billboards are prohibited throughout the state.

TOURIST INFORMATION

Both the **Vermont Travel Division** (134 State Street, Montpelier, VT 05601; ((802) 828-3236) and the **Vermont Chamber of Commerce** (P.O. Box 37, Montpelier, VT 05602; ((802) 223-3443) have free maps and travel information.

BACKGROUND

In 1609 French explorer Samuel de Champlain described what he saw from the lake that now bears his name as *les verts monts* (the green mountains). However, when the French pulled ashore, his Algonquin Indian

guides attacked their enemy, the Iroquois, and Champlain was forced to lend aid with his armed troops. Verts monts became a bloody battleground between the French, the Indians, and the colonial-minded British for the next 150 years. Only after the English defeated France at Quebec in 1759 did large numbers of colonists begin to settle in the territory.

THE GREEN MOUNTAIN BOYS

Colonial Vermont was long embroiled in a territorial dispute with neighboring New York over land beyond Vermont's present borders. Ethan Allen's Green Mountain Boys, a self-styled militia, was formed to defend Vermont's position.

The same band of intrepid fighters helped the New World colonists to rid themselves of British rule and proclaim their independence. Vermont then declared itself

Vermont farm near Peacham.

an "independent nation" in 1777 because of continuing land disputes with New York.

Vermont remained independent for 14 years, conducting affairs with the United States as with a "foreign power." Finally, in 1791, it became the 14th state.

During the Civil War, Vermont lost more men proportionately than any other state in the Union. When, during the nineteenth century, many of its settlers joined the great westward migration, Vermont seemed destined to remain a small, sparsely populated farm state, albeit a beautiful one.

SOUTHEASTERN VERMONT

BELLOWS FALLS

Bellows Falls, in southeastern Vermont on the banks of the Connecticut River, is a good place to start a visit to Vermont. The first canal in America was built here in 1802; the **Old Stone Gristmill** (paper mill) museum preserves the town's logging legacy; centuries-old "stone face" petroglyphs attributed to Pennacook Indians are carved into rocks about 50 ft (15 m) downstream from the Vilas Bridge on the Vermont side of the river; and three covered bridges can be found nearby.

The Green Mountain Flyer

The Green Mountain Flyer, ((802) 463-3069, is a diesel-engine train with authentic 1930s passenger cars that rambles 13 miles (21 km) from Bellows Falls through two scenic river valleys before stopping in **Chester**; it often continues for another 14 miles (23 km) to **Ludlow**. The train crosses the old canal, follows the Connecticut River for a distance, then twists inland up the Williams River Valley; it also traverses the deep Brockway River Gorge, and passes both the **Warrel** and **Bartonsville** covered bridges, slowing down here and there for the photographers on board.

VICTORIAN CHESTER

Fans of Victoriana might make a quick stop at Chester to explore two historic districts Main Street's stately homes along its village

green and North Street's "Stone Village" which has more than 25 pre-Civil War houses faced with gneiss ledgestone.

COLONIAL GRAFTON

Grafton, founded in pre-Revolutionary times under George III, has been called the perfect New England village. Historic buildings, high-steepled churches, old inns, specialty shops (most circa 1805), and a little creek meandering through town make it interesting for photographers and browsers alike. Grafton's historic **Old Tavern** has operated since 1801, hosting people like Daniel Webster, Rudyard Kipling, Woodrow Wilson, and Teddy Roosevelt.

NEWFANE — THE TOWN THAT MOVED

Newfane, south of Bellows Falls on Route 30, is widely recognized for its architecture. The 1825 **Windham County Courthouse**, on the elm-shaded village green, is among the finest Early Republic buildings in the East. In 1825, the entire village moved two miles (3.2 km) south to its present location. Buildings were dismantled timber by timber and moved on ox-drawn sleighs to their new locations.

Where to Stay and Eating Out

Two historic inns, the **Four Columns Inn** (230 West Street, on the Village Green; ((802) 365-7713; 13 rooms; moderate to expensive) and the **Old Newfane Inn** (Village Green; ((802) 365-4427; 10 rooms; moderate to expensive), are located on the Green. The Four Columns Inn serves Vermont lamb and veal in its restaurant, and the Old Newfane Inn has Louisiana frogs' legs on its menu.

The Inn at South Newfane (Dover Road, South Newfane; ((802) 348-7191; moderate to expensive) features traditional New England specialities.

TOWNSHEND

About five miles (eight kilometers) north on Route 30 is **Townshend**, one of the most

OPPOSITE TOP: The spacious Common at Townshend. BOTTOM: A colonial-style porch at the Old Tavern

photographed villages in Vermont. Especially handsome is the town green surrounded by historic buildings.

Townshend's **Scott Covered Bridge**, just off Route 30, is the longest single-span covered bridge in Vermont; built in 1870, it stretches 165 ft (50 m) over the West River. At **Townshend State Forest**, a very steep 2.7-mile (4.5-km) hiking trail leads to the 1,580-ft (482-m) summit of Bald Mountain. A 10-minute drive north brings you to **Jamaica State Park**, noted for whitewater rafting on the West River.

1777, one of the campaign's most important clashes. Prior to the battle, Stark told his men, "There stand the redcoats, and they are ours, or this night Molly Stark sleeps a widow".

BRATTLEBORO

One can start the Molly Stark Trail from Brattleboro, in the southeast corner of the state on the Connecticut River. Vermont's first settlement was just south of here at Fort Dummer in 1724. (The Vernon Dam and hydroelectric plant, built in 1907, flooded

ACROSS SOUTHERN VERMONT

THE MOLLY STARK TRAIL

The Molly Stark Trail (Route 9) is the main thoroughfare across southern Vermont, stretching for 39 miles (63 km) from Brattleboro to Bennington. It is a two-lane road that is often crowded even during the off-season, but it is an interesting drive that passes through several picturesque villages and reveals some of the most dramatic fall colors in the state.

Molly Stark's husband, Revolutionary War hero General John Stark, led troops against the British at the Battle of Bennington in

the site.) Brattleboro is perhaps best known as the one-time residence of Rudyard Kipling, who married a town girl and lived here (actually in Dummerston) during the 1890's. In his unusual boat-shaped mansion, he wrote the *Jungle Books* and *Captain Courageous*.

The **Brattleboro Museum and Art Center** (the old Union Railroad Station at Canal and Bridge Streets) has a fine collection of Estey organs, a nineteenth-century mainstay in those American homes that could afford one.

South of Brattleboro on the New Hampshire border is Vernon's nuclear power plant, which is open for tours.

The **Creamery Bridge**, west of Brattleboro on Route 9, is a handsome covered bridge built in 1879; from here the Molly

Stark Trail leads into high Green Mountain country.

Clinging to the top of 2,347-ft (715-m) Hogback Mountain is the **Skyline**, a well-known restaurant overlooking **Marlboro** and offering distant views of mountain ranges in Massachusetts and New Hampshire.

The town's noted music festival, directed by Rudolph Serkin, is held in July.

Where to Stay and Eating Out
For accommodations, there is the **Quality Inn** (Putney Road, U.S. 5; ((802) 254-8701; 100 rooms; moderate to expensive), and **Dalem's Chalet** (South Street; ((802) 254-4323; moderate to expensive) serves excellent Swiss-German meals.

WILMINGTON AND WHITTINGHAM

Wilmington is the gateway to southern Vermont's ski areas, including Haystack, Hogback, Dutch Hill, Prospect Mountain, Corinthia, and Mt Snow. Detour south on Route 100 to drive through some remarkable New England scenery, especially during the fall; the tiny hamlet of Whittingham has a monument marking the birthplace of Mormon religious leader Brigham Young.

BENNINGTON

Back on the Molly Stark Trail, continue west through the high mountain scenery until you reach Bennington, historic headquarters of Ethan Allen's Green Mountain Boys.

The **Bennington Museum** has a collection of Revolutionary War artifacts and "Grandma Moses" primitives. Anna Mary Robertson Grandma Moses started painting simple country scenes at 70 years of age and achieved instant fame; she continued working until her death at 101.

The **Old First Church**, built in 1805 with a three-tiered steeple, is an oft-photographed Bennington landmark. Behind the church, a cemetery contains the graves of soldiers who fell in the Battle of Bennington, and that of poet Robert Frost, whose simple white marble tombstone is engraved with the epitaph: "I had a lover's quarrel with the world."

But the **Bennington Battle Monument** dominates every view of the village. The 306-ft (93-m) blue limestone obelisk was completed in 1889 at a cost of $112,000; it marks the site of an important colonial supply point that was defended in a three-hour clash that was a turning point in the Revolutionary War. From its observation tower there are superb views of Massachusetts' Berkshires, the Green Mountains, and New York.

Bennington College in North Bennington, situated on a lovely, rambling campus, is one of the nation's leading non-traditional or experimental colleges. Emphasizing lit-

erature, dance, and the other arts, it is known for its wealthy, non-conformist students, and for innovative approaches to education.

Nearby, surrounded by the Taconic and Green Mountains, **Old Bennington** offers lovely village scenes.

Tourist Information
The **Bennington Area Chamber of Commerce** (Veterans Memorial Drive, Bennington, VT 05201; ((802) 447-3311) has any information you might want about the town and the surrounding area.

OPPOSITE AND ABOVE: Like much of New England, Vermont has remained largely a rural state.

Where to Stay

Hotels in Bennington are reasonably priced; many are in the moderate category. Always reliable are **Best Western New Englander** (220 Northside Drive; ((802) 442-6311, toll-free (800) 528-1234; 51 rooms); **Kirkside Motor Lodge** (250 W. Main Street (next to the Old First Church); ((802) 447-7596; 23 rooms); and **Ramada Inn** (U.S. 7 at Kocher Drive; ((802) 442-8145; 104 rooms).

Eating Out

For a fine French-style meal, you can dine at

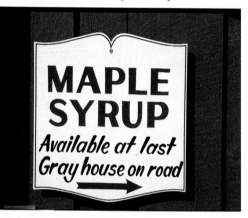

Four Chimneys Inn and Restaurant (Route 9; ((802) 447-3500; expensive). The **Publyk House** (Harwood Hill on Route 7A; ((802) 442-8301) serves inexpensive steak and seafood dinners.

NORTH TO RUTLAND

NEW ENGLAND HERITAGE TRAIL

Route 7 takes the traveler through the villages and scenic valley of the **Green Mountains National Forest**. There, in the tranquil hamlet of **Arlington**, once a gathering place for the Green Mountain Boys, artist Norman Rockwell made his home. The **Norman Rockwell Exhibition Gallery** in Arlington has hundreds of Saturday Evening Post covers and prints on display. Often, the models who posed for his works lead gallery tours.

ABOVE: There's no substitute for the real thing. OPPOSITE: The stunning Quechee Gorge and the Ottauquechee River.

MANCHESTER

Manchester, a summer resort since the 1800s, was enjoyed by Abraham Lincoln, who was drawn here by its beauty and serenity. It is a picture-postcard village nestled in the Valley of Vermont, between the Taconic and Green Mountains. Mount Equinox, the tallest peak in the Taconic Range, rises high above a town where Federal and colonial Revival mansions line its shaded streets.

Nearby, Robert Todd Lincoln, the President's son, built a 24-room manor on a large estate which he called "Hilldene". The site commands a splendid view of the surrounding countryside. He summered here from 1904 until his death in 1926 and many of the original family furnishings remain in his home **Hilldene** (admission $5.00 adults, $2.00 children; open daily, mid-May to October from 9:30 am to 5:30 pm; ((802) 362-1788).

Ernest Hemingway often tried his luck on the **Battenkill River**, one of New England's premiere fly-fishing streams. The **American Museum of Fly Fishing** (Route 7 and Seminary Avenue; ((802) 362-3300; admission is $2.00 adults, children under 12 are free; open daily 10 am to 4 pm, May to October, and Monday through Friday the rest of the year, closed on major holidays) has books, files, displays, and equipment of famous fishermen, including Hemingway, Daniel Webster, Winslow Homer, Presidents Hoover and Eisenhower.

The **Southern Vermont Art Center** is located off West Road (admission $3.00 adults, $.50 students, children under 13 free; open May 26 to October 14, Tuesday through Saturday, 10 am to 5 pm; Sunday 12 pm to 5 pm).

One of the best views in the area is found along the **Equinox Sky Line Drive**, five miles (eight kilometers) south of Route 7A. It is a six-mile (9.7-km) paved road that climbs from 600 to 3,835 ft (183 to 1,169 m) and offers panoramas from the summit of Mt Equinox.

From the **Lye Brook Wilderness Center**, hikers can follow a two-mile (3.2-km) trail leading to the Lye Brook Waterfalls, or pick up the Long Trail for a trek among the abandoned marble quarries leading to the 3,186-ft (971-m) Mt Aeolus. Maps can be picked up at the **Manchester-in-the-Mountains Chamber of Commerce** in Manchester Center, ((802) 362-2100.

Where to Stay and Eating Out

The best accommodations are in the country inns of Manchester, all of which have fine dining rooms.

The **Inn at Manchester** (Route 7A; ((802) 362-1793; 20 rooms; expensive) is a Victorian inn and converted carriage house. Nearby are the **1811 House** (Route 7A; ((802) 362-1811; 14 rooms; expensive),and the **Panther Inn** (Route 7A in Manchester Village; ((802) 362-2568; 13 rooms; expensive) whose chefs create five course dinners that usually include trout and quail.

On a slightly larger scale are the **Manchester View** (U.S. 7 in Manchester Center; ((802) 362-2739; 29 rooms; moderate to expensive), **Palmer House** (U.S. 7 in Manchester Center; ((802) 362-3600; 36 rooms; moderate to expensive), an **Willburton Inn** (off Route 7A; ((802) 362-2500; 32 rooms; expensive).

For moderately priced meals, **Chantecleer** (U.S. 7 in East Dorset; ((802) 362-1616) has Swiss Provincial dishes and the **Sirloin Saloon** (Route 11 in Manchester Center; ((802) 362-2600), as its name suggests, serves steaks.

DORSET

Dorset, just a few miles north of Manchester, is an artists' colony in a beautiful mountain setting. Its annual **summer theater festival** offers Actors' Equity productions featuring Actors Equity players from June to Labor Day, ((802) 867-5777.

Where to Stay and Eating Out

The **Dorset Inn** (Church and Main Streets; ((802) 876-5500 or 876-9392; 34 rooms; expensive), located on the green, has been in operation for 200 years.

On the outskirts of town is the **Barrows House Inn** (Route 30; ((802) 867-4455; 31 rooms; expensive) whose restaurant serves fresh fish and calf's liver and has its own bakery.

Village Auberge (Route 30; ((802) 867-5715; moderate to expensive) has a classic French-style menu.

CENTRAL VERMONT

RUTLAND

Rutland is Vermont's second largest city, with a population of less than 20,000. It was once known as the "Marble City" because of the quarries in the vicinity. The Vermont Marble Company supplied marble from these quarries for construction of the Tomb of the Unknown Soldier and the Kennedy Memorial in Washington, D.C., as well as for the Lincoln Memorial and the Supreme Court Building.

In Rutland, too, along Main and Center Streets and on Merchants Row and Strongs Avenue, there are buildings of historic significance embellished with marble. The **Vermont Marble Exhibit** in nearby Proctor has displays of marbles from all over the world, a working sculptor, and a sculpture garden with a bas-relief "Gallery of Presidents" (admission $2.50 adults with reductions for students and children; open daily late May to October, 9 am to 5:30 pm).

Rutland is also only 10 miles (16 km) from the large **Killington ski resort**, (see page 160).

Where to Stay and Eating Out

Rutland has several good motels, including the **Best Western Hogge Penny Motor Inn** (U.S. 4; toll-free (800) 828-3334; 96 rooms; moderate to expensive), and the **Holiday Inn**

Centre of Vermont (S. Main Street; ((802) 775-1911; 151 rooms; moderate to expensive).

The best dining in the area is found at **Countryman's Pleasure** (Townline Road in Mendon; ((802) 773-7141; moderate to expensive), where the veal and lamb dishes are complemented with home-baked goods.

Royal's Hearthside (U.S. 7; ((802) 775-0856; moderate to expensive) serves a standard New England fare, and the Italian sandwiches at **Gill's Deli** on Strongs Avenue are among the best anywhere.

PLYMOUTH

In the early morning of August 3, 1923, in Plymouth (about 30 miles or 48 km east of Rutland on Route 100A), Vice-President Calvin Coolidge was sworn in as the 30th president of the United States by his father in the parlor of the Coolidge homestead. These unusual circumstances arose when Coolidge was notified of President Warren Harding's death while visiting his home town; his father, a notary public, did the honors.

A visit to Plymouth, a typical rural Vermont village nestled among the Green Mountains, should include a walk through the historic district which includes the **Coolidge Homestead** and his birthplace home.

Nearby is the family cheese factory operated by Calvin's son, John. Founded by the president's father, it still specializes in the curd cheese so favored by "Silent Cal." Other Coolidge sites include the steep hillside cemetery where Coolidge and six generations of his family are buried.

Where to Stay

The **Salt Ash Inn** (junction of Routes 100 and 100A; ((802) 672-3748; 15 rooms; moderate) is an historic country inn still in operation today.

WOODSTOCK

Woodstock exudes a peaceful nineteenth-century charm. The oval-shaped town green is surrounded by fine examples of Federal, Greek Revival, and Romanesque-style homes.

The Town Crier bulletin board, at Elm and Central Streets, still informs residents of important announcements and events. Of the 87 remaining Paul Revere-made bells,

four hang in Woodstock churches; three of these continue to toll as well as ever.

The successful Gold Rush lawyer, Frederick Billings, is credited with generating an interest in village preservation in the 1870s. Sample Woodstock's nineteenth-century charm during the two-hour guided walking tours of the historic district; for information; call ((802) 457-1830. Or visit the **Billings Farm & Museum** (admission $5.00 adults, with reductions for children and senior citizens; open daily May 7 to October, 10 am to 5 pm), a living history of Vermont farm life

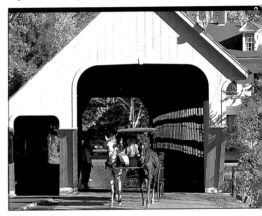

a century ago. The last covered bridge built in Vermont (1969) is in the village center.

Skiing is big in Woodstock, with **Suicide Six** and **Sonnenberg** ski areas nearby. The village is credited with the invention of the tow rope (pulling skiers up Mt Tom, powered by a "Model T" Ford engine) which revolutionized the ski industry.

Quechee Gorge, six miles (10 km) east of Woodstock on Route 4, is a sheer 165-ft (50-m) chasm dropping down to the Ottauquechee River; a steep one-mile (1.6-km)-long hiking trail leads to the bottom of the gorge. An obelisk marks the 1805 birthplace of Mormon Church founder Joseph Smith just outside **South Royalton**, 18 miles (29 km) north, and a museum there displays early church artifacts. **Brookfield's floating bridge**, built in 1812, is a structure of weathered timbers floating on 300 barrels spanning tiny **Sunset Lake**, 18 miles (30 km) north of Woodstock.

OPPOSITE: Locals seek recreation in a Woodstock park. ABOVE: A covered bridge in Woodstock. Once a common sight in Vermont, few of these bridges now remain.

Where to Stay and Eating Out

Woodstock Inn and Resort (14 At the Green; ((802) 457-1100; 120 rooms; expensive) has facilities for almost every sport imaginable and its restaurant is moderately priced.

The **Braeside Motel** (U.S. 4; ((802) 457-1366; 12 rooms; moderate), situated on a hillside, includes breakfast in the price of its rooms. There is also **The Kedron Valley Inn** (106 S. Woodstock Street; ((802) 457-1473; 29 rooms; expensive).

Parker House (16 Main Street in Quechee; ((802) 295-6077; expensive), serves French-

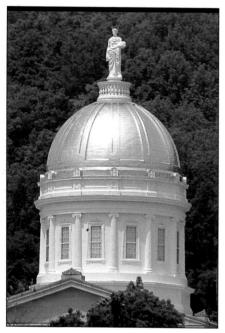

style menus, and **Prince and the Pauper** (24 Elm Street; ((802) 457-1818, expensive), also serves French-style menus.

MONTPELIER THE TINIEST CAPITAL

Montpelier, with less than 9,000 residents, is the smallest state capital in the nation. It is a pleasant town, set in a valley of the Winooski River. The gold-leaf dome of the **Vermont State House** is stunning when viewed against a backdrop of hills ablaze with fall foliage.

On the State House Lawn is the **Vermont State Museum** (admission free; opening

The gold-domed state capital building ABOVE and Ben and Jerry's ice cream OPPOSITE are two of Montpelier's biggest attractions.

times variable), fashioned to resemble the old Pavilion Hotel, a landmark demolished in 1966. Collections are eclectic and include the last panther shot in Vermont in 1881.

Those with a sweet tooth should head up Interstate 89 to the Stowe exit, then go about half a mile (800 m) to the headquarters of "the best ice cream in the world," according to *Time* magazine. **Ben & Jerry's** all-natural ice cream, ((802) 244-5641, offers guided factory tours, but most fun is the sample scoop of ice cream offered before you leave.

AROUND MONTPELIER

Barre The Granite Capital

Barre is the center of the country's granite industry. For a better understanding of just how difficult and dangerous granite mining can be, visit **Rock of Ages Quarry**, four miles (6.4 kilometers) south of Montpelier on Route 14. This is the world's largest granite quarry, 350 ft (107 m) straight down to the bottom of the open rock mine. Huge machines lift 100-ton granite slabs out of the pit, while at the Craftsmen Center, workers cut and polish the rock, then carve it into memorial gravestones or sculptures. A quarry train offers a 20-minute ride through the mining complex. (((802) 476-3115; admission $2.00 adults, $1.00 children; open June 1 to October 15, Monday through Friday, 9:30 am to 3:30 pm.)

The town's granite legacy can also be viewed at **Hope Cemetery** on the edge of town, where the headstones are said to rival the finest granite carvings anywhere.

The Green Mountains

Stretching from Montpelier south to Rutland and north to Underhill State Park, the Green Mountains offer some of the best skiing on the east coast.

MAJOR SKI RESORTS

MT MANSFIELD AT STOWE

One of Vermont's two premier ski areas, Mt Mansfield at Stowe, is about an hour's drive east of Burlington. There is always snow at Stowe, is a much-repeated refrain. The Civilian Conservation Corps built Stowe in 1933 when workers carved a trail on Mt Mansfield, Vermont's highest peak (4,393 ft or 1,339 m); since then, Mt Mansfield at Stowe has created more challenging and scenic runs, and is often called "the ski capital of the East."

Located at the foot of Mt Mansfield, the village of **Stowe** is also one of New England's most varied resort communities, with its white-steepled churches, colonial-style buildings, and Swiss chalets.

Mt Mansfield's fabled "Front Four" have been called "the toughest expert proving grounds in the East." Beginning at elevations of 4,000 ft (1,339 m), with vertical drops of 2,350 ft (716 m), these slopes challenge a skier's ability with steep, mogul-filled, tree-lined chutes.

There are plenty of intermediate slopes providing wide-open touring, and a Nordic system that meets with three other trails to offer more than 100 miles (161 km) of interconnected backcountry trails.

Stowe has several beginners' trails, so new skiers need not be scared away by its "expert" reputation. For example, the novice run called the Toll Road is more than four miles (six kilometers) long.

Year-Round Attractions at Stowe

Four-season attractions make Stowe an enjoyable summer resort. The **Mount Mansfield Toll Road** ($6.00 car and passengers) off Route 108 is a five-mile (eight-kilometer) gravel road leading to a lookout point near the summit; from there one can follow a two-mile (3.2-km) hiking path to the top. Mt Mansfield's **gondola ride** (admission $6.00; open daily June to early September, Saturday and Sunday from September to October) also provides near-summit panoramas. Nearby Spruce Peak has an **alpine slide**, a kind of warm-weather luge with wheels, that barrels down the slopes along an aluminum chute.

It is also renowned for its charming inns and lodges. One of the most famous is the **Trapp Family Lodge**, run by the family of the *The Sound of Music*. The site of their Tyrolean-style lodge is said to remind them of their native Austria.

SMUGGLERS' NOTCH

At **Smugglers' Notch Ski Area**, about eight miles (13 km) north of Stowe in Jeffersonville, the three mountains — **Morse, Sterling,** and **Madonna** — are interconnected by winding trails and lifts. Some trails run from the village center.

Smugglers' main attraction is Madonna, 3,668 ft (1,118 m) high with a vertical rise of 2,610 ft (796 m). This is expert skier territory, with giant moguls requiring a high degree

of skill. Yet Smugglers' (named after the contraband that was smuggled through the pass during the war of 1812) also has a special children's center which offers day care, ski schools, and camps — there is even a Club Med-type program headquartered in the newly completed **Village Center** with a swimming pool.

Smugglers' Notch auto road, open summers only, is a narrow, twisting road that climbs to the scenic notch (mountain pass) between Mt Mansfield and Spruce Peak.

WHERE TO STAY

Expensive

The **Trapp Family Lodge** (off Route 108; toll-free (800) 826-7000; 93 rooms) is the most prestigious of the lodges in Stowe. Breakfast and dinner are included in the price of rooms.

The **Golden Eagle Motor Inn** (Route 108; ((802) 253-4811, toll-free (800) 626-1010; 68 rooms) rents moderately-priced apartments and has every facility imaginable.

Also recommended are **Mount Mansfield Resort** (Mountain Road; ((802) 253-7311; 80 rooms) and **Salzburg Motor Inn** (Route 108; ((802) 253-8541; 51 rooms).

Moderate

Alpine Motor Lodge (Mount Mansfield Road; ((802) 253-7700; 29 rooms); **Stoweflake Resort Motor Inn** (Mountain Inn; ((802) 782-9009; 73 rooms; on the expensive end of the range); **Stowehof Inn** (Edison Hill Road; ((802) 422-9722; 46 rooms); and **Topnotch at Stowe** (Mountain Road; ((802) 253-8585; 107 inn rooms).

EATING OUT

Expensive

The **Trapp Family Lodge** (((802) 826-7000) serves traditional Austrian fixed-price menus). The **Topnotch at Stowe** (((802) 253-8585) and **Ile de France** (Route 108; ((820) 253-7751), both serve French-style meals.

Inexpensive

The **Shed** (Mountain Road; ((820) 253-4364) serves hearty hamburgers dubbed Shedburgers.

KILLINGTON

Central Vermont's largest ski resort is Killington, 10 miles (16 km) east of Rutland on Route 4. One word describes it BIG. It has six separate but interconnected mountains (Killington Peak is the highest at 4,241 ft or 1,293 m), with 107 ski trails and moguls the size of small hotels in all, twice as much skiing as any other Eastern ski resort. And it claims the longest ski lift in the world, stretching more than three miles (4.8 km) over the Green Mountains.

Bear Mountain is expert terrain, with one trail, Outer Limits, at an incline of 62 percent; it is easily the steepest in New England. Beginners should try the 10-mile (16-km)-long Juggernaut trail, the longest Alpine run in the United States.

Another Killington drawing card is the long ski season. With more than 240 inches (six meters) of snow annually and vast snowmaking capacity, the resort's season often extends from October to June.

Killington's outstanding ski school and Children's Center attract many families. Besides special programs, activities, and day care, its "family ski workshop" allows Mom, Dad, and the kids to receive lessons and ski together under the tutelage of a single instructor.

Tourist Information

Killington and Pico Areas Association (P.O. Box 114, Killington, VT 05751; ((802) 773-4181) and **Killington Lodging Bureau** (((802) 422-3711) can help find lodging and provide information of recreational facilities in the area.

Where to Stay

Specifically recommended accommodations are **Cortina Inn** (Route 4, Mendon Mountain; ((802) 773-3331; 98 rooms; expensive); **Grey Bonnet Inn** (Route 100; ((802) 775-2537; 40 rooms; moderate); **Killington Village** (718 Killington Road; ((800) 343-0762; 96 rooms, more than 600 condominiums; moderate to expensive); **Shelburne-Killington Motel** (U.S. 4; ((802) 773-9535; 18 rooms; moderate to expensive); and **The Vermont Inn** (U.S. 4; ((802) 775-0708; 16 rooms; expensive).

Eating Out

For Vermont country-style food, the restaurant at **Vermont Inn** (Route 4; ((802) 773-9847; moderate to expensive) is excellent.

Other popular restaurants, serving - Vermont lamb and fresh trout, include **Annabelle's** (Junction of Routes 100 &107; ((802) 746-8541; moderate to expensive) and **Hemingway's** (U.S. 4; ((802) 422-3886; expensive).

OTHER SKI RESORTS

Other popular ski areas include **Mt Snow**, 14 miles (22,5 km) north of Wilmington, which has old New England charm. It offers several open snow-field downhill runs, and a five-mile (eight-kilometer)-long Nordic touring trail skirting craggy ridges along six peaks of the Green Mountains, making it the highest-elevation cross-country trail in Vermont.

Stratton Mountain, about 15 miles (24 km) north of Mt Snow, has a European atmosphere, and Tyrol-style vaudeville entertainment ("better than Kitzbuhel's.")

Jay Peak lies eight miles (13 km) south of North Troy and the Canadian border.

LAKE CHAMPLAIN

Lake Champlain stretches for 125 miles (201 km) down Vermont's northwest border, separating the state from New York. Nestled in a huge valley with the Adirondacks to the west and the Green Mountains on the east, the lake is one of the most popular resort areas in Vermont.

MIDDLEBURY

An easy place to begin a Champlain valley tour is at Middlebury (on Route 7, about 46 miles, or 74 km, north of Rutland), a little town whose female academy, now **Middlebury College**, was founded in 1800; tours of the campus take in the handsome 1806 Congregational Church on the Common, and the Starr Library, with its collection of works by Robert Frost.

Just north of Middlebury in **Weybridge** is the University of Vermont's **Morgan Horse Farm**. You can watch more than 50 Morgans being put through training drills, and guided tours will take you into the handsome Victorian barns.

MAD RIVER VALLEY

Bristol is the gateway to the remote Mad River Valley, known for its rolling mountain terrain. Three ski areas and a scenic road leading to the 2,356-ft (718-m) tip of the **Appalachian Gap** are highlights of the valley. Bristol also operates the only freshwater windjammer cruises in America; here you may sail one of these tall-masted ships on Lake Champlain with Vermont's mountains in the background.

At **Charlotte**, there is an 18-minute ferry ride across Lake Champlain to Essex, N.Y., a charming nineteenth-century town.

The **Shelburne Museum and Heritage Park**, ((802) 985-3344, is five miles, or eight kilometers, south of Burlington. It has been called a collection of collections, with 45 acres (18 hectares) of Americana. The enclave includes 37 buildings: a horseshoe-shaped barn which houses more than 150 horse-drawn carriages and sleighs; the 1783 Stagecoach Inn, with its collection of American folk art; the 1840 Dorset House, featuring more than 1,000 hand carved duck decoys; and even Lake Champlain's historic sidewheeler steamboat *Ticonderoga*, docked alongside the old Colchester Reef Lighthouse.

Another fascinating stop is **Shelburne Farms**, ((803) 985-3222, a beautiful nineteenth-century agricultural estate on the shores of Lake Champlain. The old farm buildings include Shelburne House, the estate's 110-room mansion with views of both the lake and the Adirondacks in New York. The gorgeous estate grounds are attributed to landscape architect Frederick Law Olmstead. Today it is a working experimental farm and learning center.

LAKE CHAMPLAIN'S ISLANDS

The three islands in the northern end of Lake Champlain **Grand Isle**, **North Hero**, and **Isle la Motte** are sometimes referred to as "Vermont's Cape Cod." Isle la Motte is the best of the three, with its St Anne shrine marking the site of a 1666 French fort. All islands can be reached via highway U.S. 2.

There is also "Champ," the Loch Ness monster of Lake Champlain. The humpbacked creature, first "sighted" by Champlain in the 1600's, has been "seen" several times by ferry boats and pleasure craft from both Vermont and New York. However, much like Scotland's Loch Ness "monster", it has never shown itself to scientific research expeditions.

BURLINGTON

Burlington, Vermont's largest city with 38,000 residents on the shore of Lake Champlain, is the commercial and industrial center of the state. It hosts the annual **Champlain Shakespeare Festival** and the **Vermont Mozart Festival** presented by the University of Vermont (UVM) in July and August.

Some Burlington landmarks are the **University of Vermont** (founded in 1791), located at the top of a hill on the eastern edge of town, and the **Old Mill** building, which has a cornerstone laid by Lafayette in 1825. **Battery Park**, on Pearl Street, is where American guns defeated the British during the War of 1812; now it affords great views of the lake. And **Ethan Allen Park** preserves part of the Allen's historic farmstead.

You can sail Lake Champlain on the *Ethan Allen*; ((802) 862-9685, a vintage stern-

wheeler that takes in the mountain scenery along the shoreline.

WHERE TO STAY

Expensive

The **Sheraton Inn** (870 Williston, S. Burlington Street; ((802) 862-6576, toll-free (800) 324-3535; 125 rooms) is built around a central greenhouse.

At the **Radisson Burlington Hotel** (60 Battery Street; ((802) 658-6500, toll-free (800) 333-3333; 257 rooms), children stay free.

Moderate

Howard Johnson Motor Lodge (U.S. 2, S. Burlington; ((802) 863-5541, toll-free (800) 654-2000; 89 rooms) has an indoor pool and tennis court, and children stay free.

Nearby is the **Best Western Redwood** (1036 Shelburne Road, S. Burlington; ((802) 862-6421; 54 rooms)

ABOVE: A still-life in Vermont.
OPPOSITE: East Orange, Vermont.

EATING OUT

The best restaurants in Burlington are moderately priced, and include the French-style **Déjà Vu Cafe** (185 Pearl Street; ((802) 864-7917); **Ice House Restaurant** (171 Battery Street; ((802) 863-9330), which serves seafood; **Pauline's** (1080 Shelburne Road; ((802) 862-1081), which also serves seafood; and **Sweetwater's** (118 Church Street; ((802) 964-9800), the yuppie favorite.

NORTHEAST VERMONT

St Johnsbury, on U.S. 2, is the gateway to the northeast, a backwoods region travelers seldom visit. It is a land of lakes, forests, small villages — and few people.

The best time to visit the area is during the fall "color" season in September, when the woods are ablaze with color, and villages celebrate with festivals, food, and fun.

Danville, west of St Johnsbury, is the headquarters of the American Society of Dowsers, people who use willow wands to find water; their fall convention draws lots of attention. **Lyndonville**, nestled in the green hills of the Passumpsic River valley, has five covered bridges within village limits, the earliest dating from 1795.

Finally, **Derby Line** is one of the most unusual hamlets in America. The United State–Canadian border passes right through the town, resulting in houses sitting astride the border between Vermont and Quebec. In the town library, the book stacks and checkout desks are in different countries.

AUTUMN FOLIAGE TOURS

Vermont's fall foliage has been called the world's finest, attracting people from all over the world. The leaves usually begin to change in early September at higher elevations in northern Vermont and along the Canadian border. This is the least-populated portion of the state, and is noted for its sweeping, panoramic views. The color season moves progressively southward, usually ending in the final weeks of October.

The compactness of Vermont (180 miles, or 290 km long, and about 60 miles, or 97 km at its widest point) makes it relatively easy to travel. Don't be afraid to get off the main highways you will often find that the back roads with their colorful canopies of leaves, lined by old stone walls, or set off against the brilliant green pastures of rolling country-side, enhance the pleasure of fall touring.

Scores of small Vermont towns celebrate the season with festivals that might include guided tours, bazaars, live entertainment, and homemade, traditional New England foods.

colors but also a wide array of cultural activities. Vermont's northern mini-metro-polis follows the shore of Lake Champlain, and a walk to downtown Battery Park, where American guns turned away British warships during the War of 1812, reveals a setting that impressed even Rudyard Kipling.

• For color cruising, board *The Spirit of Ethan Allen* (((802) 862-8300), a recreated paddle-wheel-era boat that offers 90-minute voy-ages on Lake Champlain; you will have a magnificent view of Vermont's Green Moun-

TOURIST INFORMATION

The **Vermont Travel Division** operates a fall foliage hotline, ((802) 828-3236, and pub-lishes suggested fall color routes covering the entire state. Also remember that over-night accommodation anywhere along popular fall color routes should be made well in advance.

ITINERARIES

A few additional fall color tour suggestions include:

• **Burlington**, surrounded by remarkable scenery, not only offers brilliant autumn

tains in the east, and New York state's Adirondacks to the west.

• Back on shore, head 20 miles (32.3 km) southeast on Interstate 89 to reach the **Green Mountain Audubon Nature Center,** ((802) 434-3068, 230 acres (93 hectares) of trails winding through beaver ponds, hemlock swamp, and retired farm fields, set in a blaze of color.

• An especially colorful 124-mile (200-km) car tour follows U.S. 7 south from Burling-ton, skirts **Lake Champlain** and then enters the **Green Mountain National Forest** before reaching Bennington, near the New York/Massachusetts border.

• **Smugglers Notch State Park**, near Stowe, offers some of the most spectacular color scenery in Vermont, though you may have to fight off the crowds. From Stowe, travel west on Route 108, enter the state park, and soon you will be negotiating hairpin curves along sheer cliffs and ledges leading to the 2,162-ft (659-m) "notch," named after nineteenth-century creative capitalists who smuggled illegal goods from the United States into Canada through the natural pass in the Green Mountains.

BICYCLING IN VERMONT

Vermont's rolling hills, low-road mountain passes, country backroads, outstanding state parks, and light traffic make it a cyclist's paradise. In fact, it has often been rated as the top biking state in America.

Bicycle touring is a great way to enjoy at close range the state's emerald green landscape while discovering interesting villages and historic towns. There are several Vermont cycling groups that conduct tours of varying lengths and degrees of difficulty, from leisurely rides into the countryside to grueling off-road mountain touring. Most not only provide experienced guides who lead the way, explaining state sights and sounds, but also make all the arrangements for overnight lodging and meals.

Or you can rent bicycles and strike out on your own, following suggested state cycling routes, or those mapped out by bike clubs that create itineraries to match your interests.

BICYCLING DIRECTORY

Guided Tours

• **Bike Vermont** (P.O. Box 207 G, Woodstock, VT 05091; ((802) 457-3553), conducts inn-to-inn bicycle tours for cyclists at all skill levels. Groups average no more than 12 to 15 people, with 20 the maximum.

• **New England Bicycle Tours** (P.O. Box 26-R, Randolph, VT 05060; ((802) 728-3261), offers two- to five-day road tours and mountain bike adventures for riders of all abilities. You will stay overnight in country inns or renowned resorts; you can even choose back country camping. Tour leaders and support vans accompany all trips. Both road and mountain bike rentals are available.

• **Outdoor Tours Limited** (P.O. Box 97, Calais, VT 05648; ((802) 229-4570) specializes in northern Vermont trips which include weekend and five-day, camping and inn-to-inn tours. Rentals are available.

Vermont Back Roads Bike Tours (Box 31, Craftsbury Common, VT 05827; ((802) 586-7767), includes three-day and six-day tours on back roads, averaging 10 to 20 miles (26 to 32 km) per day using mountain bikes.

• **Vermont Bicycle Touring** (Box 711-GX, Bristol, VT 05443; ((802) 453-4811) offers easy to challenging tours for adults and

families, with special emphasis on overnighting at country inns, and sampling home-cooked meals. Two- to five-day trips; others can be booked for extended periods. A support van assists with luggage transportation, picnic lunches, and repairs on the five-day trips. Rentals and custom-planned trips are also available.

• **Vermont Country Cyclers** (P.O. Box 145-VT3, Waterbury Center, VT 05677; ((802) 244-5215) conducts two- to nine-day biking vacations for cyclists of all abilities. Country inn overnight accommodation includes some of the finest Vermont has to offer, and evening

ABOVE: Cycling in the White Mountains.
OPPOSITE: A country-store shopping opportunity in Peacham.

meals consist of gourmet cuisine. Two tour leaders and a support van accompany every group, which is limited to 20-plus cyclists.

• **Vermont Mountain Bike Tours** (P.O. Box 526, Pittsfield, VT 05762; ℂ (802) 746-8943) offers mountain adventures for cyclists who desire an out-of-the-ordinary cycling experience. Only back country is traveled, including seldom-used dirt roads, old farm lanes, logging trails, and staying overnight at country inns. Two- to five-day tours, for beginners and intermediate levels. Mountain bikes required; rentals available.

Self-Guided tours

• **Bicycle Holidays** (Road 3 Box 2394, Middlebury, VT 05753; ℂ (802) 388-7347), plan personalized self-guided tours that might include country inn or bed and breakfast overnight accommodation, attractions, and service along the route.

• **Country Inns Along the Trail** (Road 3, Brandon, VT 05733; ℂ (802) 247-3300) prides itself on custom-planned biking itineraries based on length of trip and degree of difficulty desired. Their program includes the participation of more than 25 country inns in western and central Vermont.

MORE CYCING INFORMATION

• The **Vermont Travel Division** (134 State Street, Montpelier, VT 05602; ℂ (802) 828-3236), provides up-to-date information about biking in the state, including suggested routes and material on attractions, accommodation, and restaurants along the way.

• The *Handbook on American Youth Hostels, Inc.*, provides information on budget accommodation; you must become a member to use the hostels. Send a self-addressed envelope to **Greater Boston Council, American Youth Hostels** (1020 Commonwealth Avenue, Boston, MA 02215; ℂ (617) 731-5430).

• One of the most popular information sources over the years has been *25 Bicycle Tours in Vermont*, available through Vermont Bicycle Touring, listed above.

Weathered wood at Waits River.

Connec-
ticut

FOR MORE THAN three centuries, Connecticut has welcomed travelers. George Washington visited the state a number of times; the bedroom his hosts decorated at Webb House for his visit to Wethersfield in 1781 still looks the same today.

Mark Twain stopped in Connecticut on business in 1873, and stayed for a good portion of his life, writing such classics as *Tom Sawyer* during his time in Hartford. His flamboyant "Steamboat Gothic" home still stands in Hartford.

Even P.T. Barnum, the master of hype who traveled the world with his Greatest Show on Earth, put all that aside when he returned to his home in Bridgeport. The Barnum Museum there provides lots of entertainment courtesy of the master showman.

However, travelers on Interstate 95 often pass straight through Connecticut on their way to holiday spots elsewhere in New England, missing out on a unique part of New England which is best explored along its picturesque back roads.

It is not hard to get around in Connecticut. The state is a rectangle measuring only 90 miles (145 km) by 55 miles (89 km), bordered by New York on the west, Massachusetts to the north, and Rhode Island to the east.

Its southern boundary stretches along Long Island Sound; protected by Long Island, New York, these shores have long sandy beaches and historic port towns. Both the Connecticut River, which bisects the state, and the Housatonic in the northwest provide spectacular scenery, and the Litchfield Hills, which rise in northern Connecticut, are dotted with villages perfect for leisurely touring.

TOURIST INFORMATION

Since no two places in the state are more than a two-hour drive apart, it is possible to enjoy the best of what Connecticut has to offer in a few days. The **Connecticut Department of Economic Development** (210 Washington Street, Hartford, CT 06611; ((203) 566-3385 or 566-3977) provides free maps and guides to help plan your trip. For **travel information,** call toll-free (800) CT-BOUND.

BACKGROUND

Adriaen Block, a Dutch navigator, was the first recorded European explorer to sail along Connecticut's coast in 1614. He traveled up the Connecticut River, where the Dutch later established a trading post near today's Hartford, for dealing in the region's lucrative beaver trade.

However, by 1635, English settlers from the already crowded Massachusetts Bay Colony, driven by a search for farmland, were flowing into the Connecticut River valley.

The Massachusetts colonists established three towns along the Connecticut River Hartford, Wethersfield, and Windsor known jointly as the Hartford Colony. On January 14, 1639, the colony proclaimed the Fundamental Orders of Connecticut which, some historians contend, is the world's first written democratic constitution; hence the state's nickname, "The Constitution State."

Connecticut revolutionaries played important political and military roles in the American Revolution. Among these were General Israel Putnam, who ordered troops on Bunker Hill not to fire "until you see the whites of their eyes," and the revolutionary Nathan Hale, hanged as a spy by the British, who said before he died, "I regret that I have but one life to give to my country."

Commerce, trade and manufacturing took root thereafter. Banks were established in Hartford by 1792, and the insurance industry began in Norwich in 1795. Samuel Colt

Southern Connecticut is more commercial OPPOSITE, than the northeast "Quiet Corner" ABOVE.

of Hartford developed the Colt .45; Gideon Roberts made Bristol the clock capital of the United States; everyone wore Danbury hats; and Meriden silver services were treasured.

This level of prosperity endures today, as indicated by the state's per capita income which is the highest in the nation.

HARTFORD

Mark Twain once said, "Of all the beautiful towns it has been my fortune to see, Hart-

ford is chief." The capital of Connecticut, Hartford, can look back on 350 years of history from its setting on the banks of the Connecticut River. The **Center Church burying ground** has gravestones dating from 1640. The **Old State House**, built in 1796, is the oldest in the nation, and Mark Twain's eccentric mansion still stands on a small green surrounded by skyscrapers.

The state's second largest city has recently undergone a boom that has transformed downtown Hartford into a mixture of high-rise architecture, new riverfront developments, restorations such as Pratt Street, sophisticated stores and cafés set into refurbished buildings, and Constitution Plaza.

The national headquarters of 40 insurance companies, Hartford has been an insurance haven since an eighteenth-century ship owner took out a policy on his boat and cargo. When the tragic fire of 1835 de-

The State Capitol reflects Hartford's wealth, much of which has been amassed by its numerous insurance companies.

stroyed more than 600 buildings in New York City, many insurance companies could not honor claims and went bankrupt. The Hartford Insurance Company's president visited every New York policyholder, assuring them that their claims would be quickly settled. Since then, its financial stability, despite disasters such as the Great Chicago Fire and the San Francisco earthquake of 1906, have enhanced Hartford's reputation as the insurance capital of the nation.

THE CHARTER OAK

Hartford's riverside location drew early attention. The "city" began as a Dutch trading post named Fort Good Hope in 1633. Massachusetts Bay Colony Puritans settled here two years later, and the village eventually formed one-third of the Hartford Colony, its independence guaranteed by the Royal Charter of 1662.

Legend has it that when the royal governor demanded return of the charter 25 years later, it was stolen and hidden in the trunk of a massive oak tree, the famous "Charter Oak," that stood until felled by a storm in the 1850s. (The oak's location is now marked by a plaque.) The governor was recalled, and the threat to independence overcome.

TOURIST INFORMATION

For a quick orientation and free maps and guides of the city, you can stop at the **Tourist Information Center** in the Old State House (800 Main Street, Hartford, CT 06103; ((203) 522-6766) which is open Monday through Saturday, 10 am to 5 pm.

A WALKING TOUR

The Walk is a self-guided journey through Hartford's historic sites and new landmarks. Begin at the **Old State House** in the downtown district. Tours of the handsome 1796 Federal structure, the first public building designed by Charles Bulfinch, include the restored Senate chamber with its Gilbert Stuart portrait of George Washington and original furnishings.

North on Main Street is the **Richardson**, a brownstone designed by Henry Hobson

Richardson, one of America's foremost architects of the nineteenth century. It is considered an architectural landmark, now restored to its original condition, with restaurants, specialty shops, and apartments.

Across the street, **Christ Church** is made conspicuous by its elegant spire. Then at State and Market Streets is **Constitution Plaza**, a unique, 12-acre (five-hectare) urban park where on sunny days some of Hartford's 100,000 downtown workers take café-style lunches on the green.

The plaza's two-sided boat-shaped building, home to Phoenix Mutual Life Insurance, is already a Hartford landmark. New employees are greeted with "Welcome aboard!" (The Phoenix company was established in 1851 to insure only teetotalers.)

Travelers Tower, off Main Street, has a 527-ft (161-m)-high observation deck offering splendid views of the city and the Connecticut River Valley. It is home to its namesake company, which started in 1863 by insuring Colonel James Bolter for $5,000 on his trips from the post office to his home. His premium? Two cents.

Just ahead is the **Wadsworth Atheneum** (((203) 278-2670), one of the country's first public art museums. It holds 165 permanent and visiting exhibits that include 40,000 art objects. Its collections include Egyptian and Roman artifacts, paintings by masters such as Goya and Rembrandt, and a large selection of works by American artists of the Hudson Valley School.

By far the most impressive building is the **State Capitol**, near Bushnell Park. The golden-domed capitol, with its many turrets, gables, and towers, was built 1879. The **Hartford Civic Center** (Asylum and Trumbull Streets) is home to the Hartford Whalers, the city's team in the National Hockey League.

Among other "Walk" attractions is **City Place**, the tallest office building in Connecticut, with a high-tech system of sensors, scanners, and silicon chips that automatically control most of the building's functions.

MARK TWAIN'S NOOK FARM

Mark Twain (Samuel Clemens) is perhaps America's most oft-quoted writer. Born and raised in Hannibal, Missouri, on the Missis-

sippi River, he came to Hartford in the 1870s. His home at **Nook Farm** (Farmington Avenue and Forest Street), built in 1874 for $131,000, reflects the grand style of its owner. The many gabled, orange-red colored house caused scandalous comments in its time because of its stylistic excesses.

It is Victoriana and Gothic — a tangle of gingerbread, pointy towers, intricate woodworking, even decorating gems fashioned by Louis Comfort Tiffany. It still contains much of Twain's original furnishings, including the huge hand-carved bed purchased on his travels through Europe. He became so enamored of the delicate headboard hand carvings that he often slept with his head at the foot of the bed to gaze at the head board.

Upstairs in the billiards room is where Twain did much of his writing and entertaining. He wrote *Tom Sawyer*, *The Adventures of Huckleberry Finn*, and other masterpieces here.

Twain left the house in 1891 after bad business investments forced him to embark on a quick European lecture tour to raise money. Novelist **Harriet Beecher Stowe**'s modest Victorian home is just across the lawn. For tour information, call (((203) 525-9317.

WHERE TO STAY

Expensive

The large, modern **Parkview Hilton** (One Hilton Plaza; (((203) 249-5611, toll-free (800) 445-8667; 400 rooms) and **Sheraton-Hartford Hotel** (315 Trumbull Street; (((203) 728-5151, toll-free (800) 325-3535; 400 rooms) frequently offer weekend specials to attract travelers. At the Hilton children stay free.

The weekend specials at the **Holiday Inn Downtown** (50 Morgan Street; (((203) 549-2400; 359 rooms) drop this hotel to the moderate category.

For a touch of Old Hartford, try the **Summit Hotel** near the Old State House (5 Constitution Plaza; (((203) 278-2000; 285 rooms).

For excellent accommodations outside the city, Marriott operates the **Hartford Marriott Hotel/Farmington** (15 Farm Springs Road, Farmington; (((203) 678-1000, toll-free (800) 321-2211; 381 rooms)

and the **Courtyard by Marriott Hotel** (1 Day Hill Road, Windsor; ℂ (203) 683-0022, toll-free (800) 321-2211). Both offer excellent weekend rates.

Moderate

In Hartford, the best buy is the **Howard Johnson Motel** (7 Weston Street; ℂ (203) 525-4441; 80 rooms). On the outskirts of town is the **Super 8 Motel** (57 W. Service Road; ℂ (203) 246-8888, toll-free (800) 843-1991; 104 rooms) that includes breakfast in the price of the rooms.

Close by in East Hartford are several smaller, moderately priced motels: **Executive Motor Lodge** (490 Main Street, East Hartford; ℂ (203) 569-1100; 85 rooms); **Holiday Inn** (363 Roberts Street; ℂ (203) 528-9611, toll-free (800) 465-4329; 130 rooms); and **Ramada Inn** (100 E. River Drive, ℂ (203) 528-9703, toll-free (800) 272-6232; 199 rooms).

Four Seasons International Bed & Breakfast (11 Bridlepath Road, West Simsbury, Connecticut; ℂ (203) 651-3045) is a booking service for bed-and-breakfast lodging in the Hartford area. Most of their listings are in nearby small towns.

Inexpensive

The best bargain in the greater Hartford area is **Motel 6** (Silas Deane Highway, Wethersfield, CT 06109; ℂ (203) 563-5900; 146 rooms).

EATING OUT

Expensive

Terrace on the Park (1 Hilton Plaza; ℂ (203) 249-5611) in the Hilton serves as elegant a meal as you can find in Hartford.

Moderate

Featuring Northern Italian cuisine, **Carbone's Ristorante** (588 Franklin Avenue; ℂ (203) 249-9646) is a popular Hartford eatery.

In nearby Glastonbury, you can dine in the Colonial atmosphere of **Blacksmith's Tavern** (2300 Main Street, Glastonbury; ℂ (203) 659-0366).

Inexpensive

The eating-out experience in Hartford is **Shelly's Downtown Deli** (Hartford Civic Center; ℂ (203) 278-1510) with its 300-item menu including every type of sandwich available and kosher favorites. Breakfast is served at all hours.

HARTFORD AREA EXCURSIONS

Farmington

Just 10 miles (16 km) west of Hartford on Route 10, Farmington is an elegant colonial town often referred to as "one of New England's museum pieces." Its rich eighteenth-century architecture includes the **Stanley-Whitman House**, parts of which date from

1663. The village's **Hill-Stead Museum** contains several French Impressionist paintings.

Wethersfield

In Hartford's suburban south, Weathersfield has more than 150 houses pre-dating the mid-nineteenth century, including the 1752 **Webb House**, where George Washington and French commander Jean Baptiste Donatien de Vimeur, Count of Rochambeau, met in 1781 to plan the Yorktown campaign that led to America's victory in the Revolutionary War.

Hartford mixes modern and traditional.
OPPOSITE: An Alexander Calder sculpture.
ABOVE: The Harriet Beecher Stowe house.

Bristol

In 1790, Gideon Roberts started selling his clocks here, just 18 miles (29 km) west of Hartford. Soon the town became the clockmaking capital of the United States. The **American Clock and Watch Museum** (Maple Street, off Route 6; ((203) 583-6070) displays more than 2,000 fine timepieces made in Connecticut.

CONNECTICUT RIVER VALLEY

The Connecticut River (from the Indian

name Quinnituckett or long tidal river) flows for 410 miles (660 km) from its headwaters near the Canadian border in New Hampshire to Long Island Sound, neatly bisecting Connecticut into east and west. **Essex, Ivoryton, Old Lyme, Chester** and **East Haddam**, a cluster of little towns 10 to 15 miles from Long Island Sound, are within easy reach of the area's attractions and where you can stay in one of the Valley's country inns

ESSEX

A gateway to the valley, Essex is also the terminus of the **Valley Railroad**, ((203) 767-0103, which offers 55-minute tours of the river valley aboard turn-of-the-century steam

trains to **Deep River Gorge** near picturesque **Chester**. From Deep River Gorge, riders take an hour-long **riverboat cruise** up the Connecticut River past some of the valley's best scenery, including Gillette's famous castle and the Goodspeed Opera House, before returning by rail to the Essex Depot.

GILLETTE CASTLE

A five-minute ride by car ferry from **Chester** brings one to **Hadlyme** and an eccentric hilltop fieldstone mansion dubbed **Gillette**

Castle, ((203) 526-2336. Built by actor William Gillette, a Hartford native famous for his portrayal of Sherlock Holmes, the 122-acre (49-hectare) medieval castle commands a sweeping view of the Connecticut River and countryside.

Construction of the 24-room mansion began in 1914, and took five years to complete. Built to Gillette's design, the castle has granite walls that are four feet (1.3 meters) thick at the base, and interior trim hand hewn from southern white oak. Huge oak doors are fastened by complicated wooden locks; some bedroom furniture is built into the castle's structure, and other furnishings slide on metal tracks. Electric light fixtures are decorated with bits of colored glass gathered by his friends. He could even see who was entering the house by a series of angled mirrors starting outside his bedroom door. Outside, Gillette built a large railroad, with a "Grand Central" depot starting at the entrance gate and winding to "125th Street" at the property's eastern terminus; he delighted in manning the throttle while treating visitors to rides through his estate. The train was dismantled long ago.

In his will, Gillette instructed his executors "to see to it that the property [does] not fall into the hands of some blithering saphead who has no conception of where he is or with what surrounded." In 1943, Gillette Castle was acquired by the state.

EAST HADDAM

Just north of Gillette Castle on Route 82, East Haddam is an old riverboat landing and the site of the **Goodspeed Opera House**, ((203) 873-8668. This 1876 building on the banks of the Connecticut River cuts a dashing figure when viewed from the water; inside, the beautifully-restored Victorian auditorium now offers equity productions of American musicals from mid-April to December.

The Victorian-style town is also the location of the **Nathan Hale Schoolhouse** (where Hale taught in 1773). Also available are afternoon **sightseeing cruises** and evening music excursions on the river (board in Haddam; ((203) 345-4507).

WHERE TO STAY AND EATING OUT

Part of the experience of visiting the Connecticut River Valley is staying in one of its many country inns. For centuries New Yorkers have come here to escape the hustle and bustle of America's largest city. In the summer, reservations are essential; most of these inns are in the expensive category.

Essex

The **Griswold Inn** (48 Main Street, Essex; ((203) 767-0991; 23 rooms) is almost a tourist attraction in itself. Reservations to stay in the 212-year-old country inn are made months in advance. In spite of its popularity, its rates are reasonable, at the high end of the moderate range. They do, however, include breakfast. To dine on its wild game specialties, you will

have to make reservations and those who wait till the last minute to call are often disappointed. On Sundays from 11 am to 2:30 pm, you can feast at a Hunt Breakfast for $12.00. Children under six eat free.

Ivoryton

The **Copper Beach Inn** (Main Street, Ivoryton; ((203) 767-0330; 13 rooms) is an excellent alternative to the Griswold. Food critics claim it has the best restaurant in southern Connecticut.

For a change of pace in dining, the **Fine Bouche** (Main Street, Centerbrook; ((203)

767-1277), a couple of miles away serves French meals at about the same price as the Copper Beach Inn.

Chester

The **Inn at Chester** (318 W. Main Street; ((203) 526-4961; 48 rooms) is in a lovely rural setting. This late-eighteenth century farmhouse is adjacent to the state forest and has access to miles of hiking trails.

Old Lyme

Old Lyme has two excellent inns: **The Old Lyme Inn** (85 Lyme Street; ((203) 434-2600),

OPPOSITE LEFT: The Connecticut Valley Railroad. OPPOSITE RIGHT: Gillette Castle. ABOVE: Essex.

a stately 1850's mansion with five rooms in the main building and nine in the new addition, and **Bee and Thistle Inn** on the banks of the Lieutenant River (100 Lyme Street; ((203) 434-1667), which serves seafood and duck specialties in its dining room.

MYSTIC AND NEW LONDON

Facing Long Island Sound and the sea, Mystic and New London attracted restless, venturesome Yankees, who became sailors, and sailed

them around the world in search of whales, rum, spices, and the riches of the China Trade.

MYSTIC

Since the seventeenth century, Mystic has been building boats. Its elegant clipper ships made Mystic one of the country's top whaling centers — with nearly 20 whalers in its fleet. Later, its vessels formed the backbone of America's Navy in World War II.

Mystic Seaport

This recreated nineteenth-century seafaring village and living-history museum is at the

Fog and sun at Mystic Seaport.

mouth of the Mystic River and has a whaleboat demonstration, oystering displays, and sailors tending the sails aboard an elegant whaler.

The 17-acre (seven-hectare) Seaport, begun in 1929, contains more than 60 historic waterfront buildings, 300 ships and boats, and artifacts of nineteenth-century maritime America.

America's sole surviving wooden whaling ship, the *Charles W. Morgan*, is the Seaport's master attraction. Visitors may walk the main deck, explore the cargo hold which still smells of whale blubber, and see where the crew of more than 90 men lived and worked. The 113-ft (35-m)-long, three-masted *Morgan*, built in 1841, sailed the seas for nearly 80 years, making 37 whaling voyages, some lasting up to five years. A fascinating 30-minute program on nineteenth-century whaling at the Meeting House includes rare footage of an actual whaling voyage.

You can also explore the decks of the square-rigged *Joseph Conrad*, an iron-hulled Dutch training vessel built in 1882; today it serves as a training ship for the Seaport's special sailing program. The *L.A. Dunton Fishing Schooner* (1921) illustrates the days of Grand Banks fishing aboard a two-masted Gloucester schooner. And the coal-fired *Sabino Passenger Steamboat* (1908) provides pleasant cruises down the Mystic River.

Along Gravel, Clift, and High Streets, among others on the west bank of the river, are a number of historic sea captains' homes. Especially interesting is 13 Gravel Street, an 1836 "spite house" built into the street to deliberately block the neighbor's view. (Ninety-minute self-guided audio-cassette tour tapes are available for rent or sale at Olde Mistick Village shops.)

Stonington

Don't leave the area without visiting Stonington, just east of Mystic, off Alternate Route 1A. It has been called "one of the prettiest coastal villages in Connecticut."

The **Old Lighthouse** on Stonington Point reminds visitors of Stonington's past as a whaling and sealing port; inside, a small museum contains seafaring artifacts, and the lighthouse tower has a view of three

states (Fisher's Island, N.Y., Rhode Island to the east, and Connecticut), as well as breathtaking vistas across the sound.

Where to Stay

Overlooking the harbor, atop a hill at the junction of U.S. 1 and Route 27, **The Inn at Mystic** (Route 27; ℂ (203) 536-9604; 68 rooms; expensive) is an old-style New England inn, housed in a cluster of Victorian buildings. On its spacious grounds are tennis courts, a pool, and a boat dock.

In town is another traditional inn,

Whaler's Inn (20 E. Main Street; ℂ (203) 536-1506; 45 rooms), as well as the larger, more modern **Mystic Hilton** (Coogan Boulevard; ℂ (203) 572-0731, toll-free (800) 445-8667; 187 rooms). At the Hilton, children stay free in their parents' room, and special weekend rates are often available.

Comfort Inn (132 Germanville Avenue; ℂ (203) 572-8531; toll-free (800) 228-5150; 120 rooms; moderate) and **Days Inn of Mystic** (Route 27; ℂ (203) 572-0574; 122 rooms; moderate) have less luxurious rooms at a more modest rate. The Days Inn has designated no-smoking rooms.

Just east of Mystic in Stonington, you can find bread-and-breakfast accommodations. **The State of Connecticut Tourism Division Information Center** at the North Stonington southbound exit off I-95 has a listing of these homes and will help make reservations.

Eating Out

EXPENSIVE

If you don't stay at the Inn at Mystic, you may want to dine at its **Flood Tide Restau-**

rant (junction of U.S. 1 and Route 27; ℂ (203) 536-8140) on Long Island roast duck or Maine lobster.

For a French-style meal, **J.P. Daniels** (Route 184, Old Mystic; ℂ (203) 572-9564) is the best in the area.

MODERATE

Actually three restaurants in one, **Seamen's Inne** (Germanville Avenue; ℂ (203) 536-9649) caters New England meals to suit your price range. You can have an inexpensive snack at the bar, a moderately-priced meal at the cafe, or a more expensive, larger meal in the dining room.

Nearby in North Stonington is **Randall's** (Route 2; ℂ (203) 599-4540), which serves fixed-price meals that feature New England specialties.

INEXPENSIVE

To the south in Noank is **Abbot's Lobster in the Rough** (117 Pearl Street; ℂ (203) 536-7719) where you get the best buy for your money. There are no waiters; you order at the window, pay the tab, and wait for your number to be called. In addition to steamed lobster, the menu includes whatever seafood is in season.

NEW LONDON

At one time, New London was the second busiest whaling port on the East Coast. The mansions built by her sea captains testify to their successes. Especially interesting is Huntington Street's **"Whale Oil Row"**, where wealthy seamen built four white-columned Greek Revival mansions in the 1830s. The Pennsylvania oil boom in the late 1850s ended the whaling industry's profitability.

New London is still a seafaring town; its fine deep water port is home to the **United States Coast Guard Academy**, ℂ (203) 444-8270, one of the nation's four service academies that train military officers. You can take a walking tour of the grounds; cadet dress parades are held in spring and fall, and the training barque *Eagle*, a three-masted square rigger built in 1936, is open for weekend tours when in port. New London also has several historic buildings, including the 1774 **Nathan Hale School House**, and **Monte**

Cristo Cottage, boyhood home of Nobel Prize-winning playwright Eugene O'Neill.

Groton

Across the Thames River from New London is Groton, home port of the **United States Navy's Atlantic Submarine Fleet**. You can take a one-hour submarine base tour aboard sightseeing buses, ((203) 449-4779, with the possibility of seeing docked submarines being repaired along the river.

A better way to immerse yourself in submarine lore is by climbing aboard the *SS Nautilus*, the world's first nuclear-powered submarine, built in 1954 by Groton's Electric Boat Division of General Dynamics. The ship's claustrophobic quarters were crammed with 111 officers and crew during its journeys, which included cruising under the Arctic ice cap, from the Bering Strait to the Greenland Sea, in 1958.

The **Submarine Force Library**, ((203) 449-3174, is filled with interesting displays and exhibits that trace the development of United States submarines from the Revolutionary War, through World War II, to today's sleek nuclear-powered ships.

It's also possible to take a sightseeing cruise on the Thames aboard the **River Queen II** (board at The Harbour Inn, 193 Thames Street; ((203) 445-9516). You will pass the *SS Nautilus* and other submarines at their riverside berths, sight Trident submarines being constructed at Groton, pass the submarine base and Coast Guard Academy, and perhaps even see a submarine or two returning to home port.

Tourist Information

Maps and guides of the area are available from the **Southeastern Connecticut Tourism District** (Ye Olde Town Mill, 8 Mill Street, New London, CT 06320; ((203) 444-2206).

NORTHWEST CONNECTICUT

Quiet country back roads, peaceful colonial villages, great hiking trails, including part of the Appalachian Trail, make touring in this region quite special. **Canaan**, on Route 7 near the state line with Massachussets in the north and **Kent**, further south also on Route

7 near the New York State line are the access pointes to the region. From Hartford, **Litchfield**, 30 miles (50 km) away on U.S. 202, is perhaps the best base for a visit to the region.

CANAAN TO KENT

At Canaan, just south of the Massachusetts border, one can ride the **Housatonic Railroad** along the Housatonic River through the green hill country. Board at the 1872 **Union Station** (Routes 7 and 44; ((203) 824-0339), America's oldest train

depot in continuous use. Six miles (10 km) east on U.S. 44 at Norfolk is the site of **Indian burial grounds** Nearby **Haystack Mountain** and the 34-ft (10-m)-high stone tower at the summit (1,716 ft or 523 m) offers views of Long Island Sound, the Berkshires in Massachusetts and mountain peaks in New York. A road one mile (1.6 km) north of Norfolk on Route 272 leads halfway up the mountain; a quick 30-minute hike gets you to the top. The June mountain laurel and fall foliage are spectacular.

OPPOSITE: Groton, home port of the U.S. Navy's Atlantic Submarine Fleet and the Submarine Force Library. ABOVE: Lobster, the New England seacoast specialty

Another summit pavilion, in **Dennis Hill State Park** south of Norfolk on Route 272, provides views of Haystack Mountain, the Green Mountains, and part of New Hampshire; even New Haven Harbor can be seen on the horizon on a clear day.

West Cornwall

West Cornwall, 13 miles (21 km) south of Canaan, has a **covered bridge** (Route 128) that has been in continuous service since 1837. If you are here at meal time, **Fresh-**

field's (Route 128, West Cornwall; ((203) 672-6601) serves moderately-priced meals.

Housatonic Meadows

South of West Cornwall on Route 7 and located in the heart of the rock-strewn valley of the Housatonic, Housatonic Meadows lies amid rugged hills. Tall pines shade the banks of the river, which is known for its fly fishing.

Kent

Another **covered bridge** spanning the Housatonic River is south on Route 7 in Kent, where the **Sloane-Stanley Museum** displays handmade tools used by early settlers. The covered **Bull's Bridge** also spans

the Housatonic, stretching into New York state; it is four miles (six kilometers) south of Kent.

Kent Falls

North of Kent on Route 7, Kent Falls whitewater cascades draw thousands of visitors. A gentle stepped pathway runs parallel to the waterfalls. It is also one of the most photographed natural sites in the state.

Macedonia Brook

At Macedonia Brook, north of Kent, two 1,400-ft (427-m) peaks offer stunning views of the Catskills and Taconics.

LITCHFIELD

Many historians consider Litchfield the finest unrestored colonial town in the country. George Washington and General Lafayette both visited here. In fact, the entire borough of Litchfield has been declared a National Historic District.

The eighteenth-century, white-clapboard mansions lining its peaceful, wide streets are not museums but homes. Historic buildings on serene South Street include the 1753 **home of Oliver Wolcott**, signer of the Declaration of Independence; the birthplace of the revolutionary Ethan Allen; and the **Tapping Reeve House**, the first law school in America, founded in 1774. Tapping Reeve claims as alumni two vice-presidents of the United States (Aaron Burr and John C. Calhoun), 101 members of Congress, 34 Chief Justices of the United States, 28 U.S. Senators, and 14 governors. The beautiful white-steepled **Congregational Church** presides over the town's lovely village green.

Tourist Information

Free information is available from the **Litchfield Hills Travel Council** (P.O. Box 1776, Marble Dale, CT 06777; ((203) 868-2214).

Where to Stay and Eating Out

The best accommodations in town are at the **Litchfield Inn** (Route 202; ((203) 567-4503; 31 rooms) and **Tollgate Hill Inn** (Route 202; ((203) 567-4545; 10 rooms), which was established as a tavern in 1789, but was located on a nearby hill. In 1923 it was moved to its present site. Both inns serve excellent meals and are in the expensive category.

Black Rock State Park

West of **Thomaston** on Route 6, Black Rock State Park is a hiker's paradise, with the scenery of the Western Highlands dominating the blue-blazed **Mattatuck Trail**.

Lake Waramaug and New Preston

Five miles (eight kilometers) north of New Preston, is an autumn delight, with bright hues mirrored in the unrippled surface of

For those entering Connecticut from New York on Interstate 95, it will be hard to tell just when the Empire State ends and the Constitution State begins. That's because coastal cities and villages such as affluent **Greenwich**, **Stamford**, **Riverside**, and **Darien** are more suburbs of New York City than Connecticut towns.

An endless number of New Yorkers talk about owning a little farmhouse in Darien, to

Lake Waramaug. **Mt Tom**, near Bantam, boasts hiking trails leading to a summit tower. Overlooking the lake is the **Hopkin's Inn** (Hopkins Road, New Preston; ℭ (203) 868-7295; 10 rooms; moderate), famous for its restaurant which serves Austrian and Swiss specialties.

HIKING AND CANOEING

Serious hikers might want to trek part of the **Appalachian Trail** that stretches from Kent to Canaan, while canoeists can look forward to flatwater or **whitewater adventures** on the Housatonic (contact Clarke Outdoors, West Cornwall; ℭ (203) 672-6365).

get away from the Big Apple's problems at the end of the work day. Only 50 to 90 minutes from Manhattan, some of these towns have evolved into dormitory communities.

BRIDGEPORT

Farther up the coast is Bridgeport, an important manufacturing city with a population of 150,000, and P.T. Barnum, creator of the Greatest Show on Earth, wintered in Bridgeport. He also discovered one of his greatest acts here namely 28-in (71-cm)-tall General Tom Thumb, a Bridgeport native.

ABOVE: Pig farm in Litchfield county.
OPPOSITE: Norwich Connecticut's Leffingwell Inn preserved as it was in 1735.

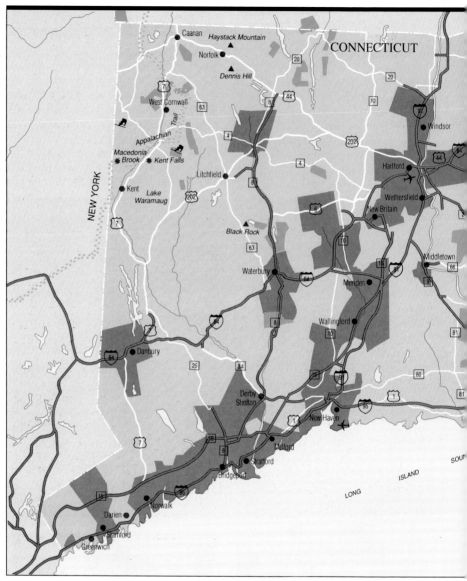

The **P.T. Barnum Museum** (on Main Street; ((203) 576-7320) has just undergone a $6 million renovation. It boasts much circus lore and many curiosities that made Barnum famous, including personal memorabilia of Thumb and others.

Bridgeport's **Beardsley Zoological Gardens** is the only zoo in Connecticut. And the city **Summer Music Festival** hosts the New York Philharmonic.

Stratford, just east up the Sound, is the home of the **American Shakespeare Theater**, which offers the Bard's plays all summer,

and pre- and post-Broadway productions the rest of the year.

WHERE TO STAY

As this area is just across the state line from New York, many visitors to New York City elect to stay in Connecticut where rates are more reasonable and train service to Manhattan is good.

Expensive
At the top of the line are the **Hyatt Regency Greenwich** (1800 East Putnam Avenue, Old

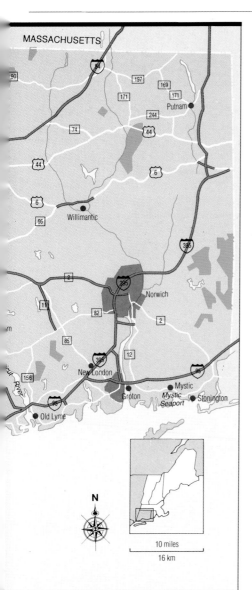

N

10 miles

16 km

The **Showboat Inn** (500 Steamboat Road, Greenwich; ℂ (203) 661-9800 or toll-free (800) 243-8511; 103 rooms) is a good medium-sized hotel.

Moderate
Bridgeport Hilton Hotel (1070 Main Street, Bridgeport; ℂ (203) 334-1234, toll-free (800) 465-4329; 234 rooms); **Howard Johnson Motor Lodge** (150 Ledge Road, Darien; ℂ (203) 655-3933; 72 rooms). **Ramada Inn** (50 Ledge Road, Darien; ℂ (203) 655-8211; 100 rooms); and **Ramada Inn** (19 Clarks Hill Avenue, Stamford; ℂ (203) 327-4300; 87 rooms).

EATING OUT

Most of the hotels in the area have their own restaurants, but for distinctive Italian dining in Bridgeport **Meghan's** (2068 E. Main Street, Bridgeport, ℂ (203) 576-1283; expensive) and **Paris Bistro** (3546 Main Street, Bridgeport; ℂ (203) 374-6093, expensive) are recommended.

Greenwich has many good French restaurants: **Cinquante-cinq** (55 Arch Street; ℂ (203) 869-5641; expensive); **Jean-Louis** (61 Lewis Street; ℂ (203) 622-8450; moderate to expensive); **La Grange** (420 Field Point Road; ℂ (203) 869-7500; expensive); **Tapestries** (554 Old Post Road #3; ℂ (203) 629-9204; moderate to expensive); and **Swan Court** (26 Mill River Street; ℂ (203) 325-1900; expensive) which serves a fixed-price traditional French meal.

NEW HAVEN

Founded in 1638 on the Connecticut coast, New Haven began as a Puritan settlement at the end of a harbor four miles (6.5 km) from Long Island Sound. Three rivers flow into the sound here — the Quinnipiac, the Mill and the West. Around the village, low meadows give way to gently sloped hills. The prominent landmarks then, as now, were two isolated peaks known as East Rock and West Rock.

The town was planned in classic fashion with nine squares. The center square today is New Haven's public Green, once a marketplace and pastureland. It is surrounded by

Greenwich; ℂ (203) 637-3691; 35 rooms) and **The Inn at Mill River** (26 Mill River Street, Stamford; ℂ (203) 1900, toll-free (800) 325-0344 in Connecticut or (800) 325-0345 outside Connecticut; 94 rooms). Both are old-style country inns.

Also in Stamford in this category are **Le Pavilion Hotel** (60 Strawberry Hill Road; ℂ (203) 357-8100; 176 rooms); **Crowne Plaza Hotel** (700 Main Street; ℂ (203) 358-8400, toll-free (800) 465-4329; 381 rooms); and **Stamford Marriott Hotel** (2 Stamford Forum; ℂ (203) 357-9555; 505 rooms).

three historic churches built between 1812 and 1815, all exhibiting distinctive architectural styles: Federal, Georgian, and Gothic Revival.

In the nineteenth century, worn out farmlands forced people into cities and towns; by the end of the Civil War, more than half of Connecticut's population lived in urban areas. After Eli Whitney created a mass-production line for manufacturing his cotton gin, New Haven gradually became a manufacturing center; that tradition continues today.

Guided one-hour walking tours of the historic campus start at **Phelps Gateway** on College Street, across from the New Haven Green, ((203) 432-2300. One of the most interesting areas is the **Old Campus**, containing Yale's oldest buildings, including Connecticut Hall, where Nathan Hale studied. One of the most unusual campus buildings among those designed by famous architects is the **Ingalls Hockey Rink** by Eero Saarinen, inspired by the shape of a whale.

The **Yale University Art Gallery**, on Chapel Street, is one of the finest small

In 1716, the Collegiate School of Saybrook, established 15 years earlier, moved to New Haven, changing its name to **Yale University** to honor a generous donor, Elihu Yale. The earliest Yale buildings were built just west of the Green; the campus now covers 160 acres (65 hectares) in the central city and dominates New Haven. The distinguished Ivy League school has nearly 12,000 students divided among its 12 colleges — each with its own library, dormitories, and dining halls. Historically, about 15 graduates each year eventually become U.S. Congressmen. Renowned alumni include Nathan Hale, William Howard Taft, Noah Webster and George Bush.

galleries in the country. In addition to a collection of French Impressionist paintings, it has on show many works by patriot painter John Trumbull, including the original *Bunker Hill* and *Declaration of Independence*.

New Haven's **Shubert Performing Arts Center** features Broadway-bound productions and road shows. The New Haven Symphony Orchestra performs at Yale's **Woolsey Hall**.

Where to Stay

At graduation and matriculation (May and September), hotels in New Haven can be completely booked. If your trip takes you here during these times, you will have to make your reservations well in advance.

EXPENSIVE
The best accommodations in New Haven, without doubt, are at **The Inn at Chapel West** (1201 Chapel Street; ((203) 777-1201; 13 rooms). In fact, the excellent service raise this above the category of expensive to luxury.

Also in the heart of downtown is **Park Plaza Hotel** (155 Temple Street; ((203) 772-1700; 300 rooms), which has a rooftop restaurant.

Less expensive and close to Yale is the **Colony Inn** (1157 Chapel Street; ((203) 776-1234; 86 rooms).

MODERATE
Children stay free with their parents at the **Holiday Inn at Yale** (30 Whalley Avenue; ((203) 777-6221, toll-free (800) 465-4329).

There are two Howard Johnson's in the area. The **Howard Johnson's** north of New Haven in Hamden (2260 Whitney Avenue, Hamden; ((203) 288-3831, toll-free (800) 654-2000) is less expensive than the more centrally located **Howard Johnson's Long Wharf** (400 Sargent Drive, New Haven; ((203) 562-1111, toll-free (800) 654-2000; 154 rooms).

Eating Out
The best restaurants in New Haven are in the expensive category and serve ethnic dishes.

For Greek dining, you won't be disappointed by **Basel's** (993 State Street; ((203) 624-9361).

Blessings (45 Howe Street; ((203) 624-3557) serves tasty northern Chinese specialties, and **Delmonaco's** (232 Wooster Street; ((203) 865-1109) prepares northern Italian-style meals.

If you want something more traditional, there is **Robert Henry's** (1032 Chapel Street; ((203) 789-1010).

Less a place to eat, and more an attraction, is **Atticus Bookstore-Cafe** (1082 Chapel Street; ((203) 776-4040), where you can have coffee and pastries for breakfast or tea and cakes for afternoon tea in the presence of one of the best selections of books in the state.

New Haven's Yale University, among the nation's most distinctive in learning and architecture.

Rhode Island

ACASUAL glance at a map of the United States reveals that Rhode Island at 1,212 sq miles (3,144 sq km), even with the many islands of Narragansett Bay, is the smallest state in the nation. But the "Ocean State," as it calls itself, with its 400 miles (664 km) of shoreline, has a variety of coastal land and undeveloped beaches. (It also claims the longest official name of any state — "Rhode Island and Providence Plantations."

It was the seacoast that brought the bluebloods of America to Newport, a harbor town transformed into a haven for the millionaires of the "Gilded Age." They built magnificent estates (referred to as "summer cottages") along the cliffs and ledges that border the ocean. Many of these structures remain today as a testament of Newport's affluent past.

BACKGROUND

The Florentine navigator Giovanni da Verrazano explored Narragansett Bay in 1524 under commission from the King of France. He is said to have named the area Rhode Island because of its resemblance to the island of that name in the Aegean Sea. One hundred years were to pass before the first colonists would arrive — from England, not from France. Among the first of these was Reverend William Blackstone, a nomadic preacher who came to Rhode Island when his lands on the Shawmut Peninsula, near Boston, were taken over by Puritan settlers.

Roger Williams, who founded Providence Plantations in 1636, had been driven out of Salem, Massachusetts, for advocating religious freedom and tolerance. His convictions were to have a benign and continuing effect on the development of the new colony. Ann Hutchinson, who helped to establish Portsmouth in 1638, soon followed, as did others anxious to be free of the rigors of Boston Puritanism. By the nineteenth century, immigrants in large numbers were coming to Rhode Island to seek a new life.

Religious freedom, rich farmlands, and sheltered harbors provided, for Rhode Island, an environment in which tolerance and liberty could prosper.

THE TRIANGLE TRADE

Providence and Newport became leading seaports and centers of the infamous, "Triangle Trade" in the New World. Their merchants sent ships loaded with rum to Africa, traded the rum for slaves, then sailed to the West Indies where they traded slaves for sugar and molasses, the ingredients from which, in home ports, rum could again be distilled. By 1760, Newport had become New England's major port for slave-trading

ships — a dubious distinction in a colony founded on tenets of religious and individual freedom.

In the same century, Rhode Island's craggy coastline, islands, and coves sheltered pirates and privateers who raided ships far out in the Atlantic; later in life, these scoundrels and their crews returned, often, to reside ashore in respectable affluence. The search for legendary pirate treasure, said to be buried somewhere in Jamestown, continues today.

STATEHOOD AND THE TWENTIETH CENTURY

In 1772, the resistance of Rhode Islanders to British rule became increasingly overt, as witnessed by the burning of the British ship, *Gaspee*. After the Revolutionary War broke out, the colony joined wholeheartedly in the long struggle for independence that culminated in the final American-French victory at Yorktown.

Boating and fishing: holiday pastimes on Rhode Island's rugged coast.

Despite its passion for independence, Rhode Island was the last of the original 13 states to ratify the United States Constitution. Subsequently, the state enjoyed rapid growth and prosperity, becoming, in time, a major industrial center. By 1793, a large-scale textile industry had been established in Pawtucket and, by the mid-nineteenth century, it was producing almost 20 percent of the nation's cloth. By the turn of the century, immigrant workers and their families accounted for almost 70 percent of the state's population. When textile factories

were drawn to the south by cheaper labor after World War II, the state was forced to diversify its economy.

TOURIST INFORMATION

Today, with nearly 950,000 people squeezed into 1,214 sq miles (3,144 sq km), Rhode Island is a bustling, energetic state and a popular summer resort in which Newport continues to enjoy preeminence. The state's compactness — only 48 miles or 77 km long, and 37 miles or 60 km wide — makes it easy for visitors to enjoy its quiet coves and beaches, wildlife-filled salt marshes, open meadows, and big cities. The **Rhode Island Division of Tourism** (7 Jackson Walkway, Providence, RI 02903; ((401) 277-2601, toll-free (800) 556-2484) has prepared numerous maps and brochures to help you enjoy your stay in Rhode Island.

Bellevue Avenue ABOVE and the Cliff Walk OPPOSITE in Newport have been the home of New England's nouveau riche since the Civil War.

NEWPORT

Dramatic cliffs rising out of the ocean, elegant mansions, expansive lawns, and baronial gardens are to be seen in Newport. The rich transformed this harbor town into their own summer resort, commissioning America's finest architects to recreate gaudy palaces, mansions, and ersatz chateaus along Ocean Drive and Bellevue Avenue.

Pre-Revolutionary southern plantation owners were the first to discover Newport's summer pleasures as they exchanged the intense heat of the south for refreshing ocean breezes. Following the Civil War, such scions of American wealth as the Astors and the Vanderbilts flocked to the town, entertaining their friends with picnics and parties, caviar and champagne, in keeping with the excesses of what came to be known as the Gilded Age.

Today, no visit to Newport is complete without a tour of a few of these mansions abandoned when income and property taxes and the Great Depression made their upkeep too expensive.

An option is a bus tour of Newport, a 22-mile (35-km) ride through the historic Colonial section, Ocean Drive and its spectacular coastline, Bellevue Avenue with its millionaire "cottages," and guided tours through two of the mansions, conducted by Viking Tours of Newport (101 Swinburne Row, Brick Market Place; ((401) 847-6921). Or you can rent a 90-minute guided auto-tour cassette tape which covers more than 300 years of Newport history and local anecdotes. Cassettes can be purchased at local gift shops or rented at The Paper Lion on America's Cup Avenue in the Long Wharf Mall.

THE MANSIONS OF THE GILDED AGE

Although scores of mansions existed during the Gilded Age, only 50 or so remain, of which eight owned by the Preservation Society of Newport County, ((401) 847-1000, are open to tours.

It is a good idea to purchase a combination ticket that allows you to visit a number of mansions at your leisure; each tour takes less than two hours.

The Breakers, on Ochre Point Avenue, is the most spectacular of the Newport mansions, and largest of the grand summer "cottages." Built in 1895 for Cornelius Vanderbilt and designed by architect Richard Morris Hunt, it replicates a sixteenth-century northern Italian palace. Seventy rooms (tended by 40 servants in its heyday) are graced with imported blue marble, alabaster pillars, gold gilt, mosaics, and stained glass, with magnificent grounds overlooking the Atlantic Ocean — all enclosed by immense wrought iron fences and gates.

sailles. Completed in 1902 for the daughter of the man who discovered Nevada's Comstock Lode, it was the scene of brilliant society balls and galas.

Hammersmith Farm, on Ocean Drive, was the site for the wedding reception of John F. Kennedy and Jacqueline Bouvier after their Newport marriage in 1953. The rambling 1887, 28-room shingled mansion, with gardens designed by Frederick Law Olmstead, was often used as a summer White House by President Kennedy, and now houses mementos from those years.

Marble House, on Bellevue Avenue, was built in 1892 as a gift for the wife of William K. Vanderbilt. Another Hunt design, it is one of the most sumptuous of Newport's "cottages," featuring a dazzling gold ballroom in the French style. (The house is thought to have been styled after the Petit Trianon in Versailles.)

The Elms, on Bellevue Avenue, was completed in 1901 for Pennsylvania coal king Edward Julius Berwind. Modeled after the Chateau d'Asnieres near Paris, it features large rooms and an awesome entrance hall, with its own fountains and formal gardens. It is perhaps the most gracefully-styled of the mansions.

Rosecliff, on Bellevue Avenue, is a 40-room mansion designed by Stanford White and inspired by the Grand Trianon in Ver-

The farm itself was established in 1640 by William Brenton of England and remains the only working farm in the city.

CLIFF WALK

To enjoy the grandeur of the mansions and the sea in a more natural setting, take the **Cliff Walk**, a 3.5-mile (5.5-km) coastal path that hugs the craggy shoreline along Rhode Island Sound. From its starting point just off Memorial Boulevard (near Newport Beach) to its terminus at Ocean Avenue, the walk is a narrow strip of public land that separates great estates such as The Breakers, Rosecliff, Marble House, and Salve Regina College from the sea.

In the nineteenth century, the rich attempted to close the path to the public. But the locals protested, and eventually the state backed them. Proceed to the end of Narragansett Avenue; there the "Forty Steps" enable you to reach the water without following the entire length of the walk.

COLONIAL NEWPORT

Among Newport's great treasures is its colonial architecture, especially evident in the Point and Historic Hill neighborhoods. The 1748 **Hunter House**, considered "one of the 10 best examples of residential colonial architecture in America," was also the headquarters of the French Navy during the American Revolution. **Trinity Church** (1726), with its tall white colonial spire, is based on a Christopher Wren design, and is a landmark visible for miles. The **Touro Synagogue** (1759) was the first ever built in America. **Old Colony House**, an eighteenth-century structure, was headquarters for George Washington as he planned the battle of Yorktown in 1781; it also became the seat of Rhode Island's colonial government. The 1699 **Quaker Meeting House** is the oldest religious building in Newport. And the **White Horse Tavern**, built before 1673, is America's oldest operating tavern.

The **Old Stone Tower**, a "mysterious" structure variously attributed to the Phoenicians, Celts, Vikings, and the Portuguese, is more probably the remains of a colonial windmill built by then-governor Benedict Arnold. The **Green Animals** on Cory's Lane in nearby Portsmouth, dating from 1880, is considered the best topiary garden in America, with 80 trees and shrubs sculpted in every animal shape imaginable.

Visitors who wish to take home a memento of Newport history should head to "**Antique Alley,**" a cluster of antique shops grouped on Thames and Spring Streets; especially good antique hunting is found on Franklin Street in the Historic Hill section of town.

THE WATERFRONT

It is not unusual to see million-dollar yachts anchored in **Brenton Cove** or sailing the waters of Narragansett Bay. Of the bay it has been written, "It is big and scenically lovely, surrounded by wooded countryside, colonial towns, big cities and history-packed shores, with sightseeing opportunities matched by few cruising grounds."

Newport and yachting are inseparable; in fact, it has often been called the yachting capital of the world, harboring countless yacht clubs, boatyards, and sail-making shops. Twenty-four America's Cup races were held in Newport waters beginning in 1851; the last Cup race held here, in 1983, saw the Australians become the first foreign country to wrestle the trophy from the United States.

Fort Adams State Park

America's Cup memorabilia is housed at the **Museum of Yachting**, worth a visit just for its spectacular waterfront location at Fort Adams State Park on Ocean Drive. It is a display of Newport's rich yachting heritage, with small craft, ship models, costumes, and photographs; the America's Cup section includes the 1930 Cup challenger, *Shamrock V*, one of the largest sailing sloops in the world at 127 ft (38.7 m) long and 160 ft (48.8 m) high. The museum also sponsors the Classic Yacht Regatta each Labor Day weekend.

Sightseeing cruises set sail daily (May to October) from Goat Island Marina, off Washington Street, and other dock areas. Cruises take you past the mansion-dotted coastline of Newport, the once pirate-infested shores of Jamestown, towering Newport Bridge, and Fort Adams, guardian of the harbor; some include a visit to Hammersmith Farm.

Another major attraction is shore surfcasting, and bottom fishing in protected bay and shoreline areas, and offshore big-game fishing for white marlin and tuna. Numerous charters are available; for licensing information, call ((401) 789-3094.

TENNIS HALL OF FAME

The **Newport Casino**, facing Bellevue Avenue, was America's most exclusive country club in the 1880s. Now it houses the **International Tennis Hall of Fame**. American lawn tennis started at the Casino some 100 years ago, and the first national championships were held on its grassy courts from 1881 until 1915, when the tournament moved to Forest Hills, New York.

Hall of Fame exhibits include Davis Cup memorabilia, historical displays, and equipment exhibits. Outside the main building, the Casino's dozen grass courts stretch across to the restored "court tennis" court, where you can see how the "sport of kings" was played in England and Europe during the thirteenth century. Each summer, a Grand Prix tennis tournament lures top international players; it is one of the few professional tennis championships played on grass in the United States.

WHERE TO STAY

The luxury **Inn at Castle Hill** (on Ocean Drive; ℂ (401) 849-3800; 9 rooms) has a beautiful view. This handsome retreat rests on 32 acres (13 hectares) of shoreline hugging Narragansett Bay and the Atlantic Ocean. Reservations should be made well in advance.

Expensive

If you prefer to stay in one of the old Newport homes, the **Guest House Association of Newport** (P.O. Box 981, Newport, RI 02840; ℂ (401) 846-5444) will help you find rooms.

Offering standard hotel and motel accommodations are **Treadway Newport Resort and Marina** (America's Cup Avenue; ℂ (401) 847-1000; 134 rooms) and **Sheraton Islander Inn and Conference Center** (Goat Island; ℂ (401) 849-2600; 254 rooms).

Moderate

There are many bed-and-breakfast establishments in the area. Contact the **Bed & Breakfast of Rhode Island** (P.O. Box 3291, Newport, RI 02840; ℂ (401) 849-1298) for reservations. Other accommodations include **Best Western Mainstay Inn** (151 Admiral Kalbfas Road; ℂ (401) 849-9880; 52 rooms); **Holiday Inn Crowne Plaza** (25 America's Cup Avenue; ℂ (401) 849-1000; 308 rooms); and **Mill Street Inn** (75 Mill Street; ℂ (401) 849-9500; 23 rooms).

EATING OUT

Newport presents a variety of dining choices.

Expensive

One of New England's most appealing French-style restaurants is **La Petite Auberge** (19 Charles Street; ℂ (401) 849-6669), with French classic and nouvelle cuisine.

The **SS Newport** (Waite's Wharf; ℂ (401) 846-1200), a restored fishing boat-turned-restaurant moored offshore at Waite's Wharf, specializes in lobster.

French-style provincial fare is the mainstay at **Le Bistro** (Bowen's Wharf; ℂ (401) 849-7778).

Interesting colonial dishes are served at the **White Horse Tavern** (Marlborough and Farewell Streets; ℂ (401) 849-3600).

The Inn at Castle Hill (ℂ (401) 849-3800), **The Black Pearl** (Bannister's Wharf; ℂ (401) 864-5264), and **Clark Cooke House** (Bannister's Wharf; ℂ (401) 849-2900) are also fine restaurants.

Moderate

Choices include plain and exotic seafood at **Scales and Shells** (527 Thames Street; ℂ (401) 846-3473); **The Mooring** (Sawyer's Wharf; ℂ (401) 846-2260), which serves great clam chowder; and **Puerini's** (24 Memorial Boulevard West; ℂ (401) 847-5506), where excellent pasta dishes are served.

For more restaurant suggestions, pick up a free *Newport Guide* at the town's Information Center at Brick Market Place.

NEWPORT AREA EXCURSIONS

A side trip to **Jamestown**, three miles (4.8 km) west of Newport on Conanicut Island, should include a drive along its southern tip; there are superb views across Narragansett Bay from Beaver Trail Lighthouse, including **Fort Wetherill** — built on 100-ft (30-m)-tall granite cliffs — and Mackerel Cove.

BLOCK ISLAND

Where do Rhode Islanders go during the summer to get away from it all? Small Block Island, 11 sq miles (28 sq km), situated about 12 miles (19 km) south of the mainland off Point Judith.

A relatively unspoiled retreat of oceanside cliffs, shifting sand dunes, and spectacular annual spring and fall bird migrations, Block Island has cooler summer temperatures than on the mainland, and great beachcombing and biking. The beaches are almost deserted even at the height of the tourist season, and some of the best deep-sea fishing can be had in the island's waters.

GETTING THERE

Most visitors to the island arrive by ferry from Galilee, Providence, or New London, Connecticut. However, you can travel from **Westerly** Rhode Island on New England Airlines, ((401) 466-5953 or 5881, which operate regular 12 minute chartered flights.

Before or after your trip to Block Island, you can stay at the **Pine Lodge Motel** (Box 562; ((401) 322-0333; 80 units; moderate) and eat at **Shelter Harbor Inn** (10 Wagner Street; ((401) 322-8883; New England cuisine; moderate) or **Villa Trombino** (106 Ashway Road; ((401) 596-3444; Italian cuisine, inexpensive).

AROUND THE ISLAND

Cycling is one of the most popular ways to get around Block Island. Bicycle rentals are near the Old Harbor and Great Salt Pond ferry docks. By bike or car, head to **Mohegan Bluffs** on the island's south shore; multi-colored clay cliffs of 200 ft (61m) in height stretch for several miles along the shore, offering a spectacular ocean vista, with the steep walking paths to the beaches that rim the coastline below.

Not far away is **Palatine Graves**, east off Dickens Point, said to be the burial grounds of eighteenth-century Dutch immigrants. **Settlers' Rock**, resting on the shore of Cow Cove, is the island's own Plymouth Rock, commemorating the arrival of the first pioneers on the island in 1661.

Much of the north shore is a bird and wildlife refuge, and an old stone lighthouse on Sandy Point can be reached along a sandy path. **North Light** is a prime spot for bird-watching and sunsets.

New Harbor is great for surf fishing and water sports. The best swimming is along the eastern shore, especially at **Crescent Beach**, but the deserted beaches along the windswept western shore can also be very appealing. (Be cautious of strong undertows and rugged surf.) You can also explore some of the 365 freshwater ponds in the island's interior.

Taxi island tours (pick them up near Old Harbor ferry) are gaining popularity with visitors who prefer to leave the driving to someone else. A round trip lasts little more than an hour, and drivers will usually let you stop for photographs.

The island's folklore is rich in stories of eighteenth century pirates and in tales of undiscovered treasure buried on the island by Captain Kidd and others.

Even more infamous than pirates is the island's reputation for shipwrecks. More than 1,000 ships have gone down off its fog-bound coast. Folk tales tell of unscrupulous islanders who lured boats to the treacherous waters, then looted, wrecked, and sank the ships. Tourists today receive a friendlier welcome.

WHERE TO STAY

Expensive
The **1661 Inn and Guesthouse** (Old Harbor, Spring Street; ((401) 466-2421 or (401) 466-2063; 26 rooms), is a luxurious Victorian hotel with ocean views. There is also the **Samuel Peckham Inn** (New Harbor; ((401) 466-2439 or 466-2567; 17 rooms).

Moderate
Historic **Spring House** (Spring Street; ((401) 466-5844), one of the best known hotels, has been greeting visitors since 1852; its veranda offers a fine view of the Atlantic. Block Island has several other moderately priced inns and bed-and-breakfast accommodation.

EATING OUT

Block Island has several fine moderately-priced restaurants: **Ballard's Inn** (Old Harbor; ((401) 466-2231; Italian and American cuisine); **Harborside Inn** (Old Harbor; ((401) 466-5504; steaks and seafood); and **Samuel Peckham Tavern** (New Harbor; ((401) 466-2439; lobster specialties).

PROVIDENCE

This handsome city, set like Rome on seven hills and bisected by the Providence River, was founded in 1636 by Roger Williams

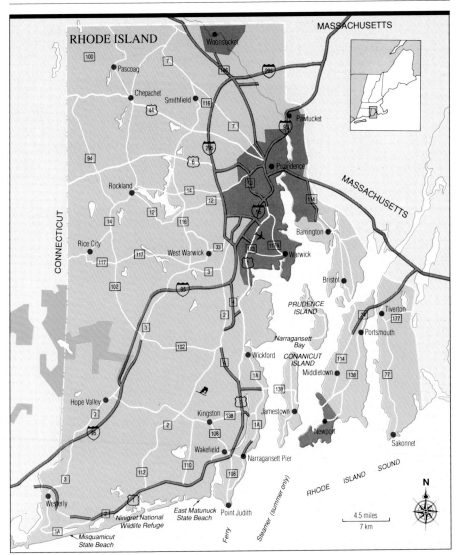

after clashes with the Puritans forced him out of Massachusetts. Williams' open, spirited humanity has endured in Providence's sunny streets and lovely homes, and in the liberal character gave rise to two of the nations finest schools, Brown University and the Rhode Island School of Design.

BACKGROUND

Early Providence earned its reputation as a seaport in the Triangular Trade (rum, slaves, and sugar). When the China Trade opened in 1781, many Providence merchants made a fortune. By 1793, with maritime fortunes declining, Slater Mill (in suburban Pawtucket) became the first American mill to harness water power to spin cotton. (Now a historic site, the Roosevelt Street mill offers guided tours with eighteenth-century machine demonstrations.)

Textile manufacture brought the city into the nineteenth century, and Providence became an important industrial center. However, with the Great Depression and the southward shift of industry after World War II, the city fell on harder times.

Today Providence, the capital of Rhode Island and the second largest city in New England, has a revitalized downtown district and streets of Federal-style homes that haven't changed much since the nineteenth century.

TOURIST INFORMATION

Providence is a good city for walking, given its one-way streets, narrow roadways, and snarled traffic. The **Preservation Society**, ((401) 831-7440, offers several guided walking tours of various city districts. And the **Convention and Visitors Bureau** (30 Exchange Center; ((401) 274-1636) has pamphlets describing self-guided walking tours.

TOURING THE CITY

City Hall, at Kennedy Plaza in the revitalized downtown district, is designed in the manner of the Louvre and the Tuileries in Paris. The old **Biltmore Plaza Hotel** (now the **Omni Biltmore**), a 1920's showplace, has been transformed into a first-class hostelry, with a grand marble staircase in the lobby.

South of Kennedy Plaza is the ornate Majestic Theatre (now called the **Lederer Theater**), a 1917 movie house that is all terra cotta and arches; it is home to the Tony Award-winning Trinity Square Repertory Company, one of the finest in the country. East of the plaza, between Westminster and Weybosset Streets, is **The Arcade**, the country's oldest indoor shopping "mall" (1828), and sole survivor of several Greek Revival-style "temples of trade," built in America in the early 1800's. Today, it is a lively marketplace with shops and eateries.

Across the Providence River at the foot of College Hill (South Water and College Streets) is **Market House**, a red brick building built in 1773 that served as the political and commercial center of colonial Providence. It is also the site of the Providence Tea Party, where on March 2, 1775, revolutionaries burned hundreds of pounds of British tea in an act of defiance against the Crown. The house is part of the prestigious **Rhode Island School of Design**. The school maintains a museum, part of which is the elegant, mahogany-panelled Pendleton House and its collection of eighteenth-century American furniture.

North on Main Street is the **Meeting House of the First Baptist Church** in America, a preserved 1775 colonial church designed by Joseph Brown; it is a tribute to Roger Williams, founder of Providence, who established the church in 1638. Continue north on Main and you come to the **Roger Williams National Memorial**, a park that is the site of the original Providence settlement in 1636.

Opposite is the **Cathedral of St John**, established in 1722, one of four original colonial parishes in the state. Its box pews and communion silver date to the Queen Anne period.

You are now approaching the beginnings of Benefit Street.

BENEFIT STREET — A MILE OF HISTORY

Benefit Street area is an impressive concentration of original colonial buildings. Beautifully restored eighteenth- and nineteenth-century Federal houses, churches, and museums overlook the city's historic waterfront. The Providence Preservation Society (headquarters at 24 Meeting Street) offers guided tours and pamphlets that describe some of the 100 historic homes (built largely by early sea captains and colonial merchants) that line Benefit and adjoining streets.

The street itself has a curious history. Once a meandering dirt path that led to informal graveyards behind family homes, it was straightened and "improved for the benefit" of the people, so the official proclamation reads.

Walking south, you will see several Federal homes, and the **Old State House**, where the Rhode Island General Assembly renounced allegiance to King George III, and signed their Declaration of Independence on May 4, 1776, more than two months before the 13 colonies gave their assent to liberty in Philadelphia.

Farther south is the **Providence Athenaeum**, an 1838 building that resembles a Greek temple and is one of America's oldest libraries. The modest clapboard, 1707 Quaker-style **house of Governor Stephen Hopkins**, a signatory of the Declaration of Independence (Benefit and Hopkins Streets) is open to visitors. It is said that he nudged other delegates at the Continental Congress into supporting that document. Next is the **First Unitarian Church**, built in 1816, whose steeple holds the largest and heaviest bell cast by Paul Revere & Sons.

The **John Brown House**, on Power Street just east of Benefit Street, was described by John Quincy Adams as "the most magnificent and elegant mansion that I have ever seen on this continent." Built in 1786, the three-story Georgian mansion once belonged to John Brown, one of the four Brown brothers. Another brother, Moses, developed the Slater Mill; Joseph was a noted architect who designed some of Providence's most enduring landmarks; and Nicholas was the founder of Rhode Island College, now Brown University. All brothers played an important role in shaping the future of Providence.

The Brown family collections include a display of early Rhode Island furniture. One of the best pieces, a block-front secretary, has been described as "one of the finest examples of American colonial furniture existent."

North of the Brown House, at Prospect and Cottage Streets, is the 133-acre (54-hectare) College Hill campus of **Brown University**. Chartered in 1764, it is the seventh oldest college in the United States. The university's **John Carter Brown Library** holds the world's premier collection of early and colonial Americana.

CONSTITUTION HILL

Across the river and west on Interstate 44 is the summit of Constitution Hill, upon which rests the **State Capitol**, its white marble glistening in the sun. The capitol was built in 1891 and its cupola is the second largest unsupported dome in the world, after St Peter's in Rome. The building houses an historic full-length portrait of George Washington by Gilbert Stuart, the original royal Charter of 1663 , and, of course, legislative chambers and the governor's office. One-hour guided tours are offered weekdays from 9 am to 3:30 pm.

WHERE TO STAY

In a class all its own is the recently restored **Omni Biltmore** (Kennedy Plaza; ((401) 421-0700, toll-free (800) 843-6664; 289 rooms). With special weekend rates, the Omni could be considered in the expensive category, but the service is always that of a luxury hotel.

In the moderate to expensive range are the 13-story **Holiday Inn Downtown** (21

Atwells Avenue; ((401) 831-3900; 274 rooms) and **Marriott Inn** (Charles and Orms Streets; ((401) 272-2400; 345 rooms). In nearby Pawtucket is the moderately-priced **Howard Johnson's Motor Lodge** (2 George Street; ((401) 723-6700; 136 rooms), where children stay free.

EATING OUT

Expensive

The best seafood in town is found at the **Bluepoint Oyster Bar** (99 N. Main Street; ((401) 272-6145).

For excellent Italian cuisine, **Camille's Roman Garden** (71 Bradford Street; ((401) 751-4812) cannot be beaten.

Pot au Feu (44 Custom House Street; ((401) 273-8953) serves excellent continental cuisine.

Moderate

Wes's Rib House (1 Robar Plaza; ((401) 421-9090) serves hearty meals of Missouri-style barbecue ribs, chicken, pork chops, or cured ham. **Alforno** (7 Steeple Street; ((401) 273-9760) features northern Italian cuisine.

Inexpensive

For an unusual dining experience, Providence has the **Haven Brothers Diner** (Fulton and Dorrance Streets; ((401) 861-7777). It is a real aluminum diner that pulls up to the curb each evening, and offers American food.

Providence, Rhode Island's capital.

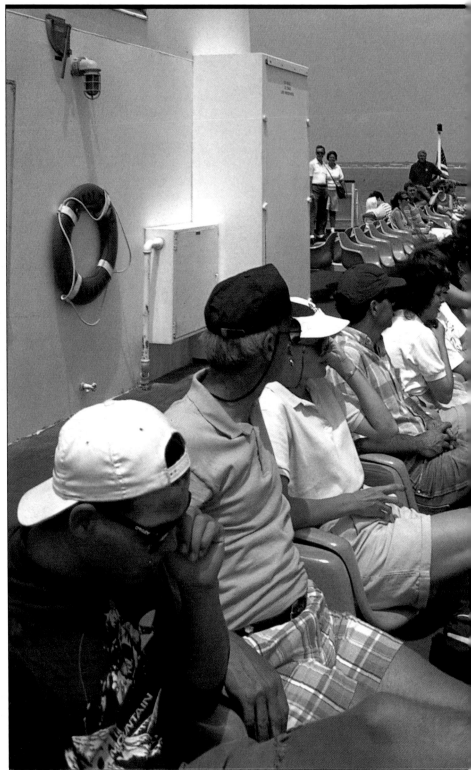

Travelers' Tips

GETTING THERE

New England is accessible by air, rail, and road. Major entry points are Boston, New York (only minutes away from Connecticut, the southernmost New England state), and Montreal, Canada.

BY AIR

Most major international airlines provide service to Boston, but fares are often cheaper to New York. Some United States carriers offer in country flight coupons at substantial savings to foreign travelers. These programs change from year to year, so check with you travel agent when planning your trip. In 1991, for example, a $50.00 coupon would allow you to fly anywhere in New England on U.S. Air. The coupons could only be purchased outside the Unites States by foreigners or United States citizens working abroad.

The following are the telephone numbers of the international carriers who maintain an office in Boston or at Boston's Logan International Airport:

Aer Lingus, toll-free (800) 223-6537
Air Canada, toll-free (800) 422-6232
Air France, toll-free (800) 237-2747
Air Jamaica, toll-free (800) 523-5585
Air New Zealand, toll-free (800) 262-1234
Alaska Airlines, toll-free (800) 426-0333
Alitalia Airlines, (617) 542-9060
American Airlines, (617) 542-6700
British Airways, toll-free (800) 247-9297
Continental Airlines, (617) 569-8400
El Al — Israel, toll-free (800) 223-6700
Icelandair, toll-free (800) 223-5500
Finnair, toll-free (800) 223-5700
Japan Airlines, (617) 262-8800
Lufthansa, toll-free (800) 645-3880
Northwest Orient, (617) 267-4885
Pan American, toll-free (800) 221-1111
Qantas, toll-free (800) 227-4500
Sabena, (617) 542-4296
Swissair, (617) 423-7778
TWA, (617) 367-2800
United, (617) 482-7900

Most domestic carriers fly to Boston and the other large New England cities (Hartford, Providence, Portland, etc.) To find economy flights to New England, you will have to consult your travel agent. Fares are variable. Competition among companies can cause sudden price wars that can make flying to New England quite reasonable. During the summer, it is advisable to avoid any discount packages that require you to fly standby. Flights are not only full but also overbooked. Make your seat reservations a week in advance to be assured of not being bumped off your flight, and do your fellow travelers a favor and cancel any unwanted reservations.

The following domestic airlines fly to New England and have offices in the Boston area:

Alaska Airlines, toll-free (800) 426-0333
American Airlines, (617) 542-6700
Continental Airlines, (617) 569-8400
Delta Airlines, (617) 567-4100
HubExpress, toll-free (800) 962-4744
Northwest Orient, (617) 267-4885
Pan American, toll-free (800) 221-1111
TWA, (617) 367-2800
United, (617) 482-7900
US Air, (617) 482-3160

BY RAIL

Amtrak, the only rail passenger carrier in the United States, connects a few New England cities. There is frequent service to Boston from Montreal and New York. On the New York–Boston line, there are intermediate stops in Connecticut. You can hop off the train from Montreal at Port Kennedy, New York, and take the ferry across Lake Champlain to Burlington, Vermont. For prices and schedules, call Amtrak toll-free at (800) 872-7245. To receive a free travel planner, write to Amtrak Distribution Center (P.O. Box 7717, Itasca, IL 60143).

BY GREYHOUND BUS

Greyhound Lines can get you to New England from within the United States or Canada. Its routes will usually take you into Boston or New York with connections to Maine, New Hampshire, and Vermont. Your travel agent or local Greyhound agent can provide information on schedules and fares, or contact Greyhound in New York (℄ (212 635-0800) or Boston (℄ (617) 423-5810).

BY ROAD

Although most New Englanders consider New England a country unto itself, there are no border crossings when driving within Unites States.

When entering from Canada, even United States citizens need to have appropriate identification (see TRAVEL DOCUMENTS below).

TRAVEL DOCUMENTS

When arriving in New England, Canadian and Mexican citizens need only show proof of identification and residence (a driver's license will do). British need only a valid passport. Other visitors need a valid passport and a United States visa. Contact the United States embassy or consulate in your country for the exact details for obtaining a visa.

Your travel agent can also be helpful in obtaining a visa. Allow 28 days for processing.

Vaccinations may or may not be required for entry into the United States. (Country of origin or recently-visited countries could alter your situation; check before you leave.)

CONSULATES

IN BOSTON

BRITISH
600 Atlantic Avenue, Boston
℄ 248-9555

AUSTRALIAN
20 Beacon, Boston
℄ 248-8655

CANADIAN
3 Copley Pl., Boston
℄ 262-3760

IRISH
535 Boylston, Boston
℄ 267-9330

IN NEW YORK

BRITISH
145 Third Avenue, New York, NY
℄ (212) 745-0202

AUSTRALIAN
636 Fifth Avenue, New York, NY
℄ (212) 245-4000

CANADIAN
1251 Avenue of the Americas, New York NY
℄ (212) 586-2400

IRISH
515 Madison Avenue, New York, NY
℄ (212) 319-2555

CUSTOMS

Customs allows you to bring in duty-free gifts valued up to $100. For more specific information, including shopping restrictions, contact your local American embassy or consulate branch. Carrying non-prescription narcotic drugs into the country may well result in a long prison sentence. When entering the United States, foreign visitors should allow a minimum of an hour to clear customs at Boston or New York. For European travelers, the close scrutiny of customs and immigration officers is sometimes shocking and annoying. During the peak summer season, foreign passport holders have had to wait up to two hours before even reaching passport control at New York's Kennedy International Airport. At Boston this rarely happens.

WHEN TO GO

There is no best time to come to New England. Summer, fall, winter, and spring all have something to offer. However, New England has a season all its own—"Colors." This arrives in early fall when the leaves change to crimson, gold, and orange. Days are warm and evenings cool. The countryside is at its best then.

New England summers are traditionally glorious and comfortable, with lots of sun and gentle cooling breezes off the ocean, although hot and humid conditions are not altogether unfamiliar to the region. Summer is the height of the tourist season, with most attractions open from late May to October.

Winters can be bitterly cold, with snow and cutting winds. But it is rarely too severe for skiers. New England has more than 100 ski areas throughout its six states. It is neither the Alps nor the Rockies, but the slopes are good and fast, the cross country runs Olympic class, and the hospitality, warm and friendly.

Spring is often referred to as the mud season: lots of rain, with warm days and cool nights. However, several airlines offer special low fares during this traditional off-season period. Your reward is the freshness of spring with its new growth and blooming flowering wild flowers and fruit trees.

WHAT TO TAKE

New England styles tend to be casual, especially in Maine, Vermont, and New Hampshire. More traditional styles rule preppy Connecticut and Rhode Island; Massachusetts has a little bit of everything. Big cities, especially Boston, may require very formal wear, especially for business meetings and restaurant dining. Men should pack a jacket and tie, and women should bring a dress or suit.

While season dictates other clothing needs, summer visitors should bring along a warm sweater or jacket in case of cool evening temperatures — especially when visiting the coast.

Regardless of season, rain gear is appropriate.

GETTING AROUND

Rail travel is the most limited means of getting around New England (see GETTING THERE below).

AIRLINES

Airplanes can get you from city to city. In addition to the domestic carriers listed under GETTING THERE above, there are small domestic airlines that provide intra-New England flights:

Bar Harbor Airlines — for Portland, Maine; toll-free (800) 343-3210.

Pilgrim Airlines — for New Haven, Connecticut, and Provincetown, Mass.; toll-free (800) 243-0490.

BUS SERVICES

Reasonable bus services are available throughout New England, provided by the following three major companies with central offices in Boston:

Bonanza, ((617) 423-5810
Greyhound, ((617) 423-5810
Peter Pan Bus Lines Inc., ((617) 426-7838, toll free (800) 628-8468 outside Massachusetts or toll-free (800) 332-8995 in-state.

Of course, bus travel is more time-consuming than air, but it does offer the advantage of being able to see the countryside at a relaxed pace.

TAXIS AND LIMOUSINES

Taxis operate throughout New England, although they are most often found in big cities rather than the small towns. Rates vary; ask if there are standard rates for airport routes.

Limousines are another way to get conveniently from airports to major cities; rates are often comparable to taxi fares. In Boston, contact:

Carey of Boston Limousine, ((617) 623-8700
Commonwealth Limousine, ((617) 787-5575
Boston Cab, ((617) 536-5010
Checker Cab, ((617) 536-7000
Red Cab, ((617) 734-5000

AUTOMOBILES

By far the best way to see New England is at your own pace and schedule by automobile. Exploring the small country roads is to find the best New England has to offer.

Most airports, major hotels, or tourist centers have offices (or can provide information) for car rentals. Renters must have a valid driver's license and a credit card (used for deposit), be at least 21 years of age, though, in certain circumstances some companies set the minimum age at 21 years. Foreign drivers may need an international driver's license. Be sure to check out liability clauses in the rental agreement; they are not automatically included, and your personal automobile insurance or credit card may cover none, part, or all of your liability risks. Check if your airline offers car rental packages with airfare. Car rental agency telephone numbers include:

American International, toll-free (800) 527-0202

Avis, toll-free (800) 331-1212

Budget, toll-free (800) 527-0700

Dollar (in Boston), (617) 569-5300

Hertz, toll-free (800) 654-3131

National, toll-free (800) 328-4567

Foreign travelers can often get better rates when booking from abroad. "Fly and Drive" packages are often better buys than booking flights and car rentals separately.

For the most adventurous travelers, consider renting a camper. Throughout New England, in state and national forests, are well-maintained and equipped campgrounds, some of the best in the United States. There are also many private campgrounds that have luxury camping facilities — hot water, showers, pool, playground, electrical hook-ups, etc. Listings of camping facilities can be obtained from the individual state offices of tourism, whose addresses are included in the opening section of each chapter.

ACCOMMODATION

Throughout New England there are many hotels and motels that all provide the standard room with one or two double or queen-sized beds, private bath, telephone, and television. As rates often change without notice, specific prices are not noted in this guide. Hotels and motels are classified in the following categories: inexpensive, less than

$35 for a double room (2 person occupancy); moderate, $35 to $85; expensive more than $80. In Boston, New Haven, and Rhode Island, there is a special category — luxury, over $200.

Also listed in the Guide are the traditional New England country inns and bed-and-breakfasts that are growing in popularity. Rates at the country inns are generally in the expensive category. However, if you book for a week-long stay or mid-week and off season, you can sometimes negotiate a more moderate price.

Bed and breakfast accommodations are in the moderate category and bring you in more individual contact with New Englanders. The bed-and-breakfast operators have a closely knit organization and will usually be more than happy to help you find a bed-and-breakfast at your next destination.

The lists of accommodations are included at the end of each destination and are not all-inclusive. State and local tourism agencies will gladly supply you with further information and help in booking rooms. On New England's backroads there are many small motels whose accommodations are good and prices reasonable. It is always best to examine the rooms before making a decision.

ABOVE: Boston's MTA subway, made famous by the Kingston Trio's lyrics in the 1950's.

EATING OUT

The most difficult thing about eating out in New England is deciding which of the many excellent restaurants to choose. Needless to say, the lists of restaurants included with each destination are far from exhaustive. Ownership, prices, chefs, and specialties do change. However, those recommended are established houses that have provided a tradition of good food over the years. Price guidelines for full meals (without liquor) are as follows: inexpensive, under $15 per person; moderate, $15 to $30; expensive, over $30. Reservations are always recommended.

TIPPING

Tips are not included on your tab. Fifteen percent is the standard. Don't hesitate to leave more if the service has been exceptional, but never leave less unless the waiter or waitress has been surly.

SHOPPING

ANTIQUES

"Antique" is generally a term bandied about in a rather casual manner. In the United States, it has often become interchangeable with the word "old." Therefore, it is best to look to United States Customs for some kind of workable definition.

In 1930, the federal government ruled that objects must be at least 100 years old to be classified as antiques and admitted into the country duty-free, and in 1966, a tariff act further ruled that there would be duty-free admission into the country of all objects 100 years old before the date of entry.

Therefore, anything at least 100 years old is "officially" given antique status, although many objects less than a century old are generally included under that term. It is to be aware of the official government distinction.

Antiquing in Litchfield County Connecticut can be a barrel of fun.

Buying Antiques

Like anything else, antique prices reflect the free enterprise marketplace. In other words, things are worth whatever someone will pay for them. You should therefore consider all antique price tags as general starting points for negotiation. You should not have to pay the asking price for an antique unless there is heavy demand or competition for the particular piece or style. (Then you might even be forced to pay more, if your heart is set on it and your wallet deep enough.)

Always attempt to bring down the price, even if you are normally a timid negotiator. Antique dealers expect you to do it; besides, the asking price probably reflects this realization.

As an educated consumer, you might want to pick up an antique price/guide book that offers background on history, styles, and general prices. One of the most consistent and respected guides is Kovel's, which can be purchased at most major bookstores.

Also remember that almost all types of Americana — whether or not they are listed in official antique guidebooks — have become sought-after collector's items.

Furniture Styles

After the wilderness was ruined and great cities sprang up along the eastern seaboard in the eighteenth century, colonial furniture took on its distinctive, elegant style. Some antiques are recognized art forms. Typical of certain time periods and much sought after today. They include:

Queen Anne (1702–1714) — walnut furniture distinguished by curved contours, often with ball and claw feet and shell carvings.

Early Georgian (1714–1745) — the Queen Anne style was elaborated with paw feet, and eagles' or lions' head carvings; a heavy baroque style came into vogue after 1735. Most of the furniture makers continued to use walnut, but mahogany was becoming increasingly popular.

Chippendale (1745–1765) — perhaps the most renowned period in American furniture styling, with the works of master cabinet maker Thomas Chippendale most prominent. Straight square legs, but a great freedom of design, with many Gothic, Chinese, and French touches, including lavish fretwork and rococo flourishes. Almost exclusive use of mahogany.

Adam Style (1760–1785) — classical, delicate with much painted decoration. This period also saw the introduction of oval and sideboard tables, and wheel back chairs. Mahogany dominated, but sycamore and other light woods were also used.

Hepplewhite Style (1780–1795) — light and graceful with much painted decorations,

shire County Massachusetts Antiques Dealers Association, and guarantee antique authenticity. Some of them are located in New England's beautiful towns, so whether you're seriously looking for antiques, just browsing, or simply wandering the region's backroads, you should have a pleasant and interesting journey.

Cautions

Be very careful about what you buy when purchasing expensive or valuable pieces. Always ask for antique authentication, or

inlay, and delicate carving that often used Prince of Wales feathers, ears of wheat, and honeysuckle motifs. Also Anglicized versions of contemporary French styles; continued use of mahogany.

Sheraton Style (1790–1810) — Thomas Sheraton was a gifted furniture designer, not a cabinet maker. His style is dominated by square back chairs, tapered legs, bow front chests and sideboards, pedestal dining tables, and much use of inlay in mahogany.

Dealer's Directory

Contact the Massachusetts State Tourism Department for a list of the antique dealers. Look out for those who belong to the Berk-

frequent dealers who take pride in their merchandise and guarantee authenticity. A simple tag description should not necessarily satisfy you unless you are knowledgeable about antiques yourself. In fact, stories are legendary about how a few unscrupulous dealers fabricate entire case histories for antiques in order to impress—and con — buyers. It is *caveat emptor* — "let the buyer beware."

HANDICRAFTS

Throughout New England are many specialty shops that sell only locally or regionally crafted merchandise. Particularly appealing are the wooden and fabric items.

One can find a variety of children's pull toys and puzzles that are as durable as they are attractive. These are not bargains because many are one of a kind, more works of art than toys.

Hand-made cotton clothing, stuffed animals, and kitchen items are also plentiful. These are usually products of cottage industries that each year play a larger role in the economies of the small New England towns.

OUTLET STORES

Until a quarter of a century ago, all the New England factory towns had stores that sold their "accidented" products. The careful, clever shopper could save enormous amounts. A family could be dressed and shod for a fraction of retail cost, and household linens were likewise cheaper. Now most of these factories are closed, but outlet stores remain. They are not the great sources of bargains they once were, but the discounts are generally 20 to 30 percent which include seconds, remaindered stock, samples, overruns of almost every name brand sold in the United States: Fieldcrest, Dior, Barbizon, Levis, Bass, Arrow, Haynes, White Stag, Nike, Adidas, New Balance, etc.

Freeport, Maine, is the best known of the outlet store shopping areas, but there are other stores throughout New England. Each spring new guides to the outlet stores appear on the New England newsstands to help visitors and residents alike find the best bargains.

MONEY

United States dollar rates have fluctuated so wildly of late it is pointless to include any specific comparative guidelines. Trends have increased the home currency value of many European and Asian visitors.

It is advisable to purchase travelers' checks in United States dollars for your money use because many banks do not offer foreign currency exchange services. Travelers' checks can be easily replaced if stolen or lost.

WEIGHTS AND MEASURES

The United States use ounces, pounds, gallons, miles, acres, etc. It does not use the metric system. Some conversions are as follows:

1 inch = 2.54 centimeters
1 foot = 0.305 meters
1 mile = 1.6 kilometers
1 gallon = 3.78 liters
1 ounce = 28.35 grams
1 pound = 0.45 kilograms.

COMMUNICATIONS

NEWSPAPERS

Pick up any local daily newspaper for the latest overview of local and national news. The *Boston Globe* is New England's leading regional newspaper. *USA Today*, a national daily, provides national news capsules. Only in Boston can you find foreign language newspapers.

MAIL

Post offices — Most post offices are open Monday through Friday from 9 am to 5 pm. There are often long lines and belligerent employees. It is just part of the system. At the time of going to press, first-class letters require a 29-cent stamp and postcards 18 cents. International rates vary with desti-

OPPOSITE: Second-hand clothing and bric-a-brac in rural Northeast Connecticut.
ABOVE: Moped rental at Martha's Vineyard.

nation, but are generally about twice the domestic tariff.

TELEPHONE

The recent breakup of AT&T has played havoc with phone users throughout the country. Now several kinds of pay phones are in operation, all requiring different steps of operation; read the directions carefully before depositing your coins. A local call is $.25 at most pay phones. To use international calling cards, you'll need to dial 0 to get the operator.

Major hotels have telefax services, at a price, as do office services stores in the larger cities.

For the electronically equipped traveler, CCITT and Bell approved modems that will work in the United States. 1200 baud is more reliable than 2400.

TELEVISION

America has four major television networks and thousands of local affiliate stations. Add cable and pay-TV to the selections, and the country becomes a TV-junkie's paradise, with scores of choices.

PUBLIC HOLIDAYS

National public holidays include the following:
New Year's Day — January 1
Martin Luther King, Jr.'s Birthday — January 15
Lincoln's Birthday — February 12
Washington's Birthday — February 22
Memorial Day — last Monday in May
Independence Day — July 4
Labor Day — first Monday in September
Columbus Day — second Monday in October
Thanksgiving Day — fourth Thursday in November
Christmas Day — December 25
During those holidays, federal, state and city offices close, and more importantly the banks. In the cities and town, stores and many restaurants are closed on Sundays,

but shopping malls are usually open seven days a week.

Other holidays such as St Patrick's Day (March 17), Easter Sunday (April), Mother's Day (May), Father's Day (June), and Halloween (October 31) may be celebrated in various ways by different states and communities.

Also, state holidays vary widely. For a calendar of state events, contact the appropriate state tourism agencies.

TIME ZONES

New England is in the Eastern Time Zone, the same time of day as New York, one hour ahead of Chicago, three hours ahead of California, normally five hours behind Great Britain, and six hours behind western Europe. There is only a five hour time differential between New England and Europe for several weeks in October and April when the Europeans switch to daylight saving time before the Americans.

Bibliography

COLLECTION, *Fifty Hikes* (one book for each New England state), Woodstock, Vermont, Back Country Publications, 1983.

JUDSON HALE, *Inside New England*, New York, Harper & Row Publishers, 1982.

JOHN HARRIS, *The Boston Globe Historic Walks in Old Boston*, Chester, Connecticut., The Globe Pequot Press, 1984.

NATHANIEL HAWTHORNE, *The Scarlet Letter*.

HENRY JAMES, *The Bostonians*.

NEIL JORGENSEN, *A Guide to New England's Landscape*, Barre, Mass., Barre Publishing Co., 1980.

HERMAN MELVILLE, *Moby Dick*.

NEAL PEIRCE, *The New England States*, New York, W.W. Norton and Company, Inc. 1976.

MICHAEL SCHUMAN, *Favorite Daytrips in New England*, Dublin, N.H., Yankee Books, 1987.

ELIZABETH SQUIRE, *Guide to the Recommended Country Inns of New England*, Chester, Connecticut., The Globe Pequot Press, 1987.

NANCY WEBSTER & RICHARD WOODWORTH, *Getaways for Gourmets*, West Hartford, Connecticut., Wood Pond Press, 1988.

Photo Credits

Ellis Klarenbeek: Pages 5 *right*, 11 *right*, 20, 22, 23, 29, 32, 41, 42 *top*, 47, 48, 61, 62-63, 68, 90-91, 101, 102 left, 106, 112, 128, 135 *right*, 140, 151 *top and bottom*, 158, 188, 189, 191, 193, 203, 205

Quick Reference A–Z Guide
to Places and Topics of Interest with Listed Accommodation, Restaurants and Useful Telephone Numbers

MASSACHUSETTS

NEW HAMPSHIRE

Illustrated Blueprints to Travel Enjoyment

INSIDER'S GUIDES

The Guides That Lead